The City as Anthology

The City as Anthology

Eroticism and Urbanity in Early Modern Isfahan

KATHRYN BABAYAN

STANFORD UNIVERSITY PRESS
Stanford, California

STANFORD UNIVERSITY PRESS
Stanford, California

© 2021 by the Board of Trustees of the Leland Stanford Junior University. All rights reserved.

No part of this book may be reproduced or transmitted in any form or by any means, electronic or mechanical, including photocopying and recording, or in any information storage or retrieval system without the prior written permission of Stanford University Press.

Printed in the United States of America on acid-free, archival-quality paper

ISBN 9781503640108

First paperback printing, 2024

The Library of Congress has cataloged the hardcover edition as follows:
Names: Babayan, Kathryn, 1960– author.
Title: The city as anthology : eroticism and urbanity in early modern Isfahan / Kathryn Babayan.
Description: Stanford, California : Stanford University Press, 2021. | Includes bibliographical references and index.
Identifiers: LCCN 2020039820 (print) | LCCN 2020039821 (ebook) | ISBN 9781503613386 (cloth) | ISBN 9781503627833 (ebook)
Subjects: LCSH: Iṣfahān (Iran)—Social life and customs—17th century—Sources. | Iran—History—Ṣafavid dynasty, 1501-1736. | Art, Safavid—Iran—Iṣfahān—17th century. | Manuscripts, Persian—Iran—Iṣfahān—History—17th century. | Anthologies—History—17th century.
Classification: LCC DS325.I7 B33 2021 (print) | LCC DS325.I7 (ebook) | DDC 955/.95—dc23
LC record available at https://lccn.loc.gov/2020039820
LC ebook record available at https://lccn.loc.gov/2020039821

Typeset by Kevin Barrett Kane in 10/15 Brill

For my father,
Hask Babayan (1929–2020)

CONTENTS

List of Maps and Illustrations   ix

Acknowledgments   xi

Note on Transliteration   xvii

Introduction: The *Adab* of Urbanity   1

1 Imperial Visions of Sovereignty   30

2 Collecting, Self-Fashioning, and Community   63

3 Disturbing the City   108

4 Cultivating and Disciplining Friendship Letters   137

5 Family Archives and Female Spaces of Intimacy   164

Conclusion: The Erotics of Urbanity   196

Appendix   207

Notes   209

Bibliography   237

Index   249

MAPS AND ILLUSTRATIONS

Maps

0.1	Early modern Eurasian cities and the mobility of characters from *The City as Anthology*	26
1.1	Isfahan's new city center in the seventeenth century	38

Illustrations

0.1	Interior wall and honeycomb arch of the new Friday Prayer Mosque	6
0.2	Panoramic view of Naqsh-i Jahan square (1590–1595)	7
0.3	A folio of the *majmuʻa* belonging to Kazim the judge (seventeenth century)	13
0.4	Muʻin Musavvir's drawing of a man holding a recipe for a talisman (1663)	15
0.5	Riza Abbasi (d. 1635), *Old Man and the Youth*	20
1.1	The Shaykh Lutfullah Mosque (1618)	39
1.2	The new Friday Prayer Mosque (1611–1630)	43
1.3	Shah Abbas I and Vali Muhammad Khan, wall painting in the Audience Hall of the Chihil Sutun (1647)	48
1.4	The politics of eros, Chihil Sutun	51
1.5	The *chub-i tariqat* ritual, Chihil Sutun	53
1.6	Submission, brotherhood, and ecstasy, Chihil Sutun	55
1.7	Female singers and cross-dressed male dancers, Chihil Sutun	56
2.1	Folio of a *muraqqaʻ* made in Samarqand (1400–1450)	69
2.2	Table of contents in Aqa Husayn Khwansari's *majmuʻa* (1675)	79
2.3	Muhammad Qasim's *Bastinade* (1650–1655)	93

2.4	Muhammad Qasim's *Youth Holding a Letter* (1635)	98
2.5	Muhammad Qasim's *Seated Man With an Album* (1640)	99
2.6	Muhammad Qasim's *Portrait of Shah Abbas and a Page* (1627)	101
2.7	Muhammad Qasim's *Boys Bird Nesting* (1650–1655)	104
3.1	Riza Abbasi, *Kneeling Youth with a Tray of Coffee* (1618)	127
3.2	Muʿin Musavvir, *A European Youth with Hat and Dog* (1687)	128
4.1	Nasira Hamadani's (d. 1620) letter to Husayn Kashi	145
4.2	Muʿin Musavvir's drawing for his friend Shafiʿa (1638)	157
4.3	*Muraqqaʿ* of calligraphy by Mir Ali (1540–1550)	159
4.4	Afzal Husayni, *Youth with an Album* (1620–1630)	161
5.1	Table of contents in the Urdubadi *majmuʿa* (1697)	168
5.2	Folio from the Urdubadi *majmuʿa*	169
5.3	Folio from the Urdubadi *majmuʿa*	170
5.4	*Dibacha* (preface) from the Urdubadi *majmuʿa*	174
5.5	Muhammad Qasim, *Woman Smoking a Pipe* (1650)	179
5.6	Muhammad Qasim, *Girls, Woman, and Dervish* (1655)	182

ACKNOWLEDGMENTS

This book project began in 1993 during my first trip back to Iran after I had left to pursue my higher education in the United States. I had made the study of Iranian history my new home in diaspora. Curious about the religious turn of the 1979 Iranian Revolution, I embarked on an intellectual journey that took me back in time to the Safavi era (1501–1722), to a period when Shi'ism was declared the religion of the empire—a move that launched the conversion of a Sunni population to the version of Shi'ism that today constitutes the faith of most Iranians. The processes of conversion and the formation of a Shi'a culture and a clerical establishment that oversaw the empire's educational, juridical, and religious institutions seemed to be the logical place to begin. After all, the clerics of today, like the men of religion of that era, were impresarios of a revolution; they successfully drew on the rituals and beliefs of Shi'ism to consolidate power after the overthrow of the Pahlavi monarchy and establish a theocracy in Iran.

Drawn to writing about Safavi social and cultural history, I had nevertheless been restricted to materials available either in print or in manuscripts housed in European libraries. Because I was unable to conduct research in Iran, these sources shaped my exploration of sovereignty and heresy in the Safavi Empire. Having recourse to court chronicles and religious treatises, I dove into accounts of popular revolts and became sensitive to the tensions that punctuated the dominant narratives as I considered these "official" sources alongside epics and poetry to gain access to the worldview of the subjects of Safavi Iran. I was of course reliant on the mediating voices of historians, clerics, poets, and storytellers to speak for the monarch, the mystic, or the messiah.

Fourteen years later, I was sitting in the University of Tehran Library reading manuscripts in a country transformed by a social revolution. Noticing the habits and gestures of the staff librarians and other readers, I was struck by how social change manifested itself in body language, in idioms of speech, and in the mannerisms of a population that had just undergone a rather different Shi'a revolution from the one I studied. Intent on finding a range of voices, I read through manuscript catalogs to see what kinds of sources had survived beyond those produced by the institutions of the imperial court and the religious seminary. It was at this point that I came across anthologies, *majmu'a*s, literally "gathered together." Anthologies are traditionally understood to be compilations of poetry or diplomatic epistles, so as I read through the catalog compiled by Muhammad Taqi Danishpazhu, the doyen of manuscript studies, I was baffled to see contents that included personal letters, essays, wills, freedom papers, and other miscellanea. Clearly these *majmu'a*s did not correspond to the anthology taxonomy I had heard of. Puzzled and fascinated by their range of content, I wondered then whether these anthologies would be the archive from which a social and cultural history of the Safavi world could be written.

That summer of 1993, I began collecting the anthologies housed in the Tehran University, Majlis, Malik, and Sipahsalar libraries, a task that has taken me nearly two decades over various visits to Iran. I began assembling my photocopied archive, printed on paper I had purchased at the bazaar, before graduating eventually to digitized facsimiles, unaware that I was mimicking the process of knowledge production that had generated those anthologies in the Safavi capital, Isfahan (1593–1722), albeit using new technology to assemble my own collection.

A daunting task lay before me. What were these anthologies? Who produced and preserved them? How were they made, and for what purpose? The process of writing this history of Isfahan has been far from smooth. Confused and lost in the multitude of subjects assembled in anthologies, I limited my research to Isfahan and the seventeenth century, when most of the extant anthologies were assembled. At least 5,000 *majmu'a*s from Isfahan in that period are cataloged in major libraries in Tehran alone. Many more are extant in private family collections and provincial libraries. Hundreds are cataloged in the libraries of Turkey, France, Germany, the Netherlands, and the United Kingdom. Others are just now being cataloged in American university libraries, such as at the University of Michigan, which houses nineteen seventeenth-century Persian *majmu'a*s. Before I could say anything about them, I had to read *majmu'a*s to get a sense of the range of material, the paleography, and the paper assembled in these collections. I have surveyed about 500 *majmu'a*s through their table of contents in printed manuscript catalogs and have closely read through several hundred others. I was lucky to be able to confer with three of the most prominent manuscript specialists who were alive during the last three decades:

Muhammad Taqi Danishpazhu, Abdul Husayn Haeri, and Iraj Afshar. They generously shared their thoughts on these anthologies, which they had cataloged for the various manuscript collections at the Tehran University, Majlis, and Malik libraries.

My graduate students, Derek Mancini-Lander, Golriz Farshi, and Shahla Farghadani, have helped me sift through some of the *majmuʿa*s during the past years in research collaboration projects. At present, together with fellow historian Nozhat Ahmadi and her graduate students at the University of Isfahan, I have begun the vast project of collecting and generating tables of contents for numerous cataloged anthologies housed in the capital's most prominent public libraries—at Majlis, Malik, Milli, and Tehran University. We have been indexing the various genres of texts included in each. Adapting our work to include reconnaissance, we have taken careful account of the content and organization of these miscellanies and have considered eventually creating a Safavi website where fellow scholars across the world may freely have access to these rich Persianate-world sources.

My dear colleague Massumeh Farhad first drew our attention to the singularity of seventeenth-century Safavi "single-page paintings." Local Isfahan artists composed these illustrations for a market of merchants and artisans who participated in the economy of the manuscript. It is thanks to the practice of collecting that they have survived. These drawings or paintings on single sheets were assembled into albums, called *muraqqaʿ*s (literally "patchwork"), during the eighteenth and nineteenth centuries, and then the *muraqqaʿ*s were torn apart and the individual paintings sold on the international auction market. Today, thousands of these paintings are housed in museums throughout the world and continue to be sold through auction houses such as Christie's and Sotheby's. Thanks to the visual archive that Farhad has amassed, I was able to bring the *muraqqaʿ* into conversation with the *majmuʿa* to think about the contemporaneous production of both verbal and visual anthologies. Massumeh Farhad's knowledge of the arts, together with her friendship, have nurtured my work. She has taught me how to read Safavi images and sent me drawings and paintings to cultivate my palate, feed my appetite, and help assemble my archive to better visualize the cultural dynamics of seventeenth-century Isfahan. Her grace and generosity have sprinkled the pages of this book with gold ink.

The City as Anthology is a long-term collaborative project that has involved many beloved friends. My writing group, the charmed circle of Artemis Leontis, Peggy McCracken, Yopie Prins, and Elizabeth Wingrove, taught me how to write for a broader academic public. With bounty they opened their hearts, their homes, and their minds to me. Although words cannot capture my gratitude, I thank you, dear friends, for your difficult questions, your curiosity, and your unwavering support during our journeys in writing, despite our crazy schedules and the vicissitudes of our lives. Valerie Traub has been an invaluable colleague and mentor from the moment we met at Vanderbilt University. Her generosity, her rigor and critical reading of my manuscript, and her insights and provocative scholarship on gender and sexuality have sharpened and challenged my "thinking sex" with seventeenth-century Isfahanis. Helmut Puff first turned me onto Alan Bray's book *The Friend*, introducing me to this stunning history of friendships in England. He has witnessed multiple stages of this book's unfolding, as we climbed mountains, walked cities, visited museums, and spent many nights in conversation about Isfahan. These precious experiences, enlivened by his depth of knowledge and refined sensibilities, fill the pages of my anthological thinking. Wadad Abed, Will Glover, Huda Karaman-Rosen, and Farina Mir have been my cherished interlocutors all the way through. They showered me with their love, wisdom, music, and delicious meals as I ventured through *The City as Anthology*. These collective gifts of friendship have carried me through the writing of this book.

To my dear colleagues, students, and friends Sebouh Aslanian, Marie Aude Baronian, Maya Barzilai, Shahzad Bashir, Yoni Brack, Craig Breckenridge, Erdem Cipa, Cameron Cross, Kobra Eghtedary, Daniela Gobetti, Gottfried Hagen, Val Kievelson, Paul Losensky, Karla Mallette, Gülru Necipoğlu-Kafadar, Michael Pifer, Amanda Respess, Janet Richards, Muhammad Sarraf, Melanie Tanielian, Terry Wilfong, and the late Michael Bonner, who left us way too soon, thank you for your encouragement and intellectual engagement.

The process of preparing a manuscript for publication is always a tedious task. Without the help of Isabel de Rezende and the editors at Stanford University Press, this book would have not taken its precise shape. I am grateful to the two anonymous reviewers whose comments and questions have made for a tighter and more cogently argued book. My special thanks go out to Kate Wahl, Editor-in-Chief of Stanford University Press, for her faith in this project and for her invaluable guidance in this process.

I would like to acknowledge the generous institutional support I received from the University of Michigan over the years to bring to conclusion *The City as*

Anthology: Spring/Summer Research Grants from the Horace Rackham Graduate School; the College of Literature, Science, and Arts Michigan Humanities Award; the Associate Professors Support Fund; the Institute for the Humanities Fellowship; the Eisenberg Institute for Historical Studies Fellowship; and the Richard Hudson Research Professorship Award from the Department of History, which provided me with a precious semester to bring the project to a close.

My deepest gratitude goes out to my parents, who have witnessed, with unconditional love, my long labor on *The City as Anthology*. I am blessed with a mother and father who have been pillars of strength and courage, even as they lost their country, their home, and their son. I dedicate this book to my father, Hask Babayan, who passed away a few months before its completion. He was an elegant human being, generous and empathetic; this book is a gift of my love in honor of his life and legacy.

Kathryn Babayan
Paris, France

NOTE ON TRANSLITERATION

I am using a simplified version of the transliteration system adopted by the *International Journal of Middle East Studies* (IJMES) to make the Persian language more accessible for a broader readership. All diacritical marks are omitted, except for the *'ayn* (') and the *hamza* ('). The Persian silent *h* is transliterated as *a*, (e.g., *nama* or *qahva*). The Persian *izafa* is rendered as *-i* (or *-yi* in words ending in silent *h* or a vowel). More common names such as Abbas, Ali, and Jafar are spelled without an *'ayn*, but less common proper names such as 'Itiqad Khan and 'Imad Khan include it. Commonly used English words are spelled following English conventions such as sharia, Shi'a, Ka'ba, and hookah. Nisbas follow the standard English spelling of place names such as I'jaz Herati, not Harati (Herat), and Aqa Mansur Semnani, not Simnani (Semnan). When Quranic terms or Arabic titles appear, they are written using modified IJMES guidelines for Arabic without diacritics, such as Khalifat al-Khulafa. I use the Persian name *Safavi* for the dynasty instead of the anglicized *Safavid*. When two dates are given, the first is the lunar *hijri* calendar followed by the Gregorian equivalent. All translations are mine unless otherwise noted.

The City as Anthology

INTRODUCTION

The *Adab* of Urbanity

Encountering the City

The history of a city can be written in infinite ways. Histories of early modern Isfahan have portrayed the city through its institutions and through its nodal function at the intersection of the arts, politics, and trade, linking it to larger imperial and global networks.[1] Isfahan's monuments and built environment—the palace, the mosque, and the religious seminary—have been privileged sites and sources in the writing of its history. Scholars have examined the Dutch East India Company archives to foreground Isfahan's political economy and the silk trade that linked the city to Europe.[2] Mercantile documents, letters, and the business correspondence of Armenian merchants from Isfahan's suburb of New Julfa connect networks of merchant families trading in Iranian silk, Indian textiles, and gems to an early modern global economy. Historians have mined these commercial documents to study the trading habits and practices that sustained a network of Julfan Armenian merchants from Madras to Manila in the east and Venice and Amsterdam to the west.[3] More recently, a multifaceted approach has focused on Georgian and Armenian slave converts to Islam who became governors and court functionaries in the Safavi imperial household. These slave elites have been studied as agents of centralization, because they were engaged in building the political and cultural life of the city through their patronage of the arts, architecture, and trade.[4]

The City as Anthology explores Isfahan through the lens of seventeenth-century anthologies. Thousands of manuscripts produced in Isfahan assembled household objects ranging from portraits and letters from friends to poems depicting the central square, marriage contracts, and talismans. Authors collected, curated, and bound together material generated by the culture of *adab*, or etiquette and conduct, to learn how to act and relate to other residents of a diverse and ever-growing capital city. The anthology, itself a medium of communication, was a new kind of book. In Persian it was called a *majmuʻa* (from the Arabic root *j.m.ʻ*), literally "gathered together," which assembled verbal texts, or a *muraqqaʻ* (from the Arabic root *r.q.ʻ*), or "patchwork," which collected visual texts. In this book I read both the *majmuʻa* and the *muraqqaʻ* as collections of city life. Both pedagogical and experiential, these visual and verbal texts anthologize the city; they preserve the material artifacts of city encounters and the conditions of communication that bring the urban scenery into focus. Moreover, anthologies accumulate histories of friendship alongside individual and family histories. They enliven the cityscape with their personal stories of love, fear and betrayal, and loss that map the emotional topography of Isfahan.

Anthologizers—as far as we know, all of them male—compiled manuals of composition and rhetoric, model letters, drawings and paintings, and essays and poems that they encountered through networks of friends, bringing together different genres to learn and take pleasure from within the domestic realm of their households. Collected in the intimate space of the home, anthologies helped fashion, and in turn were shaped by, urban sensibilities. Although authorship of anthologies was a male prerogative, the practice of anthologizing linked families of male and female readers and personally implicated them in Isfahan's culture. By archiving family histories, anthologies document how members forged social and affective bonds with kin and with friends, acts that made the city legible for themselves. Anthologies helped residents write their own place in the city or communicate the city's splendors to those not living in Isfahan, making their own journeys through its sprawling quarters legible today.

The history of *reading* the city as text goes back to Roland Barthes's engagement with urban semiotics and Kevin Lynch's visual modeling of the city as an image perceived by its residents.[5] For Barthes, the city speaks to its inhabitants in a language that becomes legible through sociability. Lynch, on the other hand, develops his concept of legibility in the relationship between the subject and the society as it is made and remade through the process of perceiving, conceiving, mapping, and moving through urban spaces.[6] I borrow Lynch's language of urban imageability and legibility to read Isfahan through the heuristic of the anthology, or fragmentary city readings assembled by residents into a codex. In addition to reading, I argue that seeing, desiring, and writing are entangled modalities of encounter that allowed residents to experience the city and to anthologize the city in complementary ways. In *The City as Anthology* I investigate how the verbal and the visual cultivate the senses to affect urbanity; residents read texts in circulation, curated them, and then wrote their own crafted works to display their city knowledge. Anthologies constitute spaces of assembly, gatherings of dispersed city texts reinscribed by authors and scribes into a manuscript. Through words and images residents in Isfahan wrote the city and performed their social relations. Their habits of collecting objects of *adab*, texts that taught them social etiquette and sexual conduct, expose city practices and can be seen as artifacts of Isfahan's urbanization as a capital. More than artifactual, the anthology is agentive. As a product of urban aesthetic, the anthology generates ways of desiring the beauty of the city of Isfahan, shaping and being shaped by styles and manners of urbanity. The intimately intertwined acts of seeing, reading, writing, and desiring the city recursively reproduce the anthology, the household, and the author in distinct and often contradictory ways.

By way of seventeenth-century anthologies, my history of Isfahan concentrates on the city as a space of urban knowledge production beyond the institution of the imperial court and the Shi'a religious establishment, which were two vital centers of training and transmission.[7] Linking practices of reading the city together with modes of writing in the city, the anthologies draw on the dissemination of urban knowledge. Like David Henkin's work on Antebellum New York in his *City Reading*, my study literally reads the surfaces of Isfahan's domes and murals to explore the roles of the written word along with the figural in the urban experience. To access the various ways in which residents imagined their relationships to city spaces, Henkin's reading of the city focuses on *actual* texts, such as newspapers, banners, and posters that take material form on the stage of public life.[8] The traffic between monumental inscriptions and writings on paper collected in anthologies is key to my understanding of how residents of Isfahan made sense of their city in a practical way. Deploying different agencies and scales involved in the act of seeing the city helps to shed light on how residents learned to read and rewrite their own experience of Isfahan. We can read monumental epigraphy, or calligraphic inscriptions on the walls and domes of mosques, to comprehend the political-religious discourse produced by the Safavi court and the Shi'a religious establishment, but we must read anthologies to understand how the imperial discourse was woven into the lived practices of Isfahan's inhabitants. Anthologies are tools for understanding state-sponsored forms of urbanity, because they are artifacts for working out ways of living in the city that negotiated with or even explicitly contested the ideal city.

Anthologies locate Isfahan's households within the urban morphology. However, generated and then collected and assembled in the interior spaces of the house, many anthologies were objects fashioned with the precise intent of traversing the spaces *between* households—as letters, paintings, and gifts. These objects were assembled in private homes and ultimately collected in households, but their first-order purpose was to forge connections outside the household. What is being archived is a record of the household's life *outside* the confines of the house. This is what makes these collections simultaneously domestic and urban—they are a record of the complex symbiosis of life in Isfahan. For the circulation of letters and paintings, I exploit what Janet Abu-Lughod has called semiprivate space.[9] Abu-Lughod was referring to features of the urban morphology and the social practices that defined them. The practice of letter and gift exchange or the performance of desire in the bazaar is found rather explicitly on the margins between public and private space. Moreover, these practices deliberately blur the distinction between the two spaces. Anthologies give us clues about how to read (make meaning out of) public monuments or spaces in personal ways—or manners that are significant for the household and its members.

Certainly, the word and the city share a long and connected history. Since the early formation of Mesopotamian city-states, the written word has been deployed to tally agricultural surplus. The very foundation of the city was contingent, in part, on the verbal. I initially focus on monumental epigraphy, designs, and paintings found on the domes and walls of the city of Isfahan; these images affected not only what residents saw but also how they read, learned to desire, and write the city. The scripting of a new program of monumental epigraphy, whereby the court and the mosque inscribed their power onto the built environment, familiarized residents with images as words and words as image(s). Blurring the verbal and the visual, Isfahan's animated surfaces solicited the gaze and authorized engagement, inciting residents and visitors to participate in its beauty. My anthologizing of Isfahan is part of this critical genealogy of city reading.[10]

The City of Isfahan

The City as Anthology tells the story of Isfahan at a moment of creation of the new capital center set in motion by Shah Abbas I (r. 1587–1629), thus laying the conditions for the making of an imperial city of rule and global trade. Writing and painting on walls and paper distributed different scales of literacy in the Safavi capital (1593–1722) during the early modern era of urbanization and state formation, which in Isfahan was contingent on the city's conversion to Shi'ism.[11] Isfahan's new urbanism attracted talent, labor, and knowledge and incited cultural production across different forms and media. This authoritative moment provides a unique context from which to investigate the mutual shaping of the social, cultural, and religious spheres of a city in transformation.

Residents and travelers to Isfahan would have been struck by the volume of traffic as well as by the vibrant turquoise, lapis, and yellow tiles of its domes and portals, the minarets of its mosques, the floral paintings on the walls of storefronts surrounding the main square and entrance to the bazaar, and especially the ubiquitous presence of the written word. Epigraphs, such as those engraved in stone exempting barbers and bathhouse employees from taxes, emblazoned the walls and domes of mosques and were visible at eye level. The ever-present medium of writing cultivated a visual aesthetic and transmitted a sense of urbane civility. Placed outside, in open spaces, the prevailing public function of epigraphy was to solicit the gaze and educate spectators as they moved through the city. With its use of monumental writing authorizing conversion to Shi'ism and encouraging innovative aesthetic forms of calligraphy and tilework developed by Isfahan's artists and artisans, this epigraphic program had a determining influence on the capital's visual culture. The use of symbolic Quranic calligraphy was a visible instrument of communication that spoke to residents with multiple registers of literacy. Graphic letters naming Allah, the prophet Muhammad, and the Shi'a Imam Ali in geometric shapes became legible icons even for the unlettered (Figure 0.1). Verses in Arabic from the Quran and Persian love poetry that evoked the garden of paradise filled the space around the new city square, known as the Naqsh-i Jahan, or "image of the world." These were accompanied by colorful paintings depicting the beauty and erotic pleasures of the "abode of the blessed" populated by delightful female and male youths. This practice of blurring letters with figures created images that infused the urban space with symbols of the divine, especially on the domes, archways, and

FIGURE 0.1 Interior wall and honeycomb arch of the new Friday Prayer Mosque inscribed with the Arabic phrase *Subhan Allah* (Glory be to Allah) on the top diamond and *Allah* on the bottom diamond of the arch. Photo by Kathryn Babayan.

walls of the central square. Carved in large calligraphic script (*thulth*) visible from the ground, the meanings of verses depicting paradise were supplemented with painted images of the heavenly garden on the arcade walls. Eroticism was inscribed into the Naqsh-i Jahan, central to the experience of Isfahan, which placed the cultivation of the sensory as a requisite for learning how to read the city square.

The bazaar and the mosque, the two lungs of a Muslim city, were separated in Isfahan by a vast open space bounded by an arcade with 200 storefronts (Figure 0.2). Developed in 1590, the Naqsh-i Jahan was designed to orient the medieval city along a new axis; it would become the site of a revolution in the function of urban outdoor spaces.[12] *Naqsh* refers to "design," in both the figurative and verbal senses of engraving and intent, and is often associated with a sheet of paper. Authors and poets came to understand the new central square as the surface of a page, a blank sheet of paper, reading a range of possibilities into its composition. Much like a scribe, the Safavi king Shah Abbas I wrote the space for his city center from dust to be flattened and filled with verbal and visual texts for his residents to experience. The double entendre in its name, *naqsh*, also cleverly links the paintings on the walls of its arcade and the bazaar entrance (Qaysariyya) to the Quranic verses, creating an analogy between rectangular space and a sheet of paper. Images and words inscribe erotic sights and rewards along the walls of the square to create paradise on earth. Fully exposed to the light of day, these elements made "the image of the world" manifest as an array of legible power scripted in calligraphic symbols of the divine across the surfaces of this new square.

FIGURE 0.2 Panoramic view of the Naqsh-i Jahan square looking toward the Qaysariyya Bazaar (facing the viewer) to the Imperial Gate (left), the Shaykh Lufullah Mosque (right), and the new Friday Prayer Mosque (vantage point of the photographer). Photo by Mohammad Sarraf.

Expressed in an idiom that drew on the Sufi discourse of love and beauty, these verbal and visual productions moved from a metaphoric space of the garden to that of the city, the new urban space where paradise was to be lived. Sufi epistemology imagines the body as the microcosm, the macrocosm as the universe, and the garden as the space that acts as a mediating heuristic between the two.[13] Once Isfahan was configured as paradise, it had to appropriate the rhetorical figure of a garden, with its metaphorical logic of excess, for spiritual union with the divine to be manifest. Much like the metaphor of the garden, Isfahan became the site of extravagance and abundance, the extension of the divine, to be desired and recognized in all its bounty and potential. As the producer of *adab*, Isfahan drew subjects, men and women from different regions and backgrounds, into the urban agential sphere to fulfill its promise, as though beckoning residents to inscribe pomp and exaggeration onto the blank folios of an anthology, and thereby to redefine, satirize, and disturb the urbane endeavor. It is not surprising, then, that writing also underwent a transformation, moving from epigraphy and the media of stone and ceramics to the realm of paper, which could then be assembled into household anthologies. Both monumental public writing and the more intimate process of writing on paper point to a larger cultural trend whereby the world was captured in poetry, calligraphy, and painting in historically and materially recognizable ways.

Passing by a commanding five-story royal building at the entry of the palace complex, a spectator would see the golden dome of a private royal mosque that signaled the intimate relationship between politics and religion. At Friday prayer, artisans, merchants, and shoppers walked from the bazaar across the 1,840-foot span of public space, where an urban economy of piety, pleasure, and politics flowed under the gaze of court and mosque. To the south, they faced a magnificent tiled portal of the first Friday Prayer Mosque inscribed with a famous testimony from the prophet Muhammad: "I am the city of knowledge and Ali is its gate."[14] Flanked by two minarets, this architectural masterpiece was built to proclaim Shi'ism as the religion of the Safavi Empire. Shah Abbas I appointed the Shi'a scholar Shaykh Baha'i (d. 1621) chief religious dignitary, the Shaykh al-Islam of Isfahan. Together the shah and the shaykh worked closely to cultivate and assemble a Muslim community of Sunni and Shi'a residents in Isfahan. The shaykh's role was to help bolster the shah's legitimacy and devise a communal platform for the inclusion of Sunni and Shi'a followers in worship. Residents of Isfahan, who were mostly Sunni, were enticed to participate in the fashioning of a singular religious collective. Shaykh Baha'i succeeded in popularizing the Shi'a religion; as part of his conversion strategy, he composed in Persian the *Jami'-i 'Abbasi* (Abbas's Collective), a manual on proper etiquette and religious obligations that highlighted shared Sunni and Shi'a rituals and beliefs.[15] In this manual he encouraged the majority Sunni population of Isfahan to enter a new communal space of worship that would, over the *longue durée*, educate and convert them to Shi'ism. Shaykh Baha'i composed the epigraphic program on the mosque's interior walls calling all worshippers of Allah to enter through the gate of Ali and pray in a hall inscribed with stories legitimizing the succession of Ali as the friend of God and Muhammad's vice-regent. By turning this Friday Prayer Mosque into a public record of how religion would elevate believers and strengthen the Shah's sovereignty, Shaykh Baha'i transformed the mosque into a space of collective worship.

The vast open space at the epicenter of Shah Abbas I's imperial creation was flattened and then covered with sand from the Zayanda-rud, the life-giving river, to stage polo games, horse races, fireworks, and mock battles against the Uzbeks, both neighbors and enemies of the Safavis. Shah Abbas I visibly flaunted his authority so that inhabitants might witness his spectacular power in the space of the central square. Commerce and traffic were engineered to flow from the medieval Seljuk center, with its markets and Friday Prayer Mosque, through the tunneled alleys of a new bazaar that opened onto the northern corner of the Naqsh-i Jahan. The bazaar rivaled not only the old commercial enterprises of the medieval city but also the regional bazaar of Tabriz, the former Mongol (Ilkhanid) capital situated on the axis of a vibrant east-west trade. Isfahan's bazaar would make Tabriz's marketplace look provincial.[16] The shah's project transformed the built environment, because he also brought merchants from Tabriz to Isfahan; they would change the physiognomy of the city as a result of this high-end migration. The forced migration of Tabrizi merchants and later Armenian silk merchants (in 1605) to Isfahan ensured the centrality of the capital in the growing global market for Iranian silk.[17] Tabrizi merchants were relocated thanks to the patronage of the shah, who ordered his chief treasurer, Muhibb Ali Beg, to build them a residential suburb named after the king, Abbasabad (the abode of Abbas), where 500 houses were constructed.[18] And for the Armenian merchant community, the shah developed a suburb on the banks of the Zayanda River: New Julfa, which was erected and named after their native city razed by the Shah's forces.

The transformation of Isfahan's built environment gave material form to new media and affective ties that, I argue, were bound together in anthologies. The imaginations that anthologizing produced and the choices behind the gathering, excerpting, recording, and ordering of texts represent different techniques of interpreting the city; they reveal a place where, among other things, the refined self was crafted on paper and performed in public. As the male collector curated sentences and verses from known works of poetry and prose, he wrote his own composition. Flaunting their erudition, residents schooled in the ways of urban *adab* actively engaged in inscribing themselves in their city. Generic experimentation with preexisting literary forms generated new compositions that melded verse with prose, mixing media and tropes together, just as it helped to translate the language of mystical love into one of urbane friendship. For instance, modes and moods embedded in the omnipresent form of the Persian *ghazal*,[19] or love poetry, were adapted to compose the prose letter to friends. Likewise, the entire cityscape became the arena of desire for the city disturber (*shahrashub*) to write about the coffeehouse, the hammam, or the central square as erotic spaces of sociability.[20] The discoursing city licensed creative acts of crafting texts and reinscribing the city in the anthology, which helps us think about the material history of writing and illustrating from a less imperial perspective. As this book reveals, urban practices related to seeing, reading, desiring, and writing were intimately related and mutually co-constitutive, informing both the lived experience of the city and its (re)assembly as domestic anthology.

The multiplication of materials for writing in and about the city is crucial to the curation of the urban self. Writing on paper entails attention to knowledge production, whereas the assembly of folios into anthologies represents different ways of desiring and seeing the city. To probe the materiality of the history of collecting, we must unpack the relationship between urban transformations and the collected experiences of city residents. First, the production of paper as a medium of communication changed the way literature and the visual arts were composed and consumed. In Isfahan paper was produced from rags, making it affordable and more readily available. Paper became the foundation of a new culture of literacy, driven in particular by the needs of an expanding and centralizing state, which required the documentation of revenues from lands (*tiyul*) granted to governors and their retinues in lieu of salaries. An economic boom generated a demand for paper to produce letters of credit, contracts, and account books that would catalog trade for a growing group of merchants—Isfahani, Tabrizi, Armenian, and Indian buyers, sellers, and agents in regional and global trade.[21] In turn, the practice of documenting benefited the literary and visual arts, because gains from trade allowed prospering merchant and craftsmen to engage in the *adab* of urbanity as authors, patrons, and collectors.

By the second half of the seventeenth century, Isfahan's population had grown to about half a million residents. According to French jeweler Jean Baptiste Chardin, Isfahan was one of the biggest metropoles he had traveled to in Europe and Asia, equal in size to London.[22] The resettlement of at least 6,000 merchant families from the two cities of Tabriz and Old Julfa, in addition to the city's draw as a new center of commerce for craftsmen, painters, poets, and students of religion, helped to produce a diverse mix of residents. Once Isfahan became established as the empire's political center, for the first time in Safavi history the entire court as well as the provincial governors built residences in the capital. If by the end of the seventeenth century the Armenian suburb grew to house 6,000 families, with a population of 30,000 inhabitants and twelve churches, the entire city of Isfahan must have experienced a similar doubling of its population.[23]

Isfahan was not just a center of an empire. It was an ideal city—to which residents, old and new, attached their sense of belonging. How did the rapid increase and mixing of populations from different confessional, sectarian, and linguistic backgrounds lead Isfahan's residents to encounter and relate to one another? Relying on new media of communication, strangers to the city assembled tools with which to connect in the making of shared and familiar experiences.

The Anthology

To participate in Isfahan's fashionable circles, men had to be versed in the culture of *adab*, a set of rules of conduct and behaviors—etiquette—that defined proper comportment through gestures and words. The Safavi court and the Shi'a clerical establishment were the impresarios of this adabizing project. As court and mosque joined forces to centralize power in Isfahan and convert residents to Shi'ism, manuals on proper social and sexual conduct, speech, and writing proliferated in unprecedented ways. Conduct and etiquette manuals, themselves the products of literacy, simultaneously produced knowledge among those who wished to advance their status. In other words, even as court and mosque deployed such manuals as disciplinary technologies, cultural how-to guides that refined and defined courtly culture, they engendered verbal and visual literacy *across* class lines.

I argue that the history of reception that the anthologies represent was integral to the state-sponsored adabizing project and the varying subjectivities it produced. Although conversion entailed the distribution of manuals that sought to discipline its subjects and control their conduct and speech, manuals also fashioned urban sensibilities. Moreover, verbal and visual products of *adab* were part of a whole range of anthologies, subjective knowledge production, and literacies attained by individual and household collectors. The letters, poetry, stories, and drawings that the anthologies stitched together point to *adab* objects shared by communities of literacy in Isfahan; they give us a sense of the household reader who encountered these diverse connected pieces, fragment by fragment, page by page, as a discrete book. Such acts of collecting and reading connect the literate experience to the spectacle of public life, shaping communication and the performance of a new urbanity that fashioned affective communities who created the city.

Every medium of communication has distinct protocols and usage styles. To embody Isfahan's urbanity, the culture of *adab* had to be learned and performed in the elite, artisan, and merchant sectors of a society in the making. Consumers of etiquette-based ideals cultivated the habits of collecting *adab* objects. Letters, proper conduct manuals, and portraits were pedagogical tools with symbolic capital for residents who aspired to participate in the creation of the new urbanism of Isfahan.[24] As a result, the agency of residents in drawing and writing, and, by extension, the author's purpose and audience, began to broaden and diversify. For example, no longer was writing limited to students or scribes copying manuscripts as functions of religious authorization, memorization, and courtly legitimacy; rather, writers wrote, copied, and collected as household author.[25] Elite households also hired their own scribes, who would procure texts in circulation for their patrons and preserve them for the family archive. However, many households did not have the means to hire scribes, so men wrote and authored their own anthologies. Occasionally male patrons and scribes are named in anthologies, but most remain anonymous.[26] They represent a range of households in Isfahan and demonstrate the breadth and popularity of these interlaced *adab* practices.

My research indicates multiple practices of collecting, copying, authoring, and producing anthologies, although the full scope of anthologizing practices found in seventeenth-century Isfahan remains to be studied by the next generation. Certainly, for seventeenth-century Isfahan, anthologies are unique sources that bring people's lives into view. This is particularly important for a city with no extant state or city archives. The rich variety of habits of collecting expose the professional and personal lives of households and their ties to generations of city life.[27] Thus part of my work here is to use anthologies to map the social space of the household in Isfahan. Characteristic of some anonymous anthologies is the legibility of the author's profession, where he records the kinds of material he uses at work. Consider, for example, the anonymous anthology belonging to a religious judge. The author collects legal documents in Persian with Arabic formulas for marriage, divorce, sales, and rent contracts—tools he used to settle the everyday cases brought before him. Along with these documents, the judge also penned a talisman to protect the health of his ailing child (Figure 0.3).[28] It is only once we turn to folio 50v of this anthology

FIGURE 0.3 The folio from the *majmu'a* belonging to Kazim the judge. Several talismans are recorded in the bottom left margin, one of which is to break the fever of a sick child. Malik Library, MS 2551.

that the name of a woman, Jahan Banu, appears in the margins. With her own hand, she identifies herself as Kazim's daughter and gifts the anthology to her son.[29] The identity of the author is revealed by his daughter, who probably inherited this anthology. Anthologists such as judge Kazim gathered their professional tools into a manuscript and mobilized devices with which to work, socialize, and behave in the city. The public life of this collector-judge Kazim is inscribed alongside his familial concerns. Although his daughter Jahan Banu did not author the anthology, she partook in the household practice of anthologizing, inheriting, and then passing her work on to her son, who himself might have learned from it and made use of its contents as an aspiring judge.[30]

Anthologies were composed of both words (*majmuʿa*) and images (*muraqqaʿ*), and although verbal and visual compositions were not bound together in an anthology, paintings and drawings were probably collected separately in households and preserved in large envelopes depicted in miniature paintings. How are we to read these two verbal and visual texts collectively? In my project I break with past approaches by bringing the understudied object of the *majmuʿa* into conversation with the *muraqqaʿ*. In the eighteenth and nineteenth centuries collectors bound together into the *muraqqaʿ* dispersed paintings and drawings that had been purchased by seventeenth-century merchants and artisans who participated in the economy of *adab* in Isfahan.[31] Drawn on single sheets of paper, illustrations could be purchased or commissioned by clients directly from the painter. Ink drawings certainly sold for a lower price than those painted with color. Many were executed with quick strokes of the pen and capture a range of urban characters drawn for a socially diverse audience. All types were portrayed—from craftsmen to dervishes and scholars—and all were representations of the men who lived and worked in Isfahan. Female subjects were sometimes depicted, but they were far fewer than male subjects. Purchased by residents from different walks of life, or gifted by artists to their friends, these images are quintessential city readings. Like words curated by authors of the *majmuʿa*s, these illustrations are images that interpret the city. Artists and clients were particularly interested in male portraits or in portraits of couples who modeled urbane gestures and postures of intimacy and sexual desire. A particular subject of collector fascination was the act of reading: male figures posing with a letter, a poem, a book, or a talisman, as in Figure 0.4. I interpret these images alongside verbal anthologies to demonstrate the different ways that Isfahan

FIGURE 0.4 A man holding a recipe for a talisman in his hand. It is signed by Muʿin Musavvir and dated 1663; whereabouts unknown.

can be seen as scenes of desire to be read and then written. They provide material evidence for the relationships between literacy, collecting, and didacticism. Together, these verbal and visual productions ground my analysis of how Isfahan's urbanity transformed the communication of social relations.

Artists and authors were keenly aware of the historical moment they inhabited. Consequently, their work bears the mark of their time. The Persian words *taza* (fresh) and *vuquʻi* (realistic) are commonly ascribed to the chronicling of history and the composition of poetry in seventeenth-century Isfahan.[32] Anthologies compiled by authors or their scribes show cognizance of the novel act of assembling household collections, just as artists knew they were creating something new on a sheet of paper, independent of the royal atelier. Free of courtly conventions around the narrative arts of the manuscript, artists could sell their work on the market. Although earlier artists did sell work in the bazaar, in seventeenth-century Isfahan many made this their primary means of livelihood. The turn to portraiture (*surat*) in painting and the naming of the beloved in poetry (*maktab-i vuquʻi*), is, I argue, correlated with the social economy of trade and *adab*, which established a clientele of collectors who valued *adab* objects and who could afford to acquire them. This turn to historicity, clearly evident in the *majmuʻa* and *muraqqaʻ*, brings Isfahan's population into distinct, even intimate, focus.

This study, which combines historiographies of the book with scholarship on urban space, intervenes in contemporary discussions about experience and materiality from the vantage point of gender and sexuality. The written word has been privileged as the site of literacy in the medieval Arabic-speaking world across a number of works that focus on histories of the manuscript or that study reading practices which connected social networks to knowledge production.[33] Literacy in these works is centered on writing, reading, and the materiality of the manuscript. But literacy is a complex matter. It was not just those who owned or had access to pen, ink, and paper and who had a gift for scribing who were literate. Lack of writing skills did not preclude one's ability to recognize, compose, or engage in the magical and auratic public presence of the word. In the chapters that follow I demonstrate how the broader habits of anthologizing intersected with urban practices of reading, seeing, desiring, and writing the city. By interpolating its differently inscribed surfaces, the city solicited the gaze, because it taught residents how to read and recognize new forms of sociability. I analyze script on the walls and domes of mosques as well as decrees engraved in stone and displayed to the urban community as creating a particular effect of sensory legibility, linking the creation of anthologies to the production of the city. The sensory and sensual stimulation of Isfahan's visual and verbal culture fostered an ethics and aesthetics of respectability, fashioning Safavi subjects into urbane and sexual selves, who in turn desired, performed, and read the beauty of the capital city of Isfahan.

The *Adab* of Friendship

The City as Anthology reads Isfahan's conversion to Shi'ism alongside its physical and cultural expansion through the anthologizing practices by which residents declared and performed their urbanity. The prohibitions against adultery (*zina'*) and sodomy (*livat*), along with brothels and wine bars, communicated the Safavi shahs' and the Shi'a religious establishment's power to enforce sharia law. Public documents signaling these proscriptions were meant to achieve order and discipline; they were visible words intended to regulate sexuality and sociability in Isfahan's various urban spaces—in bathhouses and brothels and in the streets. Just as the capital city's physical renovations generated new social formations, they also transformed affective ties between those in authority and their subjects. The social becomes a productive analytic for interpreting the transformation of the city beyond its symbolic and urbanistic features. Mystical registers of *adab* were being translated onto new urban forms of sociability, and this translation—or to put it differently, this conversion—from mystic love to urban love in the seventeenth century is documented in abundance by anthologies. In fact, the spirit-body bond between lovers and beloveds was appropriated and applied to wide-ranging performances of amity and sovereignty in the broader contexts of the city, the court, the bazaar, the hammam, and the coffeehouse. In the setting of an emerging urbanism, this new *adab* of urbanity required the cultivation of rituals and habits for communicating with other refined subjects; residents had to learn urbane mannerisms in gesture and gaze.

The ethics of friendship were of particular concern to the court and the mosque, because friends were the building blocks of sociability and community. Mystic rituals of love, desiring eros, and obedience were deployed by the court to discipline Isfahan's social order. We can visually see on a mural in the Forty Pillars Palace an image of Shah Abbas I as the beloved (see Figure 1.3). He holds the central gaze, with a wine cup in hand, while his novices are being initiated into his court through corporal punishment; they are struck by the stick of the Safavi mystical order, the *chub-i tariqat*.[34] Three decades after his death Shah Abbas I is remembered on the palace walls as the mystic cupbearer. Neither Shah Ismail (d. 1524), the messianic founder of the dynasty, nor his son Shah Tahmasb (d. 1576), the mystic lover of Ali, are cast with wine cup in hand. The imperial story narrated on the walls of the Audience Hall confirms a genealogy that had been contested during the first century of Safavi rule. Shah Abbas I is memorialized for having put an end to the second civil war (1587–1592), quashing the Nuqtavi millenarian rebellion (1593) that threatened his household's hegemony. The mural celebrates the apocalyptic figure of Shah Abbas I as the architect of a new Islamic millennium, drawing on the language of mystic love to domesticate male homoerotic desire and tame the masculine aggression of the courtly and warrior class where friendship was deployed as male rule.

The desire to delay the apocalypse conveyed in courtly and Shi'a religious discourse following the death of Shah Abbas I played on an imminent expectation of the arrival of the Shi'a Mahdi (messiah) born into the Safavi lineage. This temporal postponement was accompanied by the production of disciplinary *adab* manuals on male public conduct. In character with mystic desire edging between avowal and disavowal, the suspension of the experience of paradise, replete with promises of erotic delights, was to be relegated to the near future. Barthes has drawn attention to the "infinitely metaphorical nature of urban discourse," and in this context the erotic dimension of the city, which he uses interchangeably with sociability, is not only a place of encounter and exchange in Isfahan but also a place of anticipation, enactment, and renunciation.[35]

Different ideals of sociability—whether at court, in the bazaar, or among the literati—drew on the emotional economy of friendship. However, in the practice of *yearning* for love (*'ishq*) associated with the mystic desire (*'ishq*) for ideal union, friendship came under social, political, and religious scrutiny. Multiple practices of friendship fused love with carnal desire in a singular emotional register of love, or *'ishq*. Hence, throughout this book, I shed light on the capaciousness of love and friendship in seventeenth-century Isfahan, drawing attention to the intersection of their mutable forms with eroticism and sexuality and with practices of homoeroticism and homosociality. Only when *'ishq* is aligned with the ideals of platonic love in urban amical circles do the distinct lines between love, sex, eros, and friendship begin to be demarcated. Indeed, treatises on the protocols of friendship and manuals on composing letters to a friend abound in their disavowal of carnal love, instead stressing the importance of maintaining the secret of sexual desire. Whether they took the form of ethical essays on friendship or manuals that instructed readers in the art of writing friendship letters, these disciplinary texts were assembled in anthologies as didactic tools to learn the urban *adab* of masculinity. Anthologies archive the practices of mystic love informed by the language of urban friendships. Therefore, from the establishment of Isfahan as a capital to its consolidation as an imperial center of rule, the shifting history of friendship was bound to (and, indeed, collected by) the materiality of the anthology.

The control and display of the emotion of love and eros (*'ishq*) and its associated malady of melancholy (*sawda'*), expressed in the longing for God, the beloved, had its own history in the ubiquitous realm of Sufism, which was so integral to the daily lives of Isfahan's residents. To be a model Sufi meant that one had come under the spell of *'ishq*; love was the language, expressed in verse and prose, through which intimacy was configured. Even as the ultimate purpose was to direct the Sufi disciple toward God, in fraternal communities this was to be achieved through human guidance. And so Sufism concerned itself with the disciplining of *adab* as an entire set of behaviors meant to regulate the carnal body and align the self, through the intermediation of the Sufi master, with the celestial order.

Ritual gazing was a stage that Sufi devotees had to master on their journey toward union with the divine; its aim was to provoke the simultaneous sensations of separation from and longing for their object of desire. Boy gazing (*shahid bazi*) depicted the practitioner, often an older bearded man, contemplating a beautiful beardless youth (*amrad*), who represented the divine on earth. And because the mystic was meant to practice seeking and loving God, not the beautiful male youth, he was forbidden from acting on his carnal desire. In a typical composition, two drawings attributed to Riza Abbasi (d. 1635) materialize this state of separation between the beautiful beloved and the Sufi gazer (Figure 0.5). These drawings were executed on two separate sheets of paper and then assembled side by side in a *muraqqa'*. A grid separates them and confines each to its original state of composition. The placement of these two images, in dialogue with one another, illustrates how ritual gazing was a method of contemplation meant to help achieve the mystic lover's self-discipline and purification. Here, the Sufi

FIGURE 0.5 Composite image of two drawings by Riza Abbasi (d. 1635), *Old Man and the Youth*, with his signature: "Drawn by the humble Riza Abbasi." The two drawings are mounted on a folio of a *muraqqa'* with a line of poetry written by the calligrapher Nur al-Din Muhammad Lahiji in the second quarter of the seventeenth century. 12.7 cm × 5.4 cm. Metropolitan Museum of Art, 25.68.5. Fletcher Fund, 1925.

lover gazes and is stirred by desire, yet any actual encounter is simultaneously arrested in this activity. Desire was the emotional mechanism that made recognition and appreciation of true beauty possible, and here, on paper, erotic desire is activated.

A poem frames the diptych to guide the viewer's understanding of the image. Written by another calligrapher, Nur al-din Muhammad al-Lahiji, whose signature appears in the left margin of a third sheet of paper, the hemistich reads, "Your green line [*khatt*] is a beautiful sign." The word *khatt* here refers to the first sign of facial hair above the beloved's lip; this line is commonly referred to as green because of the way black hair is perceived as it grows on olive skin. But *khatt* means more than just a *line* of hair, or of poetry. It also means an inscription and script. A resident reading this hemistich (*khatt*) would associate it with a young beloved, an object of desire. The collating of these two images expands on that meaning of *khatt*. This is an iconic image of Sufi gazing. To absorb the ritual context of gazing, the images, together with the line of poetry, explain the rules of its practice. The green line of the beloved is both a liminal symbol of masculinity and a male fetish. But when located within Sufism, celibacy and boy gazing signify the sacred. This etiquette involves a doubled action on the part of the mystic gazer: desiring while refraining from acting on that desire by remaining celibate. In short, the very process of disciplining the gaze allows for and indeed produces more sexual desire.

The media that embody the word and the image in this patchwork are ink and opaque watercolors on paper; they were later mounted on a gold-leafed page and incorporated into a *muraqqaʿ* album. This composition makes explicit the relationship between the act of writing and the object of reading. The figure of the bearded man leaning on a staff inscribes and channels the viewer's gaze on the ground's pliant surface, which in turn points to the artist's signature (*khatt*). The drawing and writing (*khatt*) signal the other *khatt*, the line of poetry that connects the two images, and teaches the gazing anthologizer how to look for and read the green *khatt* on the beloved's face. Together the collage generates a dialogue that communicates how gazing and celibacy complement one another, because it signals to the reader where to look and how and what to see through the words, lines, and images. This composite image, part of an anthology of other writings and subjects, represents a patchwork of "lines" that gradually engross and instruct the gazer. This quintessential object of *adab*, embodied and inscribed, illustrates how the *muraqqaʿ* works heuristically to orient the reader, and it presents the reasons that such ideals produced alternative homoerotic practices, which would prove so problematic for the Safavi state's model of proper *adab* comportment.

If court and mosque marshaled literacy to discipline the social and carnal body, by the middle of the seventeenth century anti-Sufi polemics published in Isfahan suggest a historical shift characterized by the perception of homoerotic desire as a problem to be disciplined, regulated, or reformed. Sexual desire between loving men and women was deemed obstructive to efforts of stabilizing social and gender identities within the local regime of differentiation. Men, whether craftsmen, merchants, courtiers, or travelers, spent much of their day working and enjoying leisure pastimes in separate domestic and public spheres, cultivating intimate bonds that complemented familial hierarchies within Isfahan's male networks. Influential Shi'a clerics, tending to a growing heterogeneous population, began to voice their mistrust of male sociability. Anxious about its disruptive erotic potential, they identified such practices as obstructing procreation and moral probity. Under the guise of a moral campaign that relied on decrees, as well as on ethical manuals and treatises asserting the law and rule of the sharia, Shi'a scholars promoted heterosexual marriage to control spiritual and sexual practices and to cultivate subjects whose economic and sexual production would further state interests. Between 1640 and 1650 prominent clerics in Isfahan penned more than twenty treatises condemning Sufism, boy gazing, and celibacy, privileging matrimony instead. The Sufi practice of gazing came to signify *excess*, which stigmatized its practitioners as deviants in the community.

Homosexual acts (*livat*), associated in Islamic law with anal intercourse and penetration, were generally condemned as a major sin.[36] Although it is difficult to ascertain whether and how these legal injunctions were historically enforced, anxieties about sexual behavior in Sufi circles reveal that after the death of Shah Abbas I, Safavi monarchs and the Shi'a clerical establishment feared that intimacy between spiritual brothers and friends in confraternities and mystical orders could easily lead to political solidarities strong enough to resist religious, perhaps even imperial, sovereignty. The phobia around male homoerotic bonds in Sufi circles was not a Shi'a phenomenon. In contemporaneous Sunni Ottoman Istanbul attacks against Sufi rituals, dance (*sama'*), and music (*zikr*) as well as the practice of shaving the beard resulted in similar condemnations of Sufi brotherhoods.[37] The historical transformations that pushed Sufism, the original belief system of the Safavi revolution, to the outer limits of acceptable spirituality are complex. Suffice it to say here that Sufism was a popular mode of religiosity that competed with the dynastic household's newly established religion of Shi'ism and with the Safavi shahs' claims to sacred kingship.[38] An entire mystical way of life, which had permeated confraternities, Sufi brotherhoods, coffeehouses, and networks of friendship across households, was thus condemned.

Admonitions against Sufi practices in Isfahan took the form of public decrees that banned the consumption of wine, rice ale, opium, and hashish as well as the frequenting of brothels, music halls, and gambling houses. As seen in engravings on the walls of the medieval mosque in the old quarter of Isfahan, these leisurely activities had been forbidden a century before the establishment of the city as the capital in 1593.[39] Decrees prohibiting the shaving of beards were more widely published in the city's new quarters after the death of Shah Abbas I, who had transferred the capital to Isfahan. These were posted in the bazaar, hammams, and coffeehouses to inform inhabitants about the rigor with which the court intended to enforce regulations regarding public conduct and behavior. Coffeehouses were especially targeted as homoerotic spaces because the young men who served coffee also allegedly engaged in sex work. Male youths with long braided hair were barred from the public space of the bazaar. Female sex workers who had been licensed to work and walk the streets at night had their permits revoked. Seventeenth-century chroniclers include these edicts' texts and note that, even though the court had in the past legalized the practice of female prostitution, which provided sizable annual revenues (20,000 tomans) for the royal treasury, these activities were now strictly forbidden.[40] The Grand Vizier Sultan al-Ulama (d. 1660), himself a religious scholar, publicly punished transgressors; caught in a same-sex act, one male resident had his testicles nailed to a board and was then paraded through the city. In another case, female prostitution was turned into a public spectacle; a mother who had allegedly forced her daughter into the profession was thrown from a tower and her body fed to dogs. These violent displays of discipline were intended to instill fear in the public.

Reading the city of Isfahan includes reading a history of prohibitions and regulations. That the medieval mosque had been inscribed with warnings against carnal sins in the fifteenth century signals a prehistory to the constellation of interdictions that I investigate; the moment I capture is in part about shifting the culture of an urban image to different ends, namely, toward the *adab* of urbanity, of refinement in speech, manners, behaviors, and sexual desires. Technologies of power, public writings, and acts of torture clearly communicated to residents the consequences of misconduct. These mechanisms speak to the relationship between media and performance in the spectacle of public life. Edicts and the showcasing of discipline and shame accompanied manuals, handbooks, and treatises that attributed the state of corruption in the streets of Isfahan to Sufis who drank wine, listened to music, danced, and engaged in male homoerotic practices of gazing. The circulation of refutations (*radd*) against Sufis, penned by Isfahan's prominent religious scholars, alerts us to the growing importance of communicating on paper in public spaces as a new way of engaging in public discourse, enhancing many of the cultural roles played by face-to-face interactions.[41]

These ethical proscriptions were scrupulous enough not to overlook beards. The first sign of a beard heralded manhood, at which stage being penetrated became taboo.[42] According to the decrees engraved on mosque walls, sharia law would punish a beardless youth if he prostituted himself in a hammam. And if a man persistently shaved his beard, *delaying* his entry into manhood with its prescribed responsibilities of work, marriage, and reproduction, he was cast as a threat to the social order. These ways of defining the religious self are also reflected in the anthologies; conscious of the disciplinary modes of behavior, men in the anthologies censor themselves, negotiate, and speak out against contemporary technologies of power.

The anthology was the peculiar product of a discoursing city that incited people to write, curating texts and urban and sexual selves. The impulse to create new kinds of texts on new kinds of surfaces, from the walls of Isfahan to the sheets of paper that gave shape to the anthology, presented new textual and social logics and invited exploration of the capital's homoerotic culture *alongside* more normative versions of power and authority. Different "distributions of the visible" in these anthologies pushed against the rules of what could be said and shared in the city.[43] Suddenly there was not just a canon to be known and rehearsed but an opening to compare and assert the equivalence of things that had never before existed in the same frame.

Reader's Guide to the Anthologies

The incitement to expression, through the practice of writing, drawing, and collecting in the privacy of households, led to new forms and uses of word and image. To guide the reader through networks of circulating urban texts, I focus on the writing of distinct modes of communication. Manuals, model letters, and drawings and paintings are the generic urban texts that negotiated city life; they serve as actual and heuristic guides to my anthologizing the city. As we move between the imperial Safavi project, the urban media of household anthologies, and individual residents, eight resident authors act as our city guides (Map 0.1). We begin with Shah Abbas I and Shaykh Baha'i's imperial imaginations of Isfahan and then measure the reception of official visual and verbal texts in household anthologies through the alternative experiences of six other residents, as mediated by their poetry, drawings, manuals, and letters.

Chapter 1, "Imperial Visions of Sovereignty," begins with the spectacle of sovereignty in Isfahan. Shah Abbas I's imperial building project of the square was to transform Isfahan into an urban image of paradise, modeling the experience of an ideal city as the epitome of beauty and desire. To ensure that the shah's imprint on the cityscape would endure as a symbol of his jurisdiction and authority, his name and composition were inscribed across the main square. Spatially divided into four quarters and regimented into clearly defined sections, the rectangular plaza was the page the shah authored as his anthology of the city. The ways in which he and the religious scholar Shaykh Baha'i planned the built environment in and around the square, as well as the epigraphy the shaykh commissioned for the walls of the Friday Prayer Mosque, collectively reveal how monarch and shaykh wished their subjects to experience state-sponsored forms of urbanity. This chapter lays the groundwork for the making of Isfahan's homoerotic culture and its reception in anthologies.

To guide the reader around the contours of verbal and visual anthologies, I turn to the themes of collecting, self-fashioning, and community in Chapter 2. A close reading of two resident anthologizers, a religious scholar and a painter, considers the subjects of their collected words and images to show how these practices illuminate their encounter and experience of the city. The anthology of Shi'a cleric Aqa Husayn Khwansari (d. 1687) reveals shared texts that connected him with Isfahan's literary community. This agent of conversion to Shi'ism taught at a prominent seminary in the bazaar and composed decrees prohibiting the consumption of alcohol and Sufi practices of male gazing. But he collected romances and essays on love and desire. A close reading of his curatorial choices allows us to hear tensions and ambivalences that nuance this religious scholar's public face. A reconstruction of the painter Muhammad Qasim's (d. 1660) dispersed portfolio assembles a patchwork of his life and

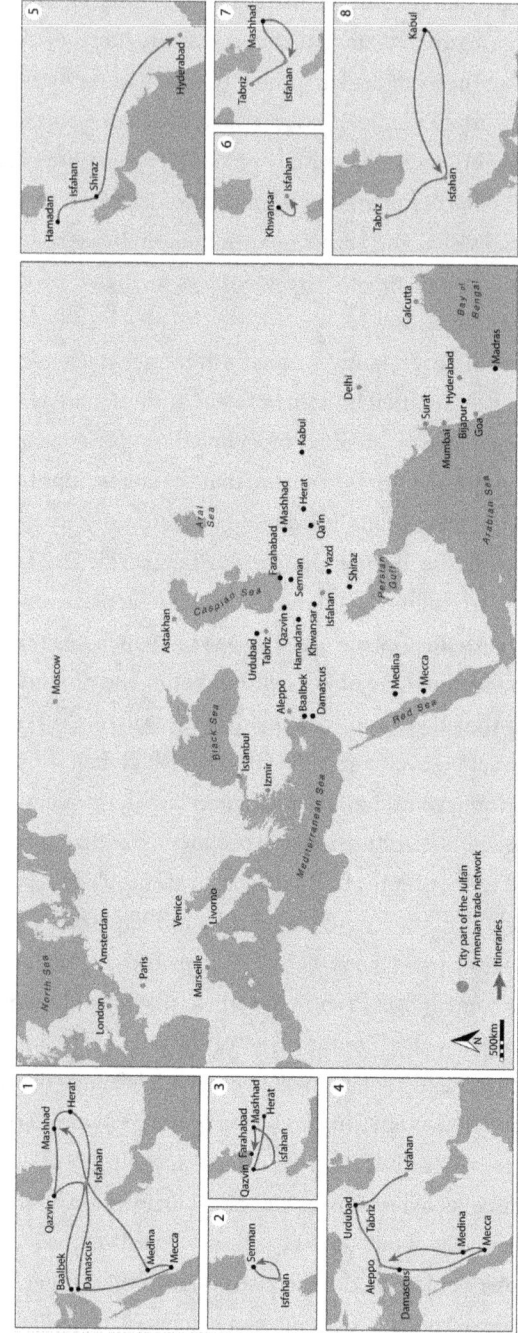

MAP 0.1 Early modern Eurasian cities and the mobility of the characters whose anthologies are studied in this book. Drawn by Matilde Grimaldi.

shows the range of his clients' commissioned works. From his self-portraits to the activities of women and men in his drawings, Muhammad Qasim created a collage of city life in Isfahan that reveals what the verbal archive conceals. The practices according to which these two migrants to the capital fashioned their urban selves guide my reading of their authorial voices and of their writing of Isfahan's habitus.

Chapter 3, "Disturbing the City," mediates the opposing views of the imperial imaginary and the city of Isfahan as allegories of the spiritual journey to paradise. For the cleric and poet Aqa Mansur Semnani (alive in 1656), the physical delights of Isfahan lay in its wealth of beautiful male youth. He visualized the city for his audience through the poetic form of the *shahrashub*, literally "city disturbance." In this chapter, then, I focus on how the effort to create ideological unity in Shah Abbas I's rebuilding of Isfahan could be unsettled by Aqa Mansur's work preserved in anthologies, and I consider the degree to which the imperial project was real, or lived, or successful. Deploying a new form of authority based on the vitality of embodied experiences, Aqa Mansur Semnani's literary experiment challenged the imperial vision, using *'ishq* (love that is desiring) and humor to reimagine the city of power as the very symbol of transcendent authority. His popular guidebook to Isfahan represents the city as a masculine space where friends are educated in the *adab* of erotic love. Moreover, Aqa Mansur identifies this city disturbance with a manual (*dastur al-'amal*) in response to a letter from his beloved friend, Aqa Rukn al-Din, signaling the poet's consciousness of manuals and letters as dialogic urban modes of communication.

Chapter 4, "Cultivating and Disciplining Friendship Letters," uncovers the archeology of sworn friendships in early modern Isfahan through the medium of epistolary practices. Friendship letters were respectable forms of social exchange collected across anthologies to model and memorialize social networks of voluntary kinship. Categorized by scribes and owners of anthologies as a genre, *rasa'il-i ikhvaniyyat*, or "fraternal" letters, were media by which to maintain social relations; they reflected anxieties around the vicissitudes of friendships. Vows of brotherhood enacted through words and images were assembled together with model friendship letters and personal letters. In this chapter I analyze the materiality and social dynamics of voluntary kinships as epistolary performances of male friendship; gifts of paintings to friends are read together with their accompanying letters to reflect on how Isfahan's urban culture transformed the grammar and aesthetics of male friendship. In particular, the most commonly assembled letters, written by Nasira Hamadani (d. 1620), provide the means to explore the affective language and sentiments of verbal communication between friends in and out of Isfahan.

In the concluding chapter, "Family Archives and Female Spaces of Intimacy," I discuss the women who have been excluded from the act of writing their own anthology to present a reading of gendered literacy and female friendship through an anthology collected in the library of the Urdubadi family of bureaucrats and poets. The anthology is a family archive, in which the sociology of the household where it was produced, from the professional occupation of its patrons to the family's public engagement with the city, is rendered legible. The decisive role of a female family member, the Urdubadi widow, whose pilgrimage to Mecca is recorded in this anthology, uncovers the connections between female members of a household and public life. As the nameless widow leaves Isfahan, she deploys dominant mystic discourses on erotic desire to write her experience in verse (*masnavi*), experimenting with realist poetics that allow her to speak about the modalities of her attachments to city and kin. In the process of writing, she also divulges her love for a female companion who was forced to leave Isfahan because of rumors circulating about their friendship. An empathetic community comes into view, established through a ritual of sisterhood, *khwahar khwandagi*, which made use of the language of mysticism to express love and friendship. A selection of Muhammad Qasim's paintings executed for a female clientele brings the visual into dialogue with the verbal, enhancing our understanding of the meanings of female friendships.

These residents' words and images relate their particular experiences of Isfahan, just as they demonstrate the larger conversations transpiring in the discoursing city. Seven men and one woman give voice and form to my own curated anthology of Isfahan (see Map 0.1). My reading of the seventeenth-century collections is but one way of interpreting these household productions. My process began with touching hundreds of folios, flipping page after page as I considered the multitude of ways the script filled the different dimensions of bound sheets of paper. Skimming my way through the paleography and guided by the writing, desiring, and reading practices there inscribed, I learned how to see, read, and write about them. The collected materials by which anthologizers gave meaning to their city life have in turn shaped my historical construction of Isfahan. The impulse behind my choice of manuals, model letters, drawings, and paintings entailed a reflection on how they figured in a set of practices that were embedded in the everyday life of a metropolis in the making. Broadening our view of Isfahan's physical, financial, and political topography to include the rich variety of anthologies and the contexts in which the practice of reading and writing took place allows us to discern new ties between seeing and desiring the city. Created at a historical moment of urbanization, these anthologies serve as new vehicles and models for communication that challenge the historiography on Isfahan, which assumes a certain familiarity with the city, whose monumental architecture has survived the passage of time. The architectural success of the central square, the Naqsh-i Jahan, as a public space in the modern city has rendered its development in the early modern era legible, as though, by merely stepping onto the ground walked by its residents five centuries earlier, we can imagine its history and the affects it produced and engaged. The turquoise, lapis, and yellow tiles of its domes and walls and the ubiquity of its calligraphy continue to draw the visitor into the square's auratic sense of aesthetics. But how did inhabitants born in Isfahan during the early decades of the seventeenth century experience their city's transformation? And how did migrants entering the new capital read the density of its words, images, colors, and people? The anthologies defamiliarize the city; they confuse our modern perceptions and reorient the historian conscious of the past's difference. In this history of Isfahan, I mine the anthologies for tools with which to weave my writing of early modern Isfahan, just as they were once assembled to help residents navigate and forge relationships in a growing metropolis. My own act of reading becomes part of writing the urban experience of Isfahan's conversion into a cosmopolitan capital city.

CHAPTER 1

Imperial Visions of Sovereignty

Staging the Spectacle of Sovereignty

For three days in the former capital city of Qazvin, from August 5 to August 8, 1593, Shah Abbas I abdicated his throne in favor of a master quiver maker by the name of Ustad Yusufi. A member of a rival Nuqtavi millenarian movement, this quiver maker had revealed a secret to the shah: One of his associates was soon to take possession of power. The traffic between concealment and revelation established the Nuqtavi secret as a powerful form of social and sacred knowledge around which alliances were forged and would be shattered.[1] Based on their reading of the stars, the Nuqtavis saw the imminent conjunction of Saturn and Jupiter as a revolutionary sign, one that would overturn the Safavi dynasty in favor of a Nuqtavi dispensation.[2] Shah Abbas I, who had frequented the Nuqtavi cloister in Qazvin and had developed a personal relationship with Ustad Yusufi, forestalled the prophecy. To align the shah's destiny with his reading of the planetary conjunction, he relinquished his authority and masterminded a mock coronation, personally placing Ustad Yusufi on the throne. He adorned master Yusufi with the appropriate regalia, dressed him in majestic attire, and placed the crown on the new king's head. This theater of sovereignty was played out for three consecutive days, with the shah directing the drama. Casting himself in the role of master of ceremonies, he stood guard, as though to authenticate the ritual coronation. On August 8, 1593, he ordered a high scaffold to be built and had the master quiver maker executed outside the palace in Qazvin. In full public view, a firing squad shot Ustad Yusufi, whose body was then hung in the central square. On the same day, at an auspicious hour determined by his court astrologer, Shah Abbas I reclaimed his throne. The secret, now publicly divulged, had revealed the social networks associated with the Nuqtavi movement, unleashing a massive campaign of persecution. Thus began a new era of Safavi dominion, which included the transfer of the seat of power to Isfahan, where yet another secret would soon be made public.[3]

The historian Mahmud b. Hidayatullah (d. 1599), better known as Afushta Natanzi, from the city of Natanz in the vicinity of Isfahan, records the story of Isfahan's inauguration as capital city, linking the move to the failed Nuqtavi revolution and forecast of millenarian change. Natanzi had witnessed Shah Abbas I's spectacular performance of sovereignty. When he wrote of the event, he depicted it as a commemoration of a thousand years of the Hijra, when the prophet Muhammad emigrated with his community of believers from Mecca to Medina, thus establishing Medina as the first Muslim *city*. It is through his eyewitness account that I write the effect of this witnessing. Although Natanzi was neither an official court historian nor indeed an admirer of the shah, his narrative interprets Shah Abbas I's entry into Isfahan as an apocalyptic event prophesized in the Quran and accompanied by natural disasters, such as floods, earthquakes, famine, and disease.[4] Like the prophet in Mecca, Shah Abbas I also was confronted with opposition in Qazvin. And like the prophet, he would have to build a new community within an already existing polity.

Natanzi associates the choice of Isfahan with apocalyptic symbols of astral conjunctions and natural disasters. Torrential storms, floods, and earthquakes had afflicted the region in the summer of 1593, the summer of the shah's abdication. These natural disasters were read as Quranic portents of the end of the world. In Isfahan dams collapsed and flooded the agricultural lands around the Zayanda River, affecting the city as well as nearby towns and villages for an entire year. Plagues spread in the spring of 1594. The community was overcome by fear, and many fled their homes, seeking refuge in less densely populated villages and towns nearby, despite attempts by the governor and alderman to prevent them from abandoning the city. Only those who had no means to leave were said to have congregated around the medieval city square and the Friday Prayer Mosque. Once the plague had eased in the autumn of 1594, residents began returning to their homes; roughly 30,000–50,000 inhabitants returned. Natanzi tells us that heavy rains and flooding were not uncommon in Isfahan, but this was a year that brought devastation and destruction the likes of which no one could remember.[5]

Shah Abbas I entered this scene of chaos in his public role as a just king poised to protect Isfahan's distraught inhabitants. The inaugural ceremonies, however, communicated more than the righteous character of the shah: These performances were a spectacular deployment of a variety of technologies, from gunpowder and pyrotechnics to the media of paint and textiles, all in the service of visually stimulating spectators' imaginations. I argue that, in this staging of the spectacle of sovereignty, the residents of Isfahan not only came to associate technologies of power with special effects but also developed a visual sensibility that would prove critical to the new city's urban development. Consider, for example, the impact of Shah Abbas I's first entry into the capital two months after Ustad Yusufi's public execution. As per customary practice, the shah was greeted outside the city for a period of three days while dignitaries, religious officials, local notables, and the city's inhabitants showered him with gifts. The shah had assembled 15,000 foot soldiers from the vicinity of Isfahan, with each group of 1,000 men dressed in a single color; together they embodied the entire color spectrum.[6] Parallel rows of multicolored soldiers armed with rifles and bows and arrows created a passage through which the shah's processional would ride into Isfahan. But suddenly rain began to pour on this grand welcoming assembly, and everyone fled back to the city. The rain fell so hard that each and every person was drenched and muddied. Some footmen fell to the ground, their clothes running with such "strange" colors as no one had seen before. As people made their way into the city, the rain stopped unexpectedly and blue skies greeted the shah into the *maydan*, the new public square that would be the site of Shah Abbas I's urban revolution.

Two days later, once the mud had dried, the shah rode in with his colorful retinue of foot soldiers. Residents were invited to congregate and stand in rows crowding the open space—the *maydan* of Shah Abbas I. The shah took a lofty position, climbing onto the roof of a seminary to watch the procession of foot soldiers.[7] He ordered the soldiers to fire a bullet each; soon the skies darkened under a shower of 15,000 bullets, giving the impression that night had fallen. To convey the awe this scene inspired, Natanzi tells us that "those holding hands with their companions were so frightened that they let go of each other and got lost in the crowd." Gunshots were fired three consecutive times; thundering reverberations and black clouds hung in the air. The chronicler captures the scene, which he associates with resurrection, in verse: "The day blackened with dust and wind, like the night of lovers' separation. Instead of brilliant stars, a thousand eyes glittered in the skies."[8]

With the *maydan* transformed into the night of resurrection, the shah took on his ritual role of generous benefactor. Storehouses had been packed with fruits in preparation for the inauguration so that the shah could distribute them. When he began scattering the fruit from the rooftop, frenzy took over the crowds, who scrambled to pick up the produce and bless him. The experience so pleased the king that he ordered another load of fruit to be dropped down. Once again, the crowds gathered around him, exaggerating their response, falling on top of each other as though they had never seen such abundance. What a sight it was, Natanzi tells us, to witness a strange amalgam of trampled fruits, mud, and dust covering the grounds of the central square!

This marvelous enactment of a savior king who delivered the population of Isfahan from ravaging floods, famine, and plague colored the imaginations of Isfahani residents, a memory that inscribed the ritual significance of the *maydan* as a space of resurrection and promise. Shah Abbas I's performative staging, coupled with Natanzi's own choices as narrator, bolster this inscription. On October 5, 1595, a repeat performance authenticated the inauguration and confirmed the new square's ritual space, replicating the first performance so as to consecrate the spectacle in the minds of witnesses. The shah once again ordered 15,000 foot soldiers from the vicinity of Isfahan to assemble, equipped in their multicolored garb and military accoutrements. Shah Abbas I mounted his horse and rode 11 miles (3 *farsang*), accompanied by his guests, who were on foot as they arrived at the *maydan*. The walls along the streets and bazaars were adorned with remarkable objects, and the entire road was carpeted with imported velvet and colorful textile. Natanzi tells us that even the creative imagination of painters and scholars had never achieved such a sight. Brilliant colors of gold and boundless jewels from turquoise to ruby bedazzled spectators' eyes. "All sorts of merchandise, the human mind could not even imagine. A lavish array of feast and battle [*bazm u razm*], no eyes had ever seen."[9]

Playing on illusion and perception, as though the colorful exhibit of crafts produced by the artisans was not sufficient for his spectacular entry, Shah Abbas I also ordered painters to illuminate the central square. In a matter of two or three months, from all over the lands of Iraq and Fars, craftsmen, artisans, and engineers were gathered together on the square. The shah provided them with whatever tools and materials they needed for their "adorning minds [*fikr-i zinnatgar*] and their educated dispositions [*tabʿ-i danishgar*]" to collectively assemble and display marvelous images. "The power of their world-adorning intellect unveiled designs and faces [*rukhsar*] hidden from human cognition, witnesses to their creativity and inventiveness. With their magical skills they made manifest their imaginings, rendering visible what was invisible."[10] In preparation, all the walls around the square were whitewashed. Then, the painters, who "possess the brush of the master painter Bihzad [*naqqashan-i bihzad qalam*], and the illustrators, who draw faces like the prophet Mani [*musavviran-i surat nigar Mani raqam*], painted pictures of wondrous creatures and strange beings on the walls. Every page from the folios of the manuscript of the *Marvels of Creatures* [*ʿAjaʾib al-makhluqat*] was reproduced on the surface of the white walls."[11]

To enter the square was to step into the strange wonders of creation, as though the reader who, folio by folio, contemplated the illustrated book of marvels now collectively experienced the marvelous built environment. Public murals conjured sights of paradise described word by word in the Quran, drawing on visual incitement to dazzle and educate the eyes of Isfahan's inhabitants. The collective creativity of regional artists patronized by the shah produced portraits of the unbelievable and the incredible, picturing the heavenly kingdom and manifesting it in the *maydan*. Although previously only royal and elite households could afford to commission or purchase illustrated manuscripts, say, of the *ʿAjaʾib al-makhluqat*, now, thanks to their sacred king, the wondrous art of painting and drawing appeared before the inhabitants of Isfahan for all to experience. The descriptive and prescriptive power of visually communicating the rewards of paradise to the population of Isfahan generated a relationship between the audience and the square, now transformed as the sacred space of the inaugural performance in which the patron-shah staged paradise. It is no wonder that the square was celebrated as the "image of the world" for those who shared in the collective experience of the city. Shah Abbas I deployed the visual power of knowledge of the occult to publicly display the arts of the book and deliver the unseen and the unimaginable for all his subjects to appreciate. There in the *maydan* the secret was revealed: Isfahan was to be the city of paradise, and the shah was not only its author but also its assembler.

The repetitive play of lightness and darkness to stage the theater of creation was a strategy for effecting verisimilitude through this mise-en-scène. Engineers mounted a twelve-wheeled structure in the square supporting a thousand oil lamps; each time one lamp was lit, its wheel refracted shimmering light on all the others. Bringing light to the murals during the night, this brilliant technology bewildered the spectators' minds. Roses, tulips, violets, narcissuses, and lilies were also planted and irrigated with the help of canals drawn from the life-giving Zayanda River. Because the inauguration took place toward the end of fall, the fruit trees were seasonally bare; empty branches were therefore adorned with colorful cloth and wax fruits, a trompe l'oeil designed to create the optical illusion of the eternally bountiful nature of paradise. "And fruits in plenty, neither out of reach nor forbidden. Lo! We have created them [mankind] a new creation, and made them virgins, lovers, and friends."[12] Quoting from the Quran, Natanzi unambiguously draws parallels between the literary depiction of paradise and its materialization in the square. The allegory of fruits in paradise "for every man a promise for what he has earned," was the promise of masculine pleasure for men to be had with virgins, lovers, and male friends. Fruits are metaphorically extended in the Quran to signify "beardless youth [*ghilman*] who amble waiting on men as if they were hidden pearls" (Quran 52:21–24). Natanzi singles out beardless youth strolling around the square, their bodies serving as physical rewards for men who uphold the tenets of Islam. The fantasy of forbidden pleasures on earth was to be experienced in carnal Isfahan—at least, such was Natanzi's reading of the promise made by the shah, patron and sovereign of the city of paradise.

The masters of the craft of pyrotechnics (*atishbar*) then staged a display of fireworks, a performance that sent rockets in the shape of halos, peacock tails, narcissuses, and lilies into the sky, sprinkling the square with heavenly flowers and iridescent special effects. The mirage of remarkable elements of nature rendered in the square was reflected through luminous fire in the night skies. A mock battle between the Uzbeks and the Safavis' Qizilbash military disciples followed the "festival of light." Four fortresses were erected on all four corners of the *maydan*, echoing the battleground of the universe. On each fortress the master craftsmen had placed a hundred effigies (*surat*) in the image of the red-clad Qizilbash; the Uzbek soldiers were dressed in purple, standing on the towers of each opposing fort. Cannons and muskets were fired, and "thick dark smoke and dust rose," covering the entire field. Then the Qizilbash burned the two Uzbek forts, which turned to dust and ash, soaring skyward. Despite all the lanterns, candles, and oil lamps that illuminated the square, the air rapidly grew pitch black; no one could see the stars, the sky, or their surroundings any longer. Again, Natanzi underscored the singularity of the experience: "Not a soul had seen such a sight. Even [as for] kings, despite their large dominions, good fortune, and abundance of accoutrements of pleasure, never did the letter of their imagination arrive at the frontiers of comprehending this innovative craft."[13] The marvelous play on reality and illusion through sensory stimulation was thus staged in the square, enacting the apocalypse in Isfahan—that is, the revelation of the square as paradise on earth—and creating a sacred space where Shah Abbas I would craft a celestial order together with his artists, engineers, and confidants.[14]

Reading the Imperial Square

For those residents of Isfahan who did not witness the inauguration, oral accounts circulated in the city and were recorded in *majmuʿa*s, or household anthologies. Whether in verse or in prose, these anthologies depicted the city as paradise.[15] The activity of hearing or reading such accounts, even while walking in the *maydan* and gazing at the animated surfaces on the walls of the arcades, ritualized the meaning of this spectacular encounter. Shah Abbas I and his artists curated words and Quranic phrases that offered a parallel between the promise of paradise and its lived experience in the new capital center. Moreover, during his nearly thirty-year reign in Isfahan, Shah Abbas I's own participation marked urban life in the city he rebuilt: The shah walked the streets of Isfahan, consumed food from peddlers, frequented coffeehouses, bought shoes from his preferred shoemaker, and had Ali Riza, his favorite barber from the hammam located in the bazaar, shave him. He lived and breathed the city together with his subjects. Shah Abbas I's presence also extended beyond his engagement in the daily life of Isfahan. Although the *maydan* building project extended into the reign of his grandson, Abbas II, Shah Abbas I's indelible mark on the city was foundational, outlasting the sovereign himself. The *maydan* is an image that Shah Abbas I crafted of his kingship, an urban portrait he commissioned to be drawn. To ensure the shah's imprint on the cityscape as an enduring sign of his jurisdiction and authority, his name was inscribed on the monumental buildings surrounding the *maydan*. The manner in which he planned the built environment in and around the *maydan* and the writings and paintings he commissioned for the walls serve as a collective display of his intention for how denizens of the city of paradise should experience his sovereignty. Let us walk through the *maydan* to visualize Shah Abbas I's Isfahan, "the fruit of [his] fertile imperial imagination,"[16] through the built environment and his program of inscriptions.

Shah Abbas I personally financed the *maydan* project, an investment that ensured the centrality of the new bazaar complex over the old commercial enterprise. Subsidizing rents and housing for merchants, craftsmen, and hammam administrators, the shah provided monetary incentives and security to participants in the imperial economy of Isfahan. He was Isfahan's primary landowner, and when he sought land for his urban project, he simply purchased it. His court chroniclers made sure to mention that these lands where sold willingly and acquired justly, endeavoring to promulgate the knowledge that the imperial development project was not an act of displacement or extortion. Moreover, Shah Abbas I sought to appease the fears of the commercial and religious networks and brokers rooted in the medieval city when he abandoned his original plan of rebuilding the old city quarters and instead built the *maydan* on an undeveloped space, which became the shah's *maydan*.[17] In a public act of gifting, Shah Abbas I endowed his entire estate for the *maydan* building project as an act of piety toward his holy family, Muhammad, Ali, Fatima, and their descendants, the Imams. Religious endowments (*waqf*) were part of an economy of piety that safeguarded private property from the vicissitudes of political turmoil; in theory, they guaranteed a long-term administration of land and its fruit, specifying the family member who was to administer the endowment and manage its revenues. In the case of Shah Abbas I, so long as his household reigned in Isfahan, the shah was assured that the proceeds generated by his endowment would be reinvested into the life and maintenance of the square and its attendant institutions.

On the square's northern corner, Shah Abbas I commissioned the Qaysariyya, a grand portal built to announce the entrance of the new bazaar; the Imperial Gate (Ali Qapu), his seat of power, was prominently situated to the west (Map 1.1). This five-story administrative complex (*dawlatkhana*) enjoyed a panoramic view of the entire square, marking the shah's vantage point.[18] Across from the Imperial Gate, on the square's eastern flank, the lofty royal perch communicated with an exquisite domed mosque. Built for the Shi'a cleric Shaykh Lutfullah Maysi, it was the first religious structure commissioned for the shah's urban project: a private mosque reserved

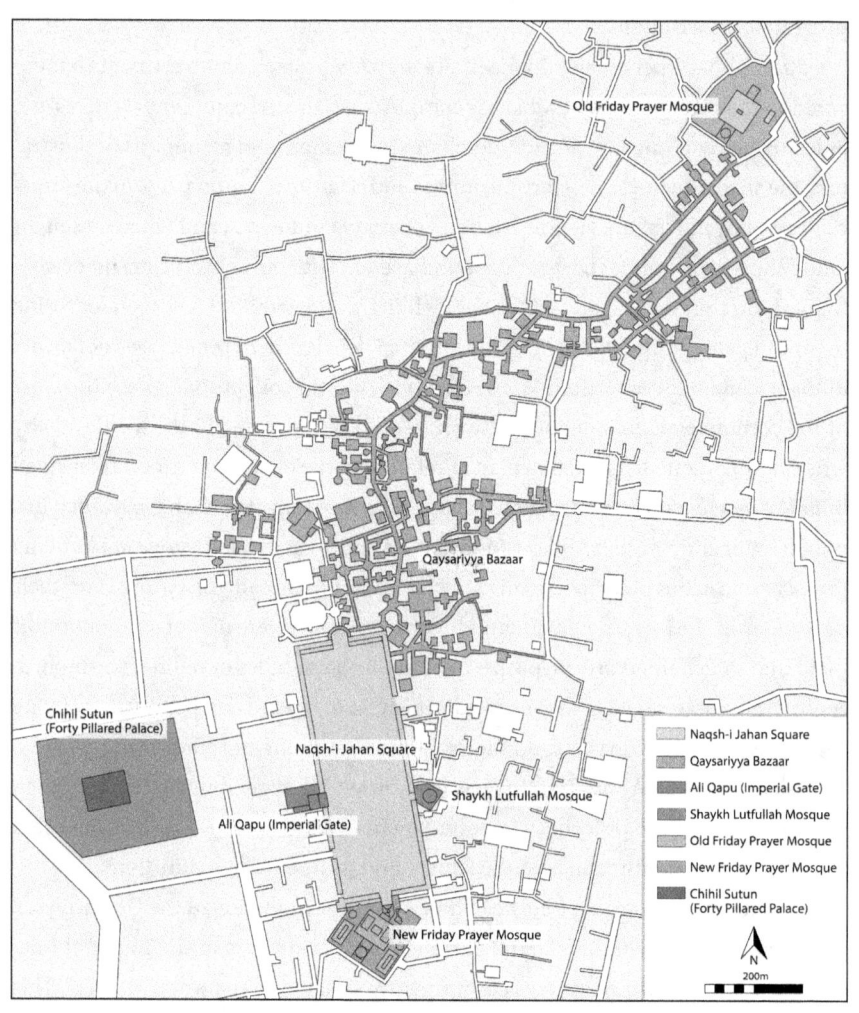

MAP 1.1 Isfahan's new city center in the seventeenth century. Drawn by Matilde Grimaldi.

for the royal family, which the community was to experience from the outside.[19] Its magnificent golden dome with turquoise floral accents visually conjured the heavenly dome. Isfahan residents, one surmises, would have been educated about the epigraphy inscribed in white script, quoting from the three Quranic chapters *Sun*, *Time*, and *Kawthar*, the river of paradise. The words, signifying belief in the Creator of the sun, the end of time, and the rewards of paradise, encircled the structure, creating a belt of lapis lazuli supporting the dome. There, from the heavenly dome, God spoke to the denizens of Isfahan, confirming that "this mosque is Allah's mosque and not a soul shall be his enemy."[20] God then revealed what to expect on the Day of Judgment, enumerating the promises of plentiful water, ambling male youth, and fine green silk embroidered with gold and silver. Below, inscribed in larger white letters, three of the ninety-nine names of God are legible. The white-on-turquoise calligraphy is discernible to the eyes of the passerby: "O Allah," "O Beneficent [*rahman*]," "O Merciful [*rahim*]," "O Generous [*karim*]" (Figure 1.1).[21] There is no trace of Muhammad, Ali, or any of the other Imams on the dome; the message of the epigraphy is clear: This is God's mosque, and all Muslims—whether Shi'a or Sunni—who believe in him will be rewarded in paradise.

FIGURE 1.1 The Shaykh Lutfullah Mosque across from the Ali Qapu (Imperial Gate) and the palace complex. Photo by Muhammad Sarraf.

At the entrance of the mosque are inscribed the names of the shah and his personal calligrapher, Ali Riza Abbasi Tabrizi, along with the date of the building's completion, 1618. The shah is cast as the greatest sultan, the "reviver of his [Shi'a] virtuous predecessors and the propagator of the doctrine of the infallible Imams." To the intimate who could enter the mosque, the shah's genealogy is disclosed, connecting him to Muhammad and Ali. The epigraphy associates the sacred space of the royal mosque with two holy shrines, one in Medina and the other in Najaf, where the bodies of Muhammad and Ali are buried. In humble reverence to his divine ancestors, Shah Abbas I takes on the reverential role of "the dog at Ali's threshold [*kalb-i astan-i Ali*]," thus creating a sacred geography linking Medina to Najaf and Isfahan. What is concealed from the populace but revealed to his intimates is that he stands guard at Ali's tomb, bringing the royal mosque into dialogue with the Ali Qapu palace gate, beyond which the shah resided. Revealed to the inhabitants of Isfahan is the epigraphy on the dome, which, through word, color, and form, conjures the sun that rises from the golden dome in the east to set at the palace gate in the west.

The epigrapher's name inscribed at the mosque's entrance, Ali Riza from the city of Tabriz, is bound to the shah with the genitive construction of his title, Abbas (*Abbasi*). Ali Riza Abbasi's story exemplifies the influx of artistic talent into the new capital and the personal relationship these artists enjoyed with the shah. He worked on the Friday Prayer Mosque in the former capital of Qazvin and copied several Qurans, mastering the art of calligraphy in the process. At the turn of the Muslim millennium in 1001 after the Hijra (1592 CE), he entered the service of Shah Abbas I. Having pioneered a new style of *thulth* calligraphy, Ali Riza was given the opportunity to exhibit his trademark in Isfahan, individualizing both the artist and the shah's signatures on the walls of the mosque. Ali Riza developed such an intimate relationship with his patron that he became known as the Shah's artist, *shahnavaz*. When Ali Riza was at work in the mosque, the shah is said to have held a candle for him, bringing light to the work of crafting holy letters from the Quran in his signature script. The spirit of the engraver is embodied in his epigraphy, and with the shah's efforts and care, he too comes to underwrite the integrity of the illumination.

Shah Abbas I's imperial project culminated in the construction of the first Friday Prayer Mosque on the *maydan*'s southern corner, an act whose pious intention was the formation of a collective community of worshippers, albeit one that was highly debated by the clerical establishment. More than 100 treatises were penned by the

Shi'a clerical establishment around the permissibility of building a Friday prayer mosque in the absence of the twelfth Imam.[22] According to Shi'a theology, the Mahdi (messiah) was to be the singular leader of Friday prayer. Political leadership of the community was the hidden Imam's prerogative, and Friday prayer was reserved for the political moment when the Mahdi emerged out of occultation to lead the Shi'a, the true community of believers. With the religious knowledge and eminence of the Shaykh al-Islam of Isfahan, Shaykh Baha'i, the shah was able to circumvent this theological obstacle. In his book, dedicated to Shah Abbas I, the *Jami'-i 'Abbasi* (The Abbasi Collection/Mosque), Shaykh Baha'i writes:

> The jurisconsults [*mujtahids*] are in disagreement about the obligation of the Friday prayers during the occultation of the Imam, upon whom be peace. The most correct [opinion] is that the individual has a choice between performing the Friday prayers and performing the noon prayers [on Friday]. But since the spiritual benefit [*thawab*] accrued from Friday prayers is greater than that of the noon prayers, it is preferable to perform the Friday prayers in place of the noon prayers.[23]

The judicious legal ruling declared by the chief religious dignitary of Isfahan encouraged the city's majority Sunni population to enter a communal space of worship that was, in the *longue durée*, to educate and convert the population to Shi'ism. Shaykh Baha'i's recommendations for the mosque's epigraphic program act as public records of how religion was to elevate and strengthen the shah's sovereignty by turning the mosque into a space of collective worship. Miracles were also deployed to bolster the legitimacy of building the mosque. For instance, a marble quarry discovered in the vicinity of Isfahan was read as a fortuitous omen, a clear sign of support from God for Shah Abbas I's pious act of building the Friday Prayer Mosque. The marble was extracted and transported to the site where God's miracle would be turned into the foundation stone of the mosque. The artisan, merchant, or bureaucrat who entered the shah's mosque would be familiar with this story as he faced the foundational text composed by the Shaykh al-Islam and engraved in tile on the mosque's marble portal.

> The construction of this congregational mosque [*al-masjid al-jami'*] was decreed, purely from his own money, by [he who is] the most eminent in lineage and the most noble in descent of the sovereigns [*khavaqin*] of the earth, the

greatest in stature and worth, the strongest in argument and proof, the most complete in justice and beneficence, the dust of the holy threshold of the prophet, and the sweepings of the virtuous court of Ali, Abu-l-Muzzafar Abbas al-Husayni al-Musavi al-Safavi Bahadur Khan.

The name of Shah Abbas I, engraved in white *thulth* script on lapis tile, identifies the ruler as the endower of his personal property intended for the blessing of his grandfather, Shah Tahmasb, the consolidator of empire and the Shi'i religion. The Safavi genealogy is visibly spelled out, tracing its descent through the seventh Imam, from Musa al-Kazim to Husayn and Ali, and thus establishing Safavi claims to 'Alid legitimacy. The master calligrapher's inscribed name brings the foundational text to a close; he is none other than Ali Riza Abbasi, another Riza Abbasi attached to the shah, the calligrapher whose ascribed work circulated in collections of household anthologies. Along with the names of the architect, Ustad Ali Akbar Isfahani, and the building project's overseer, Muhibb Ali Beg, the chief eunuch of the shah's slaves and his royal treasurer, painters, calligraphers, and engineers are visibly inscribed as participants in a major revival of monumental epigraphy. Beyond supervising the mosque's construction, Muhibb Ali Beg was a co-donor and administrator of the endowment holdings; he was a lover (*muhibb*) of Imam Ali, who shepherded the project to completion.

On the portal, a chronogram (*madda-yi tarikh*) inscribed in a Persian hemistich, reading "the second Ka'ba has been built," embeds the time of construction within the holy space of the Ka'ba.[24] In accordance with the numerological system (*abjad*) announcing the mosque as the second Ka'ba, the date 1621 emerges from the collective calculation of each letter. Through this process, another public secret is revealed. Worshippers entered the community mosque knowing that they were stepping into the second Ka'ba (Figure 1.2). On both sides of the portal they could see and hear the prophet's words: "I am the *City of Knowledge* and Ali is my gate."[25] Isfahanis entered the Friday Prayer Mosque where page by page, wall by wall, they would be educated in Twelver Shi'a history and doctrine, a process of conversion that would lead them from the gate of Ali all the way to Ali's prayer niche facing Mecca. Calling on the worshipper to utter the principles of the Muslim faith, the two minarets flanking the portal read "God is Great" (Quran 37:35), "There is no god but Allah, and Muhammad is the messenger of God. He is God the One and Only."

FIGURE 1.2   The new Friday Prayer Mosque. Photo by Muhammad Sarraf.

These verses are accented with the repetition of "Allah is Great" spiraling downward as they declare God's unity and oneness (Quran 112:1–4).[26] The mosque can be read as a book, a collection of religious texts from the Quran to the Hadith, written on the minarets, portals, walls, and the inner prayer niche; it is an assembled manual educating worshippers into proper Shi'a etiquette and belief.[27]

Epigraphic poetry, together with the foundation inscriptions and Quranic verses, blend genres and draw on different levels of literacy in Persian and Arabic. The verse informs a Persian-speaking audience that the prophet was illiterate (*ummi*); though he could not write, he was nevertheless the medium through whom God spoke. And in Arabic, Ali is referred to as the manifestation of the unknown (*mazhar al-'aja'ib*), further mystifying his stature for the Persian speaker who might recognize Ali's name thanks to a shared alphabet but may be left wondering about the meaning of his Arabic epitaph. It is only as we enter the interior chambers of the mosque that the two holy figures, Muhammad the prophet (*nubuvvat*) and Ali his vice-regent (*wilayat*), act in concert as our guides. The epigraphy gradually educates the worshipper about their intertwined histories, moving from the prophet Muhammad's death and succession to his confirmation of the veracity of Ali's vice-regency, voiced through a famous Hadith (*Ghadir Khumm*) in which the practice of friendship is called on for believers to create community. "Whoever befriends them [the prophet's family] befriends me, and whoever holds enmity for them is my enemy." Because knowledge and friendship mark the terms of community making, brotherhood is evoked with another Hadith in which believers are invited to pray together in the mosque to attain God's grace and benefits, for "they are brothers in their faith in God the Glorious and the Mighty."[28] The Shi'a creed is chiseled onto the mosque's interior, thereby creating a new community of viewers, readers, listeners, and performers: a collective of friends and brothers of Ali.

As the believer is reminded of the universals of Shi'a Islam, another decree by the shah comes into sight in the western veranda (*ayvan*). In this text, all bathhouse (hammam) employees—washers, masseurs, and shavers—are exempted from city taxes. Interestingly, they too are designated as belonging to the shah. We will return to this decree; suffice it to say here that piety of spirit and purity of body connect worshippers with the institution of the mosque and with the hammam.

As believers move further inside the mosque, God speaks as the Creator of mankind and the Judge of its destiny. The northern veranda prepares the worshipper to enter paradise within, God's eternal City of Knowledge.[29] The entirety of the Quranic chapter 76, *Time* (*Dahr*), is recorded.

> As to the Righteous,
> They shall drink
> Of a Cup [of wine]
> Mixed with Camphor
>
> And because they were
> Patient and constant, He will
> Reward them with a Garden
> And garments of silk
>
> And the shades of the Garden
> Will come low over them
> And the bunches [of fruit]
> There will hang low
> In humility

And they will be given
To drink there of a Cup
[Of wine] mixed
With ginger

And round about them
Will [serve] male youths
Of perpetual [freshness]
If thou see them,
You would think them
Scattered Pearls[30]

For the faithful of Isfahan, the Quranic chapter *Time* evokes the inaugural festivities linking the interior of the Friday Prayer Mosque with the golden domed mosque across from the Imperial Gate and the *maydan* itself. In time, rewards will be plentiful for the righteous; fruits, wine, silk, and fresh male youth await Isfahan's believers. Epigraphy and ritual reinforce each other, as letters, words, and stories usher Isfahan's inhabitants into performing paradise. Repetition carries the epigraphic sequence further into the prayer niche, where the secret is divulged time and again: the truth of Ali's succession of the prophet and his friendship and authority (*wilayat*), which is inseparable from Muhammad's prophecy (*nubuvvat*). Graphic names of the prophet's family members, from Fatima to Ali and their children, all the way to the twelfth Imam, who will soon appear to restore justice, become recognizable to the unlettered. Ali is cast as the primordial light; together with Muhammad they are divinely created of a single luminous essence, that is to say, Light. Letters buttress the dome as sunlight enters through lattice screen windows; the visual effect is powerful as words, colors, and patterns complete one another.

A fascinating story inscribed on the wall below the central dome relates a Hadith from Abdullah ibn Abbas, the prophet's cousin and companion. During a gathering in Muhammad's presence of Ali and his two sons, Hasan and Husayn, the angel Gabriel descends bearing a red crystal cup (*jam*). He hands it to Muhammad, stating, "God bestows his peace upon you and welcomes you with this salutation, and orders you to salute Ali and his two sons." When the prophet takes the cup in his hand, it begins to speak, uttering the formula, "There is no god but God and God is great," three times. And when the prophet gives the cup to Ali it utters, "Your true friends [*waliyyakum*] are God, his Apostles and the fellowship of believers, and those who establish prayers and charity while bowing down humbly in worship" (Quran 5:58). The symbolic cup of wine, which Gabriel carries from God for the prophet and his family, synchronizes mystic rituals of initiation with the succession of Ali. Cupbearers are the inheritors of mystic authority, reminding the audience of Shah Abbas I, master of the Safavi spiritual order who shares Ali's blood. Just as Ali is God's friend and beloved cupbearer, so too is Shah Abbas I. The presentation of the metaphorical cup that has been passed down from God to Muhammad to Ali and then all the way to Shah Abbas I endows the sovereign with a sacred object in the holiest of spaces: the sanctuary where Ali is the *qibla*, the prayer niche toward whom all believers turn, in the direction of the sacred mosque, the Ka'ba in Mecca. The order of guidance and leadership in the community is made evident. Shah Abbas I's role in the city of paradise is to fulfill a promise to end the history of injustice inflicted on the prophet's family and create a community where those who are true lovers of Ali are protected. The shah, however, stops short of declaring himself the Mahdi![31] The inscriptions on the dome's exterior confirm the secret, scripting God as the divine architect and Shah Abbas I as the architectural patron of the Friday Prayer Mosque.

Two decades after his death, Shah Abbas I's image as cupbearer would be memorialized on the walls of the Audience Hall built in the palace complex by his grandson, Abbas II. Moving from Ali's gate at the Friday Prayer Mosque into the Imperial Gate (Ali Qapu), it is Shah Abbas I who holds the cup passed down to him by Imam Ali. This image would be seen only by courtiers, dignitaries of the Safavi Empire, and foreign ambassadors. Thus it was through whispers and the poetic accounts depicting the Audience Hall collected in household anthologies that residents of Isfahan would hear and read accounts of their sovereign cupbearer.

The Image of the Sovereign Cupbearer

In the palace complex Sufi idioms of love and devotion fashioned Safavi sovereignty to enable Shah Abbas I to be cast as the singular beloved. His grandson, Shah Abbas II (r. 1634–1666), commissioned wall paintings depicting his three ancestors—Ismail, Tahmasb, and Abbas I—and included himself on the fourth mural to assemble a visual history of Safavi kingship, ultimately drawing his lineage back to Ismail, the founder of the empire. But it is only Shah Abbas I who is figured as the singular cupbearer. Three decades after his death, Shah Abbas I is enshrined as the beloved.³² The altered social order at court is documented on the wall; we no longer see the red headdress of Qizilbash tribal chiefs and disciples, as they have been replaced by Turkman lovers of the shah and Caucasian slaves of the household (*ghulam-i khassa-yi sharifa*), whose loyalty rested absolutely with their beloved.³³ Two window openings bordering paradise on the mural signal Shah Abbas I's sacred authority, which radiates beyond the court onto the entire city of Isfahan. Furthermore, no members of the Shi'a clerical establishment are present at Shah Abbas I's feast. The other cupbearer, Imam Ali, is present in the city, standing at the gate of the Friday Prayer Mosque, and is visibly inscribed in the prayer niche.

To enter into the Audience Hall of the Forty Pillars Palace (Chihil Sutun) beyond the gates of the palace precincts (Ali Qapu) was to enter into a picture gallery of historical events that, according to the poet laureate Sa'ib Tabrizi (d. 1676), illustrated "colorful scenes of feasts and battles [*bazm u razm*], imparting life to the frozen walls."³⁴ Above eye level the murals are large enough for invited guests, such as a foreign ambassador or a provincial governor, to have been mesmerized by the painted characters participating in the splendor of courtly banquets and by the bravura of Safavi victories in the battlefield. Dignitaries on official visits to Isfahan were invited to walk through a monumental narrative of Safavi diplomatic history. The first set of four paintings commissioned by Shah Abbas II portrays historic episodes: a battle scene depicting Shah Ismail's victory over his Uzbek rival in 1512 and three royal feasts where Safavi shahs are entertaining Mughal and Uzbek princes.³⁵ These three feasts and the singular battle display an authorized dynastic history in which the twin prerogatives of feast and battle are highlighted to endow Safavi shahs with a sacred aura. Three shahs hosting three respective renegade princes from the Mughal and Uzbek courts are figured with distinct physical characteristics: portraits that aim to historicize and provide evidentiary weight to these paintings. Such remarkable images would be part of the tales that ambassadors brought back to their respective courts, recognizing Safavi shahs as protectors of the eastern frontiers of Central and South Asia.³⁶ At eye level, along the Audience Hall's four walls, figural representations of love frame history with romance, creating two temporalities and intertwined registers of the mystic language of sovereignty and love.³⁷

The feasting scene visually documents an event recorded by court historians that marked the occasion when the shah gave refuge to the renegade Uzbek prince

FIGURE 1.3 Wall painting in the Audience Hall of the Chihil Sutun depicting Shah Abbas I and Vali Muhammad Khan. Photo by Hamidreza Bani.

Vali Muhammad Khan. The painting complements the written accounts (Figure 1.3). With color and image, it authenticates and celebrates the encounter between the sovereign and his protected subject, the Uzbek prince. Wine, fruits, dishes of rice, and stews are ready to be served as music is performed and beautiful male and female dancers entertain the feasters. At the Safavi court, eros and mystical love have been turned into an authoritative language of transcendence, with Shah Abbas I, the most prominent figure, at its center. In scale and stature, he raises a cup of wine in his right hand. Like Ali in the Friday Prayer Mosque, the shah holds the mystic cup of wine to personify divine perfection, the embodiment of Beauty on earth, an action that figures him as the beloved at court. Encircled by rows of courtiers, guests, and servants, the shah/beloved gazes at his audience and draws viewers into his eminence. To his left, Safavi functionaries form a semicircle of loyalty and devotion to their sovereign; they invoke the master-disciple paradigm that governs both craft and mystic brotherhoods. Despite its compositional arrangement of rank and stature, the mural resounds with music and movement. Through its traffic of gazes, gestures, instruments, and dances, the mural brings to life the politics of eros at court. Mirroring the idealized social and sexual order dominant at court, two windows flank the painting, reminding viewers that the city of Isfahan lies beyond the feast. Floral and animal figures fill up the space between the windows, linking the court with the images that grace the Friday Prayer Mosque in the city of paradise.

Sitting at the center of the painting, amid an assembly of courtly men, Shah Abbas I is endowed with the thickest, longest mustache—a sign of his potent masculinity. He bears a cup in one hand and a sword in the other. Symbols of mystical love are fused together with royal regalia and masculinity, reinforcing the sense of the shah's military prowess, virility, and status as a sanctified patriarch. The other figures' spatial location in relation to the shah, as well as facial and martial likenesses to him, signify proximity and membership in his intimate circle. All the senior courtiers to his left sport full mustaches, whereas to his right sits the more sparsely hirsute Uzbek prince submissively receiving the divine favor of wine and succor. His facial hair, like that of his retinue, is different in style and far less endowed. Throughout the banquet, triangulations are drawn for the viewer to recognize constellations that constitute larger collectives at court. The shah's position is central as he holds out his cup of wine. His gesture provokes a response from the Uzbek prince, who humbly offers his left hand of service to the shah. Behind the shah two jugs of wine sit on a shelf, as the *saqi* (wine bearer) grips his jug. Standing at the threshold of the banquet in erotic anticipation, he tilts his wine jug toward the shah's cup.[38] Clothed in identical textiles and colors that match the shah's, he casts his eyes down in humility. Paralleling the gesture of the Uzbek prince, the *saqi* extends his left hand in readiness to serve his beloved. Together they reaffirm and submit to the values of the feast.

The triangulation of eros and submission intersects with multiple circles of men at court. The two *saqi*s, who seductively grip their wine jugs, create an arc around the shah, emphasizing his supremacy. On the shah's left sits the grand vizier, grasping his handkerchief, which casts him as the lover ready to blot his tears of longing. He offers his right hand of service to the shah as he too gazes at the audience. Such hand gestures signify servitude, connecting the grand vizier with the *saqi* and the Uzbek prince. Loyalty and obedience toward the shah are signaled by parallel gestures as another triangulation comes to light. On the left of the wall painting, the semicircle of Safavi courtiers, endowed with thick mustaches, represent men in authority. One general grips the pommel of his sword, and another caresses his long mustache. They gaze at us, demanding attention and respect from the audience. One courtier in the front row of sitting men stands out. He is young and smooth-faced. Enticing the senior notable sitting by his side, he engages in the politics of eros. Although the mustached general extends his left hand of friendship toward the male youth, he maintains his gaze at the audience. Even the youth in intimate service to the shah, stands behind him holding the accoutrements of sovereignty: the jug of wine, the bow and arrow, and the sword. Their gazes are aimed at the audience. The pages serving dishes for dinner, like the rest of the participants in this feast, look elsewhere; they have other interests and duties. Their gazes move in multiple directions, as they bring motion to the banquet and ignite sexual politics that have the potential to disrupt order and expose the vulnerability of seniority and sovereignty.

Mystic poetics and rituals provide the imperial model of *shahsavani*, or shah loving, where men perform acts of courtly *adab* as part of the process of state formation. On the far right of the mural, amid the Safavi circle of courtiers, a singular mustached official has turned away from the audience, as though to signal to a scene transpiring further at the margins of the banquet (Figure 1.4). He is the spiritual representative of the shah (*khalifat al-khulafa*), performing his disciplinary role with a stick, a ritual function that the Safavi royal household inherited from their Sufi ancestors.[39] Three vignettes marked visually by action are unfolding below the horizontal line of the stick, collectively illustrating the Sufi mix of discipline and

Imperial Visions of Sovereignty 51

FIGURE 1.4 Close-up of the right-hand side of the wall painting in the Audience Hall of the Chihil Sutun illustrating the politics of eros, with the *khalifat al-khulafa* on the far right, disciplining novices in accordance with court *adab*.

eros. They translate mystical rituals of initiation inherited from the days when the Safavis were a Sufi brotherhood onto the present theater of sacred kingship. The vignettes depict three significant stages of transcendence: (1) beating the disciple into obedience, (2) the disciple's embrace into a brotherhood of friends, and (3) the disciple's intoxication, culminating in ecstasy and union with the beloved.

Placed on the mural's right margin, the vignette reiterates a Sufi ritual that Shah Ismail's son and successor, Shah Tahmasb (r. 1524–1578), practiced on an imperial scale one century earlier. Shah Tahmasb's ritual of choice for initiating the Qizilbash into court society was the *chub-i tariqat*, or "the stick of order." The Venetian Cypriot merchant Michele Membré, while on a visit to the imperial court in Tabriz, described this ritual during the winter of 1540. Membré, who spoke Turkish, the court's language, had been sent on a diplomatic mission to convince the shah to join an alliance with Venice against the Ottoman Sultan Sulayman, who was their mutual enemy. Membré compared the rituals he witnessed to confraternities' in early modern Florence, observing similar ritualistic practices of sworn friendships. "None of the *qurchi*s [members of the imperial military retinue] were to marry without the permission of the shah, who makes the rules for the *nozze* [Italian for wedding]," he wrote. Membré recounts that the ritual took place in a large room at Shah Tahmasb's court, where his courtiers sat in rows. After they publicly praised God and Shah Tahmasb, for an hour or so, the devotees were led by the *khalifat al-khulafa* in *zikr* and in singing Ismail's and Tahmasb's poetry.[40] "They all come one by one for love of the shah to the middle of the room and stretch themselves out on the ground," Membré described. When his name was called out, each devotee came forward and confessed his sins, whereupon the chief deputy would grant absolution. Then the chief deputy beat the initiate's back once or twice with a stick and kissed his head and foot; the initiate in turn kissed the stick. The purpose of the ritual *chub-i tariqat* was twofold: to sanction Tahmasb's role as the divine intercessor who absolves the sins of his military corps and to discipline masculine aggression among the warrior class.

In this scene (Figure 1.5) three novices are being initiated by the *khalifa*, who strikes them with the Safavi order's stick, the *chub-i tariqat*. Stick in hand and sword in another, he strikes an intimidating pose: Two novices heed to his authority, fearing him and taking refuge against the wall. Hands up, perhaps after having been whipped on their palms, their faces express pain. The novice above has shut his eyes, whereas the one below has raised his eyebrows in distress. The one facing the *khalifa* raises his hand in readiness to be whipped. His face is lit with a grin that verges on conceit before he is struck. The vignette affirms the hierarchy being established between the senior mustached *khalifa* and the beardless novice youth (*amrad*). But cultivating obedience, love, and loyalty is a process. And so time is compressed on the margins as the viewer's eye is guided to the next stage of the ritual, which assumes a camaraderie between sworn brothers, grouped in units of two and three, who belong to the larger collective of friends in love and service to the shah. Two brothers hold their drunken friend; both look at him with desire, as one holds onto his robe and the other grabs his belt, deliberate sites of disrobement. All three are in an exchange

FIGURE 1.5 Close-up of the lower right-hand corner of the wall painting in the Audience Hall of the Chihil Sutun showing the *chub-i tariqat* ritual.

of amorous gazes, gestures, and touches; they encapsulate the vicissitudes of friendships animated by the erotic potential of disruption.

The final stage of ecstasy (Figure 1.6) carries the novice into the arena of the celebratory feast, where participants witness his ultimate submission, which will grant him access to court society. Stretched out on the floor, he is losing consciousness. Under the scrutiny of a triangle of patriarchs at whose apex sits Shah Abbas I, he has capitulated to sexual temptation. Manifest ecstasy proves the devotee's love and obeisance to the ultimate beloved, the shah, through whom the devotee can attain union with God. Only once he has exhibited singular devotion can the youthful subject enter court service to perform the functions of page, or jug bearer. Disciplining sexuality here also reproduces the sexual charge associated with the Sufi practice of gazing, but it cleanses it of its erotic possibilities in friendship. In the triangulation of three men around the semiconscious youth, the standing thick-mustached courtier clad with a sword is standing guard; his arms are resolutely crossed as he gazes at the audience. With his right hand on his chest, he signals his love and devotion to the shah, whom he is serving full-heartedly. Another mustached notable with a distinct royal feather on his headgear holds his right "finger of description," in awe at what is transpiring before his eyes. His gesture is in conversation with the cupbearer, who is just as astonished as he tilts his jug of wine toward the ecstatic youth, reminding the viewer of the centrality of the ultimate cupbearer, the beloved shah. The youth has unfolded himself on the lap of a clean-shaven courtier, the chief eunuch, under whom pages are trained for court service. Embracing the head of the fainted youth with the palm of his hand, the chief eunuch offers him fruit, another symbol of love in mystical poetics. The youth also holds a finger of astonishment toward his mouth, while his other hand rests on the chief eunuch's thigh. All three knots of his belts have been untied, a visual sign for sexual concourse. In the moment of drunken ecstasy the youth has laid his desire onto the lap of the master eunuch.

Eros, the love that is desiring, is the emotional apparatus that makes possible the appreciation and recognition of beauty. The shah is embraced by his senior courtiers, who stand in control, ensuring his position as the singular object of desire; they police sexuality even as they desire the ecstatic youth. The youthful courtier's devotion for his beloved shah, for instance, allows him to engage in the rules of courtship, itself a highly ritualized form of political sociality. The scene we witness of the beardless courtier flirting with his mustached neighbor is, for this reason,

FIGURE 1.6 Close-up of the lower right-hand corner of the wall painting in the Audience Hall of the Chihil Sutun showing submission, brotherhood, and ecstasy.

didactic. If such a youth is able to navigate the etiquette and protocols of the politics of eros, the novice, after several years of usefulness and loyalty to king and court, may rise to the position of general or grand vizier. Under the disciplinary gaze of his officials, so long as love is directed toward the beloved shah, a ritualized system of coy gestures and sexual innuendos are permitted. These rituals of *adab* simultaneously test, taunt, enable pleasure, and cultivate male sexuality.

The courtly sexual economy is further elaborated with the performance of cross-dressed male dancers and three female entertainers at the forefront of the feast (Figure 1.7). The bodies of the cross-dressed male youth and the three women are figures of social otherness; they are socially marginalized and separated from the court's rank and file and inscribed as entertainers. This social marginality enables the conflation of professional marginality with fantasies of homoeroticism. Two female singers form a couple. Their heads tilt toward each other in an amorous embrace. One smiles at the audience while she offers her partner a cup of wine and rubs her groin with the other hand. This gesture, along with the female

FIGURE 1.7 Close-up of the left-hand side of the wall painting in the Audience Hall of the Chihil Sutun showing female singers and cross-dressed male dancers.

musician playing the tambourine, associates these three women with *tribadism*.[41] The Persian term for tribadism, *musahiqqa*, has the Arabic root *s.h.q*, and the word *sihaq* literally means "rubbing and pounding." The tambourine is a metaphor for the surface on which the rubbing of genitalia takes place.[42] The licentious potential of one woman pleasuring another allows the painting's male viewers license to both enjoy female-female sex and subordinate it to a mimicking of the male prerogative of foreplay. The masculine imagination is being trained to fantasize its way into the climax of the erotic narratives depicted in the mural. The painting therefore reveals a central contradiction of the sex-gender system underpinning early modern patriarchy at the Safavi court. Male sexual "apprenticeship" in the vignette is permissible through asymmetries of age and rank, but at the forefront of entertainment it licenses the possibility and visibility of behaviors subversive to that order—even if male eros is being cultivated for heterosexual or camouflaged male homoerotic desire.

A mix of political and religious veneration, erotic titillation, and sexual discipline make this wall painting part history, part mirror for princes, and part erotica. Each term is brought to bear on the other, arriving at a located ideal, a courtly rehearsal of romanticized mystic love. The representation of love and eros is disciplined as the shah comes to embody immanent authority. It is Shah Abbas I who bedazzles and confounds the banquet. He is the mighty beloved who commands total authority. Longing for the shah and anticipating the encounter with the beloved transpires in the privacy of the palace and in the presence of courtiers and official visitors to Isfahan. Mystic rituals of initiation and love deployed to shape the social order are familiar cultural vehicles exercised to tame courtly masculinity. Drawing on the ubiquitous language of mystic love, the masculine aggression of the courtly and warrior class is being visually domesticated at the Safavi court. But as we shall see in the following chapters, these forces can also be mobilized to cultivate an alternate masculinity in the city.

Disciplining Carnal Isfahan

Different technologies were deployed under the sovereign's gaze to discipline both the body's sexuality and homosocial culture in the streets of Isfahan. Although paintings on the arcade walls of the *maydan* and epigraphy inscribed on the Friday Prayer Mosque celebrated the carnal rewards of paradise, contradictions of the sex-gender system similar to that portrayed on the palace mural were operative beyond the Safavi court. The concept of beauty idealized in the figure of the male youth was central to Isfahan's aesthetics and the cultivation of masculinity. Men were to be socialized into the practice of homoerotic "apprenticeship" permissible through asymmetries of age and rank, even as possibilities for behaviors subversive to that order existed. But celebrating such ritualized, courtly *adab* practices while simultaneously disciplining men who sexually desired other men as subversive to the rule of the shah would prove a delicate balance to sustain. The Shi'a religious establishment would play an increasingly significant role in policing the sexual order in Isfahan. Scholars, such as Shaykh Baha'i (d. 1621), who was appointed by Shah Abbas I as chief religious dignitary to help provide a religious platform for the communal inclusion of Sunnis and Shi'as in worship, played a key role in launching a century-long process of conversion and confession building. Shaykh Baha'i composed manuals on proper etiquette and handbooks on Shi'a religious obligation (which he wrote in simple Persian), yet the consumption of wine was never officially prohibited nor was sodomy publicly banned during his lifetime. Consider, for example, Shah Abbas I's own performance of the homoerotic promise of his city of paradise. The shah regularly visited his Georgian beloved, who worked at his favorite coffeehouse, the Qahvakhana-yi Arab; he also frequented the Armenian quarter of New Julfa and took pleasure in drinking wine with his hosts. Shah Abbas I's public enactment of male homoerotic desire was unique and not easily replicated by his successors; he would be memorialized as the sovereign cupbearer capable of performing both the ideal and the exception.

It was Shah Abbas I who personally commanded the social, sexual, and moral economy of his city. He exercised the virtuous performance of the Muslim duty to command right and forbid wrong. God's charge, "Let there be one community of you, calling to good and commanding right and forbidding wrong," developed into a divinely imposed obligation for Muslim rulers.[43] To be marked, or to mark a community, as Muslim, rulers ordered right and wrong, deploying a variety of strategies to enforce what was politically expedient for the purpose of governing. For example, the office of the *muhtasib*, the censor of morals and commercial practices, appears in Safavi administrative manuals at the end of the seventeenth century.[44] But in Shah Abbas I's Isfahan, the *muhtasib* controlled only the price of goods to guarantee fair pricing based on the quality of commodities and the value of labor; his jurisdiction was restricted to the bazaar. Instead, it was the shah's chief spiritual representative, the *khalifat al-khulafa*, who extended his disciplinary role into the city's streets and bazaars to regulate moral and sexual misconduct. However, his dominion stopped at the door of the hammam, for the *khalifat al-khulafa* was an extension of the shah, and neither would subject their bare bodies to the public gaze.

With the death of Shah Abbas I in 1629, a decree exempting barbers along with male and female bathhouse employees from city taxes was written in stone and hung on the marble wall inside the mosque.[45] The edict, issued by the shah's successor, Shah Safi (r. 1629–1642), confirms that in accordance with his grandfather's practice, barbers (*salmaniyan*),[46] masseurs (*dalakan*), cloakroom staffers (*jamdaran*), circumcisers (*khitnagaran*), and other bathhouse attendants would be exempt from paying city taxes.[47] Singling out the entire membership of the barber's corporation (*jama'at-i salmaniyan*) on the walls of the Friday Prayer Mosque, the decree names Shah Abbas I's personal barber, master Ali Riza, as the official in charge of the group.[48] Even though barbers and bathhouse employees were exempt from paying city taxes, Shah Abbas I's barber was ordered to continue collecting dues and ensure supervision and order in bathhouses across the city of Isfahan. Meanwhile, in the hammams of Isfahan, master Ali Riza monitored the sexual order of this semipublic space, located between the street and the home. Religiously tied to the mosque, every Muslim had the canonical duty to perform ablutions before prayer. Public hygiene linked to ritual purity thus was an important civic function, which the shah entrusted to his personal barber. Where the king himself would not enter to display his body, his barber acted as the shah's eyes and ears. Irrespective of rank, in the baths men and women socialized and forged networks, their bodies exposed in close proximity to each other, with only a towel tied around their waists. The baths provided occasion for men to have their beards shaved and their bodies scrubbed and massaged; consequently, such contacts, whether physical or social, produced anxiety in view of the erotic potential they provoked.[49]

By the mid-seventeenth century, under the auspices of the imperial court, the Shi'a religious establishment initiated a project of normative regulation that scrutinized male public behavior in particular. Although Shah Abbas I's representation as cupbearer in the mural of the Audience Hall drew on paradigms of romanticized mystic love to fashion a language of sovereignty, toward the second half of the seventeenth century, and against the backdrop of competing claims to intimacy with God and his subjects, Shi'i scholars devoted much ink and paper to curtailing mystical forms of sexual and spiritual expression. Their polemics cast the practice of boy gazing and celibacy as contradictory to the prophet's teachings and hence inimical to God's will. The sacred came to be legitimately conjoined with sexual activity only in holy matrimony. In the rising politicosexual discourse on social disorder, Shi'i clerics castigated gazing, cleaved the ritual from mysticism, and rendered it an earthly, erotic pastime. Drawing from the Muslim sacred texts of the Quran and Hadith, they offered up marriage as the worldly, sanctified path to God. This shift in attitudes toward eroticism outside heterosexual marriage bolstered imperial efforts to centralize and govern. In the new paradigm of love and friendship, the shah represented the ideal mystic who reinvigorates love with purity and cleanses it of profaneness.

Heterosexual conjugality received such voluble advocacy from members of the Shi'a clerical establishment because men beyond the court were eschewing the unions of marriage to female mortals in favor of union with men through the practice and aesthetics of Sufism, which provided a language of love and friendship drawn from the more rarefied, transformative unions with God. And these unions, which they so ardently pursued, undermined the project of making socially, sexually, and spiritually disciplined and productive Safavi subjects. Part of the imperial design was to thwart and obstruct, by denouncing as anti-Muslim, relations of collective solidarity, brotherhood, and community formed between men in various intimate settings, such as the hammam or the coffeehouse—that is, outside the specific rituals of court life. By remystifying and, in this context, desexualizing love and desire between men, both the court and the religious establishment hoped to restrict the exercise and consolidation of social power to a select group of courtiers and clergymen. And yet this is represented as happening at court. An upstart youth, such as the one depicted in the wall painting of Shah Abbas I's banquet, who successfully seduces a well-connected mustached superior, might circumvent the hierarchical route to success and fortune. Cast as a transgressor, he disturbs the social order.

Along with this shift, wine was prohibited in taverns; Armenians also were forbidden to sell the wine they produced to Muslim customers. In fact, all Armenians were ordered to move out of the city proper and were confined to their suburb of New Julfa. Such practices of inclusion and segregation endeavored to create a new communal identity in Isfahan. In the process of demarcating confessional boundaries, Sufis were particularly marked as a contagion that required cleansing. The shaving of the beard was singled out as a symptom of contamination. By the end of the seventeenth century, the set of moral significations ascribed to beards and their removal became a prominent subject of discussion in manuals penned by clerics. Devoting fourteen chapters to various aspects of daily life, a famous manual on Shi'i mores and ethics, penned by another Shaykh al-Islam of Isfahan, Muhammad Baqir Majlisi (d. 1699), delineated the proprieties of dress, makeup, eating, sleeping, marriage, prayer, fasting, and pilgrimage in detail. Although Majlisi wrote that it was well known that clerics had forbidden the shaving of beards, he nevertheless included a section on the different ways to trim the beard and the mustache. There was clearly an art to trimming facial hair that signified sexual virility and masculine power. Majlisi confirmed the ban on shaving and created a genealogy going back to Genesis, referring to an episode related by the prophet Muhammad himself: "On the day God accepted Adam's repentance for having tasted the apple of knowledge, Adam declared, 'O, God, make me more beautiful.' So, God gave him a thick black beard. But, having never seen a beard before, Adam asked God, 'What is this?' 'This is your ornament,' replied God, 'and that of your sons till eternity.'"[50]

In his chapter on the virtues of marriage and the vices of celibacy, Majlisi reiterated the norm of cross-sex conjugal affiliation based on the authoritative report that the prophet Muhammad, exemplar for all humankind, loved women. He proceeded to list examples that established the Imams' desire for women, an obligation that constituted one-half of a believer's religious duties. This late-seventeenth-century manual of mores showed the prophet Muhammad as having demarcated Muslim men's faith and religious beliefs on grounds of sexuality; a true Muslim could not have sexual intercourse with members of his sex, bearded or not. When some women allegedly complained to Muhammad that their husbands abstained from sexual relations with them, the prophet condemned the men: "They are not of my followers."[51]

Sufi spirituality's fundamental tenet, that union between the human and the divine can be attained through a man's mystical love and friendship for his male beloved, effectually collapsed the distance between God and the believer, something that the rationalist clerics had been attempting to create. For Majlisi, only marital union appears to be consistent with the divine and temporal order. Marriage, the figure of speech at play here, is one of inversion, where sodomy negates both the world and the sharia. The relationship between sodomy and marriage is also mutually constitutive.[52] The religious treatises on ethics that legitimate sexual acts in marriage are differentiated from illegitimate, extramarital acts of adultery and sodomy that transgress the command of what is right. Majlisi attempted to redraw the boundary between the sacred and the sexual by advocating marriage. The sacred was to cohabit with sexual activity in matrimony. A religiously exemplary life became compatible with sexual activity in marriage, extending the expectation of a marital mode of life to groups that had formerly been exempt from marrying, namely, Sufis.

To experience Isfahan during the first decades of the seventeenth century was to encounter the city of God. Built on the heel of devastating floods and famine, Shah Abbas I's ideal city was erected on the promise of material delight and homoerotic pleasure that awaited pious Muslims in paradise. Collectively, the colorful splendor of the *maydan*, with its bright yellow domed mosque on the eastern horizon, the magnificent lapis tiled portal of the Friday Prayer Mosque, which called believers into Imam Ali's gate of knowledge on the south, and the paintings of beautiful male and female youth displayed across the arcade walls, flanking the gateway into the bazaar—all materialized the magical aura of divine beauty for residents of Isfahan. Stepping into the central square was to enter a space where Quranic and poetic depictions of paradise became visible. Regardless of whether the generation born after the floods of 1593 remembered Isfahan's natural disasters or whether those who had migrated to the city to take part in its revival had heard about the spectacular inaugural rituals, the graphic aesthetics inscribed in word and image created a habitus where erotic desire was the emotional apparatus that made the recognition of Isfahan's beauty palpable. The concept of mystic beauty and romantic love, idealized in the figure of the male youth, together with its aesthetics infused Isfahan's politics to cultivate urban masculinity.

By the middle of the seventeenth century residents of Isfahan continued to be accultured in the *adab* of urbanity but under a new regime of public scrutiny. Different technologies were deployed by the Safavi court to discipline the body's sexuality and homosocial culture in the streets of Isfahan. Shifts in imperial and religious attitudes toward homoeroticism that came to monitor collective solidarities broadcast a paradigm change in love and friendship. The mystic language of romantic love commissioned by Shah Abbas II (d. 1666) for the wall painting of the Forty Pillars Palace reserved love and eros for the person of his grandfather, Shah Abbas I (d. 1629), memorializing the sovereign cupbearer, now deceased. Mystic rituals of initiation and discipline deployed love to shape the political and social order at court; mobilized as vehicles to tame urban masculinity, these practices recalled male homoerotic desire. Contradictions of the sex-gender system that promoted the early modern Safavi patriarchal system allowed for male sexual apprenticeship through asymmetries of age and rank while licensing the sensibility of behaviors subversive to that order, simultaneously cultivating hetero- or male homoerotic desire, whether camouflaged, aestheticized, or regulated. The ubiquitous language of mystic love stimulated the capital's homosocial culture *alongside* more normative versions of power and authority as homoerotic desire produced heteroerotic phobias.

In the following chapters, we enter Isfahan's households to explore the *longue durée* of the history of reception of the Safavi state's adabizing project. I trace the ways in which friendship came under public scrutiny, how love between male and female friends would be reassessed in this process, so that intimacy between friends would require the disassociation of love from the taint of erotic desire. The production of decrees, paintings, epigraphy, and *adab* manuals all served to discipline subjects, controlling their desires, speech, and conduct, even while fashioning a range of urban sensibilities. This activity gives needed historical context to the rise of anthologies, in which individual and household collectors displayed their city knowledge and practices, thereby forging new textual and social logics that archive what could be said, shared, and resisted in Isfahan.

CHAPTER 2

Collecting, Self-Fashioning, and Community

Urban Habits of Collecting

> In the garden, the anthology [*majmuʻa*] of colorful flowers
> recalls, Saʼib, pages of your poetry book[1]
>
> Saʼib Tabrizi (d. 1676)

Saʼib Tabrizi, the poet laureate of Isfahan, conjures the Persianate trope of a garden—a space of reflection, sociability, and delight—to call to mind his poetry. Yet he also extends the symbolism of the garden, as an allegory of paradise, to the beauty and refinement of his composition, which he collects in the physical folios of his anthology.[2] I argue that habits of collecting in Isfahan are curating acts that associate the city of paradise with the household anthology. Like the garden, the city and the anthology are places of contemplation and conviviality; they are sites of learning, discovery, and sensual pleasure. But in Isfahan, idioms of love (*ʻishq*) transport practices of experiencing gardens to the city; whether strolling through or writing the city, love anticipates an urban reality. Collecting letters, verses, drawings, or manuals therefore serves as a social, heuristic tool. In this chapter, after providing some necessary context on the production of graphic works and manuscripts in Isfahan more broadly, I turn to two resident anthologizers, a religious scholar and a painter, both of them migrants to the city. My close reading of their work considers the subjects of their collected writings and drawings to show how these practices illuminate links between households as verbal and visual modes of navigating the city and fashioning the self.[3] First, the anthology of Aqa Husayn Khwansari (d. 1686), a Shi'a religious scholar, foregrounds shared *adab* texts that connect him with Isfahan's literary community, just as these texts archive his aesthetic choices and public persona. Second, my reconstruction of the dispersed portfolio of renowned painter Muhammad Qasim (d. 1660) assembles a patchwork of his portraits and gendered compositions. Muhammad Qasim represents himself, through self-portraits of a painter working outside the royal atelier, as the craftsman poised to fashion his patrons as refined subjects. Whether focused on the royal court or the religious seminary, the act of interpreting the curatorial choices of these two residents allows us access to an archive of urban knowledge that is overlooked in the historiography of seventeenth-century Isfahan (see Map 0.1).[4] Like the *majmu'a* of flowers in Sa'ib Tabrizi's garden/poetry book, these anthologies not only provide sites of reflection but also mediate our encounter with early modern Isfahan in particular ways, departing from the epigraphic program assembled by the city's designers.

In such historiography the arts and sciences of belles lettres, calligraphy, history, painting, poetry, philosophy, theology, and law have often been studied separately, as discrete disciplinary formations.[5] These categorizations reproduce Western Enlightenment thought that not only obscures the affinities that bind these bodies of knowledge with one another but also ignores the shared logic that inspired literary and visual material subjects of study. These taxonomies suggest a disciplinary hierarchy, situating religion and state as centers of knowledge production. The royal court and the religious establishment certainly enjoyed the financial and political power to create, reproduce, record, and transmit knowledge in the medium of manuscripts. These institutions possessed the infrastructure to manage resources and to deploy the people and materials necessary to implement the production of manuscripts. The court and the seminary were a critical conduit for communicating knowledge, as masters orally transmitted their craft to their apprentices from within the walls of the palace or seminary and beyond into the city, the provinces, and across imperial boundaries. But other spaces, such as the bazaar or the elite and merchant household, also participated in the production of knowledge and, in particular, in the writing and dissemination of urbanity. Thus bazaars and private libraries served as productive sites that are vital for the study of urban literacy, as they bring to bear the curated choices of patrons and scribes, drawn from the very objects that shaped and were shaped by their habitus.⁶ The practices according to which Aqa Husayn Khwansari and Muhammad Qasim performed their urbanity guide my reading of their authorial voices, which simultaneously demonstrate the acts of curating the urban self and creating city knowledge.

In Isfahan's built environment, clear correspondences materialize among the graphic arts, book production, and city building. To read Isfahan's conversion to Shi'ism alongside its physical and cultural expansion, we turn to the collecting practices by which residents declared their urbanity. The culture of *adab*, or etiquette, had to be learned and embodied across elite, artisan, and merchant sectors of a society in the making. The processes of cultivating urban subjects transformed the function of writing from a bureaucratic, religious, and commercial practice into a medium for communicating and educating the self. To develop the skills to write and speak with eloquence and wit, residents collected tools for learning and exhibiting their *adab*. Some did this in their homes, whereas others bought anthologies from booksellers in the bazaar and the central square to be read by members of their family. Whether an anthology was bought as a discrete manuscript that became a treasured household commodity or was assembled in a private household, these curated troves shaped the material and symbolic experience of Isfahan. Every collected object had its own history of encounter, recording and negotiating ways of living in the city or even explicitly contesting state-sponsored urbanity. Thanks to habits of collecting, these anthologies, prized and preserved as household archives, have been passed on to us.

Thousands of anthologies are dated to the seventeenth century and bear the inscription of Isfahan, where they were assembled. The process of disseminating urban knowledge happened through anthologies; scribes or authors most probably used anthologies to first copy texts on loose paper and then selected segments from them to author their own compositions. From among this vast corpus, I have selected anthologies produced in Isfahan's households, where families and professions are clearly identifiable from the content of the material collected and recorded in the manuscript. Household anthologies archive city writings once in circulation; they illustrate the particular practices of urban knowledge and their valorization by communities who took possession of them. To investigate household anthologies as mediums of self-fashioning, of reception and negotiation, we move between institutional spaces of knowledge making and household libraries to explore the individuals, practices, and aesthetics that illuminate the linkages between the making of the city and the assembling of an anthology.

As we have seen, when Shah Abbas I began his project of renovating Isfahan, he invited the best artists to fashion his capital city into the image of paradise. Parallel methods of production at court, in the central square or *maydan*, and in the bazaar made the arts and crafts visible to Isfahan residents. It is no wonder, then, that contemporaneous poets and historians deployed the metaphor of an illustrated manuscript, or a sheet of paper, to conjure the image of the *maydan* as it materialized in the built environment. The shah's head librarian, Sadiqi Beg Afshar, lists the names of eleven calligraphers and ten painters working at the royal workshop, the *kitabkhana*, in 1610.[7] The calligraphers Mir 'Imad and Ali Riza Abbasi, the master painter Riza Abbasi, and the historian Iskandar Beg Munshi stand out for their participation in visualizing and memorializing paradise in the *maydan*. These four individuals imagined, wrote, inscribed, and colored the built environment. From the walls and portals of mosques and arcades onto the pages of the world-adorning history of the reign of Shah Abbas I, they made public a graphic culture that would cultivate a taste for the visual among Isfahan's inhabitants. The undertaking of creating the public square was organized and managed as a macro-library; tools and materials were provided by the court to artisans and architects, who collaborated to translate their book arts into monumental epigraphic programs of buildings that configured the *maydan*.

Calligraphy and paintings ascribed to Ali Riza Abbasi and Riza Abbasi appear in hundreds of single sheets and illuminated manuscripts commissioned by royal and private patrons. Countless freestanding paintings bearing these two painters' signatures are objects that speak to patronage beyond imperial workshops. Even though these artists share the patronymic Abbasi, marking them as affiliates of Shah Abbas I, their clientele reached beyond the court. Consider, for example, Hajj Hasan Beg, a merchant and bibliophile in Isfahan who commissioned Ali Riza Abbasi to copy the epic *Garshaspnama*, composed by the medieval poet Asadi, for his private library collection.[8] Or, consider 'Itiqad Khan, another wealthy merchant who collected the works of master calligraphers Mir 'Imad and Ali Riza Abbasi in his library.[9] These calligraphers and painters worked at court, in the bazaar, and in homes. They were hired by Isfahan's residents—who covered the cost of paper, ink, and natural elements for making pigments—to produce specific projects for private libraries.[10] Their students, their paintings and drawings, and even their forged signatures all circulated in Isfahan, cultivating an appreciation for a graphic culture that illuminated the new city center. The collected lives and works of these painters were dispersed throughout household libraries in seventeenth-century Isfahan and bound in anthologies by collectors well into the nineteenth century. As shared repositories, they mark the moment of their creation in Isfahan, simultaneously connecting patrons and households to their community, just as they provided the material from which individual collectors could fashion their own visual anthologies (*muraqqa'*s).

The most visible act of collecting in the Persianate world was the textual practice of memory making, whereby stories were assembled to create a life. Referred to by the Arabic *tazkira*, or collection, the term semantically signifies the act of remembering, citing, and reporting. The *tazkira* is a biographical genre that collates stories about professional men, bureaucrats, scholars, poets, painters, calligraphers, or mystics. The idea of collecting a life story gave way to an early version of an anthology (*mukhtarat*) anchored in the practice of "choosing the best" (*ikhtiyar*) samples of these men's work.[11] A noteworthy life was recreated according to curated examples patched together to fashion an image of the biographical subject. Although anthologies of poetry (*majmu'a*), with or without illuminations, were the most common and valued collectibles before the fifteenth century and although the assembly of single-page paintings, drawings, and calligraphy for the purpose of album making (*muraqqa'*) appear on the Persianate scene in Timuri princely workshops, we have no extant albums of paintings before the fifteenth century.[12] One of the earliest anthologies was produced in Isfahan and was deliberately dated: "Tuesday evening, 21 June 1413, in Isfahan," with the name of the patron inscribed as Iskandar Sultan (d. 1415), the Timuri prince and governor of the southwestern province of Fars.[13]

Although royal albums and household anthologies share a collective genealogy, by the seventeenth century the production of literary anthologies and single-sheet paintings had become a popular urban practice in its own right in Isfahan. Religious judges, bureaucrats, merchants, and artisans participated in the habit of collecting. The art historian David Roxburgh understood the compilation and proliferation of *muraqqa'*s in the fifteenth and sixteenth centuries as cultural repositories of former artworks that produced sites of memory.[14] The ritual of compiling and making anthologies heightened the awareness of history, making a history of

Persianate art manifest for the first time through acts of mobilizing past drawings and paintings, reflecting on them, and writing prefaces to elucidate the vision of the painter who created the album. Albums also performed a didactic function in teaching past drawing and painting traditions to a new generation of artists, as in the collage from a Timuri *muraqqaʿ* assembled in Central Asia around 1400–1450 (Figure 2.1). Roxburgh suggests that the purpose of this large-format anthology was as an active learning tool to be discussed and reflected on by a private audience, usually consisting of the master painter and his disciples, who would congregate around it. Authors of household anthologies display parallel techniques of reflection and mimesis when they select and arrange their choices of different city writings. The effect of these curated choices is distinct from royal albums, in that household anthologies are agentive—they too shape the city and its experience. The label of the patchwork associated with a particular configuration of anthologies, the *muraqqaʿ*, encapsulates this sense of anthologies as family archives and assemblages which illustrate urban knowledge-in-the-making in the context of Isfahan's private households.

For the private collector, the medium of the anthology opened a space of recognition where knowledge was compiled through praxis. Similar to the apprentice of an artist who eventually masters the designs and techniques of his craft, the student did not merely imitate the drawings of his teachers. Instead, once the apprentice mastered the tradition, he added his personal touch in composing his own work of art and display, his refinement of and departure from the model.[15] In this training process, painters developed a sensibility as they drew on a genealogy of masters' expertise, adding their literary and visual interpretation of key scenes, from, say, commonly illustrated epic poems such as Ferdowsi's *Shahnama*. Such mimetic didactics were practiced widely across disciplines. Paul Losensky demonstrates how these techniques were celebrated in Persian poetry through the practice of welcoming (*istiqbal*) an old composition through a new poem, which receives the creative spirit of the past and then greets it with an innovative response.[16] The culture of *adab* that produced anthologies (*majmuʿa*s and *muraqqaʿ*s), portraits (*surat*s), and artist's signatures (*qalam*s) participated in similar acts of learning, inscribing, and reiterating. In concert with the proliferation of memoirs (*tazkira*s) of kings and mystics who wrote verse and prose in the first person, anthologies are visual and literary spaces for the unfolding of the self to be constituted and displayed.

Collecting, Self-Fashioning, and Community   69

FIGURE 2.1   Folio from a *muraqqa'* made in Samarqand between 1400 and 1450. Assembly of Drawings, Topkapi Museum, TSMK, H.2152, fol. 86v. Presidency of the Republic of Turkey, the Directorate of National Palaces.

Household anthologies share a genealogy with court and elite anthologies, though they are compiled by individual authors or scribes, gathering together families' professional and intimate writings and readings. Anthologies belong to the general category of the discursive practice of writing.[17] By choosing and rearranging selections of works from a larger corpus, anthologists created images of a poet and models of epistolary practices that were shaped by the curatorial choices and interpretations of their compiler. Over the centuries this Persianate tradition of collecting produced a wide variety of single-subject anthologies of poetry, composition, letters, and philosophy, known by interchangeable generic labels such as *jung* (Chinese for "boat"), *bayaz* (copy), *safina* (Arabic for "boat"), *majmuʿa* (anthology) or *muraqqaʿ* (patchwork). A range of anthologies from seventeenth-century Isfahan are available to us; some of these are more systematic and public in their design, perhaps denoting a practice peculiar to the manuscript market in Isfahan. Especially relevant to this market is the example of the *Safina-yi Saʾib*, compiled in mid-seventeenth-century Isfahan by the poet laureate Saʾib Tabrizi (d. 1676). Saʾib had a scriptorium where he produced his own private manuscripts and sold his signed copies on the market. Saʾib's anthology is a selection of poems and verses from the history of Persianate poetry that proposes a canon and endorses both Saʾib's own literary practice and the poetics of his "fresh style." Saʾib wrote, collected, and published his own well-crafted image in Isfahan (see Map 0.1).[18]

Household anthologies, regularly referred to as *majmuʿa*s, were bequeathed from one generation to the next and were either recorded as a gift to a son or daughter or otherwise registered in wills that are preserved in anthologies. An heirloom list of household goods inherited by the son of Hajj Muhammad at the end of the seventeenth century characterizes the location of the anthology within the household unit.[19] Included in the category of copper vessels and utensils (*misina*) that Hajj Muhammad's son was to inherit, we find two large cooking pots, one large Quran, three *majmuʿa*s, and an ewer. The inclusion of the Quran and the *majmuʿa*s along with copper vessels suggests the utility of these objects; copper pots, ewers, and manuscripts are distinguished from other household possessions (*tarkakhana*), such as a comforter, two down pillows, a hookah bowl, and two sheets of paper, and even from valuable objects, such as a woodblock print (*qalamkar*) curtain and a silver inkpot cover. The owner's title, Hajj or Hajji, indicates that he had gone on the pilgrimage to Mecca, a designation often associated in this period with a merchant who had enough money to pay for the Hajj pilgrimage. To practice his Muslim duty, Hajj Muhammad recited the Quran with his family as a symbolic object signaling the family's piety, and through the *majmuʿa*s household members also learned the ethics and aesthetics of urbanity. Two sheets of paper and an inkwell imply the son's continued practice of writing—perhaps of letters or even a *majmuʿa*. Although literacy in the seventeenth-century *majmuʿa* was mainly an attribute of Isfahan's erudite and eloquent residents—poets, bureaucrats, religious scholars, and the like—the entire corpus of anthologies provides enough evidence to argue that merchants also engaged in the habits of collecting, learning poetry and ethics, and practicing epistolary techniques as part of their cultivation of urbanity.

Manuscripts were sold in the bazaar and the central square, where booksellers displayed their collections, much as a blacksmith or a halva maker would. Those residents of Isfahan who could not inherit or purchase manuscripts might have been able to see them on display and flip through them. The Huguenot jeweler Jean Baptiste Chardin remarked that there were no printing presses in Isfahan during the time he lived there between 1655 and 1677. He had heard different reasons as to why; some argued that the weather was too dry or that the paper produced in Isfahan would break under the pressure of the press. But Chardin noted that these were excuses, because residents of Isfahan in fact loved their hand-copied manuscripts. They were "by nature lovers of knowledge, of the art of calligraphy and manuscript culture";[20] for them, calligraphy was an art form. Chardin saw their appreciation of manuscripts as the reason for a flourishing culture of manuscript production in Isfahan. Although the cost of a manuscript was greater than a printed book, manuscripts were abundant in Isfahan; paper and utensils were purchased by patrons, and scribes charged for every thousand lines they copied.[21] The thousands of surviving manuscripts copied in Isfahan are evidence of the enormous energy invested in their production.[22] Hundreds of scribes must have been occupied with copying manuscripts for court, seminaries, and private and commercial use. Consumers were of all ages; Raphaël du Mans, the Carmelite friar who resided in Isfahan from 1647 to 1696, informs us that "from childhood until their elder age they [inhabitants of Isfahan] pursued knowledge, while we in France, once we attain the age of 18 or 20, and that by force, we no longer continue the pursuit of knowledge."[23]

Manuscripts could also be borrowed from booksellers if a reader could not afford to purchase them. A fascinating note recorded in a *majmu'a* belonging to an anonymous bookseller in Isfahan lists 179 manuscripts in his inventory.[24] The date of this record, 1722, corresponds to the Afghan invasion of Isfahan; perhaps this is a coincidence. Nevertheless, the record establishes the practice of cataloging books in a collection for the purpose of accounting and creating inventories that document sales and rentals. In the last folios of the *majmu'a*, the anonymous bookseller had crossed out several titles with notations made under each one, stating that they either had been sold or loaned out. Names of borrowers appear, such as the brother of Hajji Fazlullah Beg and Aqa Qanbar Ali Khwaja. Hajji Fazlullah Beg, another merchant, who had made the pilgrimage to Mecca, and Aqa Qanbar Ali Khwaja, whose name bears social markers that distinguish him as a former slave, probably a eunuch, were avid readers and trusted clients of this bookseller. The variety of subjects in this inventory reveals the range of consumers' curiosities. From the collection of 179 manuscripts, 34 were on the subject of the religious sciences: a children's version of the Quran in two volumes, religious manuals on proper Shi'a rituals and behavior written by such early-seventeenth-century scholars as Shaykh Baha'i, Hadith collections, and commentaries on medieval works by Twelver Shi'a scholars. Works on medicine and basic manuals of prayer, purity, ethics, conduct, and inheritance laws are mixed in with dictionaries and historical chronicles, such as Iskandar Beg Munshi's history of the reign of Shah Abbas I. Twenty volumes of anthologies, *majmu'a*s of poetry, sit alongside these works on religion, history, and medicine; they speak to a range of reading interests and to the reach of knowledge by the end of Safavi rule in Isfahan.

Scholarship has focused on the libraries of religious seminaries; thanks to endowment deeds, we have lists of manuscripts housed in seminary libraries as well as records of the canonical texts that were taught. Students engaged in the production of knowledge, from paper making to recording and memorizing prominent religious works. For each text they mastered, seminary students received permission, or *ijaza*, from their teacher to copy and teach that particular work. However, reading, learning, discussing, and teaching were not restricted to the space of the seminary library. Students could borrow books from the library, take them home, read them alone or in the company of family and friends, and then return them. An endowment deed preserved in a manuscript copy of the mystic philosopher Mulla Sadra's (d. 1650) *Sharh Hidayat al-Hikma* notes that the book was endowed to the Chahar Bagh seminary in Isfahan, built by the last Safavi shah, Sultan Husayn (r. 1694–1722).[25]

> This volume is to be accessed by the Twelver Shi'a who seek religious knowledge. It is a legal, or *shar'i*, condition that whosoever needs this volume may have access to it. He must obtain permission from the superintendent, the *mutavalli* to read it for a period of six months, and whenever he checks this book out for longer than six months, he must renew his permission with the approval of his master, who must reinstate the request for the allotted period of

use. He shall not take the book outside Isfahan. Anyone who tampers with this legal contract [*sigha-yi shar'i*] will be cursed by the prophet.²⁶

Students of religion and other patrons of seminary libraries benefited from the rich holdings in the religious sciences that were financed through pious endowments. Some manuscripts had been donated by the Safavi shahs, who gifted them from their imperial libraries as acts of piety.²⁷ Other manuscripts came from less obvious sources. For instance, revenue from the hammam in the *maydan*, adjacent to the Friday Prayer Mosque, was allocated for the production of manuscripts in the seminary, materially linking practices of piety and purity to the creation of religious manuscripts. Another policy, buttressing the state's project of conversion to Shi'ism, allowed believers who were not seminary students the right to access religious works. The endowment deed from the Chahar Bagh seminary stipulates that Shi'a believers who wanted to read codices but were not seminary students could obtain permission from one of the seminary teachers. After receiving the seals of a teacher and head librarian, nonstudents could borrow manuscripts and even leave the city of Isfahan with them, so long as they were borrowing appropriate manuscripts to take to pilgrimage sites or for the purpose of prayer. Trusted individuals guaranteed by seminary teachers could also deposit a surety (*rahn*) and take the book outside Isfahan for a designated amount of time. This practice of lending religious works or manuals for prayer and pilgrimage required the believer to return the manuscript physically to the library every six months to make sure it was in good condition. After inspection, the manuscript loan could then be renewed.²⁸ An economy of trust and oaths governed the traffic and value of manuscripts as a medium of conversion to Shi'ism, shaping the practice of lending and borrowing books from public seminary libraries.

Whether compiled in household libraries, inherited as heirlooms, borrowed from seminaries, or acquired in bookstores, most of the extant anthologies are anonymous. That they were not inscribed with the owner's name speaks to their private use as household "utensils," valued possessions of the owner; like a copy of a Quran or a copper vessel, they were not shared publicly and would travel with the family in life and in inheritance. Numerous *majmu'a*s assemble an array of material on a range of subjects, including medicine, composition, and rhetoric, or contain legal documents (*sigha*), such as contracts, marriage and divorce papers, wills, and freedom papers (*azadnama*). These anthologies are sprinkled with talismans, love poetry, and recipes that blur the lines between professional and private lives. Such practices of selecting materials communicate the profession of the collector; they are notebooks used for the purpose of their vocation. That a state functionary, a bureaucrat, or a religious judge considered their workbooks as private property conveys the subjective value embodied by anthologies. But many household *majmuʿa*s defy the single-subject format; instead, they are composite manuscripts that assemble and preserve meaningful pieces, segments of texts on a variety of topics of interest to the owner and his family. Whether poetry, letters, or essays on love and friendship, what makes these miscellanies personal are the individual choices of materials handpicked by the author. Some items are written down for pragmatic reasons, such as to keep track of a personal debt or a loan. Others are motivated by sentiment, such as the insertion of a mother's death date accompanied by a poem lamenting her loss. Similar to private libraries that both create and shape the collector's mind, anthologies encapsulate bits and pieces of everyday materials that mattered to their owners; they are condensed memories fashioned by the experiences of the collector, the city he lived in, and the engagements he had.

Although the anthologies' heterogeneity displays a range of choices, professions, and levels of literacy, reading tastes and collecting preferences sometimes converged among Isfahan's households. Anthologies materialize the people and things that tied communities of literacy to one another: paper, pen, poetry, friends, lovers, mothers and fathers, teachers, and slaves. Some *majmuʿa*s contain formulaic decrees of repentance, including written confessions of sins committed against the sharia from drinking wine to engaging in adultery and sodomy; these anthologies bear the impact of the state project of repression and conversion. The dissemination of conduct manuals in Isfahan that publicized the religious duty of commanding the right and forbidding the wrong (*al-amr bi-l-maʿruf wa-l-nahy ʿan al-munkar*) suggests that these exhortations were clearly heard; we also see their import preserved in household anthologies.

But even as anthologies exhibit a growing conservatism in the religious sensibility among literate Isfahani communities, they also celebrate carnal pleasures and the erotic delights of city life. A taste for romance and an appreciation of beauty inform the poetics and aesthetics of anthologies; so too does wit and humor infuse their pages. We find myriad forms of reflection on the urban landscape, offering a visualization of a populace that enjoyed strolling through the bazaar, the royal square, and the tree-lined avenue of the Chahar Bagh, which linked the medieval city to the new residential quarters and the public gardens. The most commonly anthologized materials that connect households in Isfahan include mystic love poetry (*ghazal*), friendship letters (*ikhvaniyyat*), poetic representations of Isfahan (*shahrashub*), manuals on writing and proper speech (*insha'*), talismans, copies of declarations of repentance (*tawbanama*), and freedom papers (*azadnama*). These materials could also acquire different meanings in the anthology or perform manifold roles. For instance, talismans infuse these collections with formulaic prayers, magic numbers, and squares. Sometimes talismans took the form of inscriptions to guard households from theft, recipes to shield loved ones from fever, or stopgaps to prevent men from having "corrupt thoughts and lustful dreams." Out of these written and visual spaces, members of households speak, implicitly expressing their desires, hopes, and anxieties. So, too, in a fashion, do the anthologies exercise their own agency, marshaled by the talisman into the service of shielding the household from dangers within and without.

In short, the anthology is capacious, even in its most common forms. In the following pages, I explore the contents of a *majmu'a* belonging to a religious scholar alongside the self-portraits of a painter whose work was collected in household *muraqqa*'s. Each text represents a model for thinking about habits of collecting and self-fashioning. Whereas the clerical self unfolds through his curated choices bound in a discrete manuscript preserved in his family library, the painter's self-portraits address a clientele who conserved his works in their homes. These two authorial voices exhibit the mastering of the arts of writing and performing city *adab*, as they illuminate their experiences of Isfahan. Each requires a different method of reading, however, one that distinguishes between the cleric as an agent of curating and the painter as the subject of curation.

Reading Aqa Husayn Khwansari's *Majmu'a*

We have little information about the procedures of collecting, copying, and producing household anthologies such as the one assembled in Aqa Husayn Khwansari's library. A clearer picture emerges in the palace and the seminary, which were major workplaces that employed artists, historians, scribes, and scholars to create and transmit their craft to a new generation of students in the arts and sciences well into the seventeenth century. The court operated as a minicity, producing much of its own material needs through a network of artisans and craftsmen who moved between the bazaar and the palace. From blacksmiths to tailors to a variety of laborers who were employed to cut down trees to be used as pillars for building projects, imperial workshops mirrored the organization and specialization of the crafts represented in the bazaar.[29] Thirty-three workshops were housed at the palace complex in Isfahan.[30] Moreover, the court and the seminary were archival spaces where past knowledge was collected in libraries in a range of forms, including court chronicles, illustrated manuscripts,[31] treatises, letters, paintings, calligraphy, decrees, and fatwas; each of these provided models to be taught, recorded, and rewritten for imperial and religious purposes. Historians, accountants, painters, and religious scholars collaborated with each other to create their composition on paper. Seminary students and scribes copied manuscripts for purposes of religious authorization and memorization, and calligraphers, painters, gilders, framers, and bookbinders produced illuminated manuscripts for imperial legitimacy and cultural capital. In the seminary, as in the royal court, masters and craftsmen invested in a generation of apprentices to create new technologies for knowledge dissemination. Paid for with revenues accrued by the royal treasury or by religious endowments, the transmission of knowledge from master to apprentice parallels the economy of labor and education in the bazaar. Bazaars provided the tools and the crafts for private households to participate in the manuscript market. Every major urban center produced paper (*kaghaz*) from rags and sold manuscripts (*sahhafi*) in the marketplace.[32] Paper was made in Isfahan from rags boiled in water with a mixture of paste and was available for a clientele eager to participate in the culture of *adab*.

Isfahan's private libraries are difficult to reconstruct. Many were looted during the Afghan invasion of the city in 1722, divvied up by inheritors, or lost to the elements. However, surviving manuscripts from Isfahan's households were purchased by Iran's national manuscript libraries. An example is medieval poet Saʿdi's *Bustan* (1257), which belonged to the library of the merchant ʿItiqad Khan, who had commissioned the famous calligrapher Mir ʿImad to execute this versified work on ethics.[33] Seals of owners and names of scribes or patrons transmitted in prefaces and colophons help to identify some family library collections. Reassembling fragmented libraries is a challenging task. A study of public and private libraries remains to be conducted for the city of Isfahan in particular and for the early modern Persianate world more generally.[34] We know of nineteen private household libraries from seventeenth-century Isfahan. Bureaucrats, generals, and merchants owned eight.[35] Eleven notable library collections belonged to members of the religious establishment.[36] Consider, for example, Shaykh Baha'i, the renowned Shaykh al-Islam of Isfahan. He inherited his library from his wife, the daughter of another famous cleric, Shaykh Ali Minshar al-'Amili (d. 1576).[37] Theirs was a voluminous library, considering the inherited collection included more than 4,000 volumes purchased in India. In fact, manuscripts were collected in Isfahan from across the Persianate world. A noteworthy library belonged to the scholar Mirza Abdullah Afandi, who sent his students throughout the Iranian plateau to help build his library of Shi'a scholarship. Afandi's manuscript library was the source for his own voluminous biographical dictionary on the lives and works of contemporaneous Shi'a scholars. He often noted that he possessed a copy of any given biographical subject's work. Another collector of books, Shaykh Hazin, who lived through the 1722 Afghan invasion of Isfahan, writes that, in order to survive the siege of the city, he sold everything of value save for his 2,000 manuscripts, which he refused to part with. Ironically, it was not the Afghans who would loot his library but local thieves, who, not unlike Shaykh Hazin himself, were striving to make ends meet.[38]

One of the nineteen private libraries is a collection that belongs to the Khwansari family of religious scholars, who trace their ancestry back to seventeenth-century Isfahan. Five anthologies number among the manuscripts housed in this private library; read and preserved for over four centuries, these *majmu'a*s are prized objects that continued to have meaning for the family. Attentive to the minutiae of form and content, my reading of one of these anthologies explores habits of collecting alongside the curated choices of the original owner, Aqa Husayn Khwansari (d. 1686), as I reflect on the objects he assembled, each with its own narrative, its own symbolic and affective association. In aggregate, the objects in Aqa Husayn Khwansari's collection and his mode of curation offer a guide to his experience of the city, both as a migrant from the village of Khwansar and as a student of religion (see Map 0.1). The imaginations his anthologizing produced and the choices behind the gathering and ordering of texts represent different ways he read and wrote the city. They reveal a place where, among other things, his religious and urban self was fashioned on paper and performed in public. As a collector, Aqa Husayn mastered *adab*, curating sentences and verses from known works of poetry and prose in circulation, which he complemented with his own compositions. His daily encounters with words and images from the city's various surfaces—no less than the instruction he gave at a seminary located in the bazaar—shaped what Aqa Husayn recorded in the folios of his anthology, which served him as an exemplar for studying and practicing both Shi'ism and city *adab*.

This Khwansari anthology, currently housed in the Tehran University Library, is 11 inches long and 6 inches wide and contains 250 folios bound in a handsome leather cover (Figure 2.2). It is written on local Isfahan paper (*tirma*) in the *nasta'liq* script, the style of Persianate calligraphy preferred for writing court histories, epistolary, and poetry and for the majority of anthologies assembled in Isfahan.[39] Aqa Husayn, the first noteworthy Khwansari family member, compiled the *majmu'a* fourteen years before his death in 1686, and he was joined in this labor by a scribe who recorded his name as Riza Quli.[40] This anthology bears the trace of three hands: the owner Aqa Husayn, the scribe Riza Quli, and the scholar Navvab Isfahani, who appears in a copy of a letter he authored and recorded for his friend, Aqa Husayn. The owner and his scribe chose to include an "original" copy of Navvab Isfahani's letter, written in his hand, so as to authenticate his authorial voice. The fact that hands and eyes certified a facsimile reminds us of the sensory processes of archiving that configure this anthology. Many other *majmu'a*s also bear the evidence of multiple eyes and hands; they chronicle the continued value and circulation of anthologies well into the twentieth century.[41]

Aqa Husayn's relocation from his village of Khwansar, 100 miles north, to settle in Isfahan is a success story. Like many who were drawn by the possibilities offered by this new center of politics, religion, commerce, and the arts, Aqa Husayn left his village to explore the big city. His contemporaneous biographer Mirza Abdullah Afandi stresses Aqa Husayn's early poverty; with little more than a blanket to warm him during the winter months, he managed nonetheless to navigate the exigencies of urban life in the new capital on a seminary student's stipend. Thanks to his diligence, and because he studied with the most distinguished teachers of the religious sciences, he was assured a place in the echelons of a growing Shi'a clerical establishment and became a prominent teacher in his own right. Aqa Husayn participated in the state project of conversion, translating the Quran into simple Persian; he instructed Sunni residents in Shi'i exegesis and on the stories of succession to the

FIGURE 2.2 Aqa Husayn Khwansari's *majmuʻa*, Tehran University Library, MS 7116, fols. 1v and 2r.

prophet Muhammad, his daughter Fatima, his cousin and brother-in-law Ali, and their male descendants, thereby creating a habitus in Isfahan with a distinct Shiʻa identity. He also taught at one of the principal seminaries, the Madrasa-yi Jadda, located in the heart of the bazaar, where he was the superintendent (*mutavalli*). This seminary was established as a pious foundation by the grandmother of Shah Abbas II (r. 1642–1666), Huri Khanum; his position allowed him the financial facility to support his students, granting them stipends as well as room and board.[42] Aqa Husayn trained a new generation of religious scholars who would disseminate Shiʻa religion and law throughout the Safavi dominion.[43]

But for this station and role in Isfahan to be realized, Aqa Husayn first had to acquire the words, gestures, and manners of etiquette to communicate and participate in city life. His anthology assembles texts to showcase what I have termed urbanity, that is, to flaunt and display his grasp of the city, of which he envisioned himself a part as he mastered the arts of *adab*. And, indeed, Aqa Husayn came to be recognized for his writing skills. Notably, his epistolary collection and famous preface (*dibacha*) circulated in Isfahan and were reproduced across many *majmu'a* collections. Aqa Husayn also innovated the formulaic text of religious endowments, fusing *adab* with prescribed paradigms in the composition of his family endowment, which his scribe archived in the anthology. In other words, *adab* literacy did not mean simply reproducing other texts but rather engendered new generic possibilities. Hence, even though Aqa Husayn's religious scholarship illustrates his public persona, his anthology provides a more intimate insight into his engagement with city *adab*.

The Khwansari anthology bears the distinguishing feature of a table of contents, *ma fi hadhahi al-majmu'a* (that which is in this anthology), in which the scribe lays out the selection of material, folio by folio.[44] Most anthologies do not include a table of contents. They usually begin with a text that does not always have a title. A collection of selected text fragments follows, characterizing the structure of the household anthology. They are not random choices, as Aqa Husayn's table of contents exemplifies. There is a conscious ordering of material; contents are deliberately chosen to give meaning to various urban texts circulating in the city. Aqa Husayn's anthology preserves networks of the texts and intersecting lives that mattered to his household. Moreover, Riza Quli states the exact date when he began to assemble the anthology, 1083/1672–1673, and the date of its completion three years later, 1086/1675. Such details distinguish the Khwansari anthology, but they also provide a conceptual map, a collective sense of the many other anthologies I have consulted. Written in the same hand and using the same method of ordering information on paper, the folio opposite the table of contents presents an actual map, not of Isfahan but of the city of Istanbul with the title "Some Neighborhoods and Mosques of Istanbul" (*ba'zi mahallat va masajid-i Istanbul*). The map marks the divisions between the city's ethnic neighborhoods, including its Muslim, Christian, and Jewish quarters, just as it enumerates the population of each in Arabic numerals and Persian words. A list of congregational and local mosques, soup kitchens, Sufi cloisters, waterworks, bathhouses, wine bars, and coffeehouses fills the pages as they sketch in the city of Istanbul. Thus two early modern capital cities, Isfahan and Istanbul, are placed in implicit conversation with one another. The spatial logic of mapping Istanbul anticipates the conceptual map of the contents of Khwansari's anthology to help readers visualize the city of Isfahan.

The Khwansari anthology opens with a series of manuals on divination, associating its owner with the power to see and tell the future. Aqa Husayn collected manuals on bibliomancy, which allowed him to practice at home and then act as a public intermediary for believers who sought guidance in their daily lives. The first manual is *Falnama* (Book of Divination), ascribed to the sixth Shi'a Imam, Jafar al-Sadiq (d. 765). Aqa Husayn provides an introduction revealing its provenance: The text had allegedly been concealed until the eleventh century, when the Abbasid caliph sent a copy as a gift to Sultan Mahmud Ghaznavi (d. 1030), who had recently established his hegemony over the Islamic world's eastern frontiers. Selected stanzas from twenty-nine chapters of the Quran are written on the right side of the folio in the *thulth* script reserved for sacred texts, along with interpretative phrases written on the left in the Persianate *nasta'liq* script. The two scripts divide the text, visually and linguistically, into the sacred and the revelatory. The Persian translations are not literal but rather interpret Quranic verses as prognostications.[45] The practice of reading the language of the Quran for signs and portents was common in the Persianate world.[46] Images, both figural and literal, were deciphered to signify the present; these images were symbols that were believed to contain the potency to affect the future. The subjects of divination in this manual anticipate an audience from a cross-section of society; all walks of life in the urban capital are considered: the shah and his courtiers, slaves and students of religion, merchants and craftsmen, wives and daughters. Prized associations and relationships with family, friends, lovers, business partners, and the king are evoked. In other words, this book of divination must have served Aqa Husayn as a personal guide to bibliomancy, deploying the sacred text of the Quran to perform auguries (*tafa'ul*) that concerned the populace of Isfahan.

The ethos of the occult and the social world of Isfahan's residents are encapsulated in this Persian translation of the hidden signs and symbols of the Quran. We can imagine Aqa Husayn Khwansari, a religious scholar steeped in philosophy, law, and theology, engaged in the economy of the occult, making use of this *Falnama* to guide Persian speakers into the mysterious world of the Arabic Quran. That the manual was ascribed to the sixth Imam, Jafar al-Sadiq, confirms Aqa Husayn's Shi'i authorial voice. Traditionally, in sixteenth-century Safavi Iran, mystics acted as saintly vehicles of social insurance in both life and death. Mystic brotherhoods, such as the Safavis, contributed to their members' spiritual and material needs, as devotees gave gifts in exchange for the Sufi shaykh's *baraka*, or spiritual and material protection.⁴⁷ The exchange of gifts for blessings and protection was part of an occult economy of social and religious negotiations designed to assuage the vagaries and uncertainties of the times. That divinatory manuals stand at the forefront of Aqa Husayn's collection suggests his participation in this popular practice, revealing the habitus that shaped him and his followers in Isfahan. The divinatory materials he assembled are fragments connecting him to the social networks in which he taught and lived. Divination and the occult were part of the knowledge that ordered and gave meaning to everyday life experiences, where the quotidian was marvelous. Importantly, these manuals do not appear in the list of books enumerated in the endowment deed of the seminary library where Aqa Husayn taught; rather, placed in his anthology, they were personal texts that fashioned him as an authority on the occult.⁴⁸ Aqa Husayn's published works implicate him in the state-sponsored project of conversion and discipline, but his anthology reveals his personal affinity for a body of knowledge on divination, talismans, and amulets.

The corpus of works authored and translated by Aqa Husayn make his engagement with the conversion of Isfahan's residents to Shi'ism public. Aqa Husayn's biographers tell of his dedication to the translation of religious texts from Arabic into Persian, starting with the Quran, major Shi'a prayer books, and manuals on pious behavior. He was the first to translate from Arabic a book of prayers ascribed to Imam Ali (*Sahifat al-Kamila*), consisting of fifty-four prayers to be recited for many reasons: to release the believer from sin and sickness, to ensure the well-being of children and friends, to ward off Satan, or to request rain. This range of supplications gives a sense of both the audience and the daily preoccupations of Isfahan's residents, here framed through the intercessory role of Imam Ali and his representative, Aqa Husayn Khwansari. The *Sahifat al-Kamila* was an instant hit, and many manuscript copies of it survive; our anonymous bookseller, mentioned earlier, recorded it among his collection of books sold in 1722. As revealed by these different textual productions, Aqa Husayn was both reproducing state power and employing practices that competed with those of Sufis. For residents of Isfahan, the implications are profound: Instead of consulting with a Sufi master about the auspiciousness of a daughter's wedding, the circumcision of a son, or a commercial transaction, the believer had the option of consulting Aqa Husayn. Contending over devotees, members of the Shi'a clerical establishment launched a defamation campaign against mystic brotherhoods, inscribing Sufis as immoral men who languished in ethical and sexual corruption.

Aqa Husayn witnessed this religious competition unfolding in the capital; he studied and employed occult practices, which through their circulation and consumption encapsulate the power of magic in harmony with its practitioners in Isfahan.[49]

As we turn the folios of Aqa Husayn's anthology to the essays on divination, we come across an almanac (*taqvim*). This is another work of translation from Arabic to Persian, but this one is attributed to the prophet Muhammad. The almanac places each day of Muharram, the first Muslim lunar month, within an Abrahamic cosmology. From the first of Muharram, when Adam was supposedly created, days are given cosmological signification and then associated with auspicious or inauspicious everyday activities.[50] For instance, success in agriculture or hunting is guaranteed on Abel's birthday, whereas Cain's birthday is an inauspicious day and portends faulty transactions and troubled amorous relationships. Transformative moments in the believer's life cycle, such as the birth of a child, the ceremony of sworn friendships, or marriage and death, are linked to larger cosmic temporal revolutions. These cyclical rhythms of change are aligned with the movements of stars and planets, seen as directly affecting daily life, whether in political or social matters, religious upheavals, or floods, plagues, and ill-fated investments in property or friendships. Celestial, terrestrial, and human experiences were envisioned as intimately intertwined in the Muslim cosmological order. The almanac is followed in the anthology by more almanacs—these ones, however, are Shi'a variants ascribed to Imam Ali, as though to perform the succession of authority, from Muhammad to Ali and the Shi'a Imams, in a genre itself marked by the passage of time.[51]

Aqa Husayn's education awarded him access to the most powerful spaces in Isfahan, including the seminary, the mosque, the bazaar, the Safavi court, and even the cemetery. When Aqa Husayn died, his popularity in Isfahan prompted Shah Sulayman (r. 1666–1689) to build him a mausoleum adjacent to that of his teacher, Mir Findiriski (d. 1640). Master and disciple were interred side by side in the space of the graveyard at Takht-i Fulad. Shah Sulayman commissioned the building of a bridge to link the two banks of the Zayanda River that divided the center of Isfahan—including the *maydan*, the bazaar, the palace, and the mosque—to the cemetery, allowing residents easy access to the cemetery, located on the southern outskirts of the city. The burial grounds were a popular site of visitation for itinerant dervishes, who lingered among the dead, and for disciples, who revered dead mystics at their shrines, such as that belonging to the famous Baba Rukn al-Din (d. 1490). By the middle of the seventeenth century, the cemetery was being transformed into a sacred space for Shi'a religious scholars; through rituals of tomb visitation, Shi'a men of religion competed with Sufis in life as in death, appropriating the same Sufi practices of tomb visitation that tied master to disciple in a relationship of love and devotion.

This relationship is also on display in the anthology. A cluster of curated letters follow the series of divination manuals and the almanac, as Aqa Husayn moves from being a reader of divine signs to a communicator of words in letters.[52] The first epistle is authored by Aqa Husayn himself. Sample form letters, regarding requests for a rosary and a pair of eyeglasses, register his daily routine of reading, writing, and praying. Personal and model letters do not just demonstrate the importance of the epistolary genre in Isfahan's *adab* culture; they inscribe Aqa Husayn's valued relationships with friends and teachers. And here we find that the original matters in the practice of archiving household anthologies. Although the centerpiece of this sampling of letters is the epistle composed and scribed by Aqa Husayn on the arrival of spring and the Persian New Year, the master-disciple relationship between Aqa Husayn and Mir Findiriski is celebrated in a copy of a letter written by another prominent scholar, Navvab Isfahani.[53] Aqa Husayn's scribe, Riza Quli, makes sure to note when the hand of his patron and that of Navvab Isfahani authenticate the letter's copy (*raqaʿ*). The author's hand confirms the accuracy of its contents. These letters are followed by an entry from the scribe, who records his name and the date 1083/1672, perhaps indicating the end of the first year of archiving. Time and again, Riza Quli makes his appearance as he collects and archives material for his patron. In one case the scribe tells us that he consulted a copy of a preface to a work on composition and rhetoric with his own eyes in Isfahan in 1083/1672,[54] confirming the habit of collecting material in the city to assemble a household anthology. Consider another example in the margins of folio 238v, where the scribe records the month and day of copying (Safar 1082/June 1671) and notes that he reproduced the almanac (*maʿrifat-i taqvim*) word for word according to the original and that, since he is not an expert on the subject, he replicated the exact version (*muvaffiq-i nuskha qalam kishida*).[55]

Sample letters in praise of spring were commonly recorded in seventeenth-century anthologies; they were new year's greetings to be exchanged by friends and family, serving as places where the author could exhibit his literary skills and eloquence. Aqa Husayn's letter celebrating spring displays his ability to participate in the prized art of writing, in particular, crafting prose to visualize spring. His spring greetings circulated in Isfahan's households as a fine model, to be collected and consulted when writing one's own composition.[56] Aqa Husayn opens his letter in praise of spring to an unknown addressee with a rhetorical gesture; speech is inadequate, unable to conjure the season's splendor: "Truth be told, if I were to evoke the beauty of the new spring with the eloquent witness of speech and deploy one hundred watercolors to draw the rosy cheeks of the exalted bride [spring], I could not do justice [to it]."[57] For Aqa Husayn, speech acts as a witness, the written evidence derived from vision. Words are associated with color. The writer, like the painter, draws with the pen of color to depict a scene where the fullness of nature bursts into being, a creation that is impossible to conjure. Visuality intersects with cognition and the power, or weakness, of words and color to depict the spring's beauty, personified in the figure of the bride.

As a student and a teacher of *adab*, Aqa Husayn takes this occasion to reflect on pedagogy. Speaking of his own students, he writes that the "parrots of speech have, for years in the school of the rose garden, assembled the lesson between the palms of their hands, bound like volumes, [and] they recite their lesson." Children are likened to parrots that mimic what they have been told; time and again they recollect what they have learned from their assembled lesson, bound as though in a book, clasped by hands that have come to know the blows of their teacher's disciplinary stick. The childhood memory of learning a lesson by heart is inscribed in Aqa Husayn's mind. "[The] children of speech [*takallum*], who, through their lily-like tongues [long tongues], have grown acquainted with a medley of words that award them the ability to communicate." Word by word, students learn how to construct sentences collected together in a volume that gives voice to their thoughts. Armed with his embodied, anthologized knowledge, Aqa Husayn asserts, "I am the weaver of words, with the stature and gracefulness of [male] youth." He then explicitly flaunts his command over his learning, drawing attention back to his letter, written on gold-sprinkled paper that is evocative of calligraphy or fine painting, though it was also used in the art of letter writing. Aqa Husayn's skillfulness, embodied in a beautiful male youth, is punctuated with rhetorical words of humility that elicit a response in the *adab* of epistolarity. The letter is a medium of communication in which the author can boast of his mastery of composition; dexterity inspires a reaction. But he must perform modesty as he wonders whether his "ordering of one or two paragraphs merits his coveted answer." In a different vein than the disciplinarian with a stick, he hopes that his "sweet words" are capable of effecting "similar words in return." As he writes to his unnamed addressee, "Since I must remain separate from you, the only choice is to write an eloquent letter in the hope that I will be honored to receive your response." This letter is dated 1030/1620.[58]

Aqa Husayn taught himself the epistolary craft from the model letters and essays on composition he collected in his anthology. The epistolary art of *adab* was not part of the education he would have received in the seminary. His seminary training had introduced him to the trivium of rhetoric, grammar, and logic in Arabic, a curriculum that provided him with the rudimentary tools of composition and speech. And although he did compose letters in Arabic, Aqa Husayn took pride in his engagement with the Persianate literary field. His letter in praise of spring is exhibited in the anthology as proof of his mastery of rhetoric and subtle wordplay. In his anthology he also included a select sampling of his favorite manuals, each of which offered literary tools of communication, such as the preface to a popular manual on composition, the *Gulzar-i Ibrahimi* written by Mawlana Zuhuri Tarshizi (d. 1618). Zuhuri weaves together aesthetics of composition, fashioning ways of seeing and hearing that train readers to comprehend graphic signs, implicitly moving from the page of an anthology to the built city. Although Zuhuri wrote this preface in praise of his patron, Ibrahim 'Adilshah II (d. 1627), who ruled in the Deccan region of southern India, it was widely circulated in seventeenth-century anthologies assembled in Isfahan, which suggests that Zuhuri was immediately recognized by his contemporaries as a master of Persianate composition.[59] In fact, the poet laureate Sa'ib Tabrizi composed a verse recognizing Zuhuri as his source of inspiration for the composition of a *ghazal*.[60] *Majmu'a*s clearly connected communities of literacy in and beyond the city of Isfahan; they helped residents such as Aqa Husayn socialize in the city and communicate the city's splendor to others. In his preface Zuhuri deploys the metaphor of a library as a place of travel through knowledge and the arts (*fazl u hunar*). He evokes metaphors of paper and pen to describe, line by line, the translation of individual words into whole compositions, the assembly of script into paragraphs that come to indelibly mark the page.[61] Zuhuri draws on the relationship between painting, calligraphy, and poetry, associating the arrangement of a beautiful stanza with a painting or the drawing of a face. Words and images, Zuhuri instructs his audience, must be well proportioned (*mizan*), following the sound and rhythm of a melody (*zarb u nutq*) as they inscribe parallel beats. A cultured man, writes Zuhuri, should be familiar with music, painting, and calligraphy in order to craft a well-balanced composition.

Following the *adab* of speech that Aqa Husayn embodied (and assembled) to communicate his urbanity, his anthology then turns to a series of essays on love, focusing in particular on the carnal body and homosocial bonds. Aqa Husayn's selection on the subject deploys the language of mystic love, providing the vocabulary and the moods to convey and sustain intimate male friendships. Whether sociability was affected through a letter to an absent friend, in an essay on the ethics of friendship, or in a libretto from Vahshi's romance *Farhad and Shirin*, love was an ideal state of being. For residents of Isfahan, everyone, old and young, was to have fallen under the spell of love.

In an excerpt from an essay on love (*'ishq*) authored by Husayn ibn Nimatullah Tabib, a contemporary physician living in Isfahan, Aqa Husayn records that "love is the most beautiful emotion, for in the workshop of the revolving universe, there is nothing more pleasant than the work of loving." His is an ethical engagement with the necessities (*asbab*), the signs (*'alamat*), and the remedies of love, but the physician assumes the object of love to be the human friend. Love, he says, is the emotion that guides the lover (*muhibb*) to the beloved (*habib*). The physician uses indistinguishable language to express divine love and urban friendships. His quotation of the medieval mystic Ibn Arabi (d. 1240) particularly encapsulates the common language of love: "Love came and turned into the blood that ran within my veins and under my skin, until it emptied me and filled me with the Friend. My entire existence was consumed by the Friend, only in name do I exist, the rest is all Him." Even though Ibn Arabi was writing about divine love, the physician translates the mystic's discourse from the realm of metaphysics into a context of everyday sociability in Isfahan.[62]

According to Husayn ibn Nimatullah, love was a malady that generally struck the youth and the bachelor. But love could also afflict the elderly, particularly when love had been experienced in youth; then, love became an inclination, a trait that was ingrained in an individual's disposition (*tabi'at*). Love (*'ishq*) and friendship (*dusti*) are interchangeable sentiments in his essay, which delineates the stages of love through its disclosure: "If one is in love and the beloved is unaware, if the beloved is in the know, or if the lover does not know that the beloved knows."[63] He casts friendship as an opening of the heart, the act of making oneself vulnerable to the friend. Once love for the friend is revealed, whether through a letter or a gift, speech acts perform the work of loving. The physician maintains that love is not a one-sided vow (*payman*). Sworn friendships are assumed as the practice that ties two lovers together through a public oath-taking ceremony. In this light, he explains, chivalric codes of behavior, bravery, generosity, and forgiveness in particular are cultivated through the practice of friendship. Friendship is the place where communal ethics are tested. And loyalty is the obligation of the friend: "If you have but one talent and a thousand flaws, the friend is the one who sees no more than your talent," the physician quotes from the famous Persianate medieval poet Sa'di.[64]

The mystic language of love and a shared ethics tie friends together to create community; however, men still had to learn how to control their bodies, conceived of as self-regulating systems composed of four humors. An essay included by Aqa Husayn in his anthology encapsulates these bodily techniques. The essay is a commentary on the famous Arabic medieval compendium of pleasure on sexual delights, the *Jami' al-lazzat* by Ibn Samsamani. The essay foregrounds the need to control and moderate carnal desire, with a recommendation for sex-obsessed male believers, and then enumerates Galenic remedies for their condition. The male, imagined to be the more rational of the sexes, was hotter and dryer than the female, and so he had to regulate his bowel movements, limit his walking and even running for that matter, and avoid warming his back against a heater in order to control his sexual desire. He must not stay awake too long at night or go horseback riding. All these daily activities were to enhance the humoral equilibrium of a male body and prevent it from producing excess passion.[65] The essay goes on to describe the most excellent sexual positions for men and women, with men on top, as this allegedly facilitated the best orgasm for both. In a Galenic sexual economy, men need not concern themselves with celibacy; on the contrary, the proper road to health and piety is a desire controlled by dietary and physical acts of moderation.

Hair was the most public and visible sign of sexuality in Isfahan. Beards, moustaches, and pubic hair were central to the semiotics of masculinity that marked the (a)symmetries among men, women, boys, and slaves. Quoting from Ibn Sina's *Canon*, the *Jami' al-lazzat* declares that "cutting pubic hair makes for a larger penis, just like shaving the head makes for a thicker neck."[66] Bachelors were thus advised not to cut their pubic hair in order to be shielded from the dangers of lust (*shahvat*). Aqa Husayn, as a public religious scholar, authored several fatwas banning the shaving of hair, which circulated in multiple copies through Isfahan's anthologies;[67] he did so not because of the consequences of a thick neck but rather as a moral ban on men who delayed their Muslim duties to marry and procreate. The anxiety around men who shaved their facial hair had to do with the fear that they would continue to submit to the erotic advances of older men or continue to prefer young beardless men as sexual partners. The beard was a sign of adulthood, accompanied by a series of responsibilities and sexual desires. As discussed in Chapter 1, an asymmetry of male homoerotic desire—structured by age and rank—was not only tolerated in Islamic law but also celebrated in mystical poetry that generated a ubiquitous culture of boy gazing. The fatwas proclaimed by Aqa Husayn that forbade the shaving of beards, read alongside his manuals on proper Shi'a behavior and conduct, implicate him in the imperial program of disciplining gendered subjects in Isfahan and regulating the practice of male homoerotic desire.

Aqa Husayn's collection on discourses about love and desire ends with the romance of *Farhad and Shirin*, whose author is known by his pen name as the "wild man" from the city of Bafiq, or Vahshi-yi Bafiqi (d. 1583).[68] Even though Vahshi did not complete his tragic romance that pitted the sculptor, Farhad, against his rival king, Khusraw, in a competition over their mutually beloved Armenian princess, Shirin, it nevertheless circulated in Isfahan through household anthologies as an unfinished work.[69] Aqa Husayn includes the preface to Vahshi's romance with a scribal note in the margins of folio 119r indicating that many versions of *Farhad and Shirin*'s introduction exist; however, they all speak of the benefits and detriments of worldly love. This is the version that the scribe (*katib*) has chosen to inscribe on the page of existence (*vujud*), because there is no escaping (*la budd ast*) such a fate. Vahshi begins his preface by addressing God, asking him to grant the poet a burning heart (*atish afruz*), for the heart that has not experienced love and longing is not alive (*dil nist*) and it cannot write affectively. As love for God and the prophet Muhammad are expressed, Vahshi introduces the idioms of love that will collide in his romance. The two conflicting concepts of love, one chivalric and the other erotic, configure the terms of the debate over unrequited and all-consuming love, relishing the very notion of the annihilation of the self through love that Ibn Arabi's fragment collected by Aqa Husayn evokes. This tension captures the ethos of the contested ethics and aesthetics of love in the city of Isfahan.

As the cleric who issued fatwas banning the consumption of wine and the shaving of the beard, Aqa Husayn's discursive patchwork is a performance that illustrates the contradictions between his public role and his private life, held together in tension by the assembled fragments that shaped his attitudes and experiences. We will never know for sure why Aqa Husayn was drawn to Vahshi's romance, but in thinking about the lines of force that exist among collecting, self-formation, and community, Aqa Husayn's taste for Vahshi's romance speaks to the tensions that sexual desire and its discipline elicit; these contradictions must be felt in the body to bring about the promise of abstention. Without the allure of pleasure, repression alone is never sufficiently effective.[70]

Aqa Husayn's curatorial choices offer historians access to urban bodies of knowledge—manuals on divination, epistolary practices, writings on love and friendship—that weave the lived city together with the imperial imaginary but are never fully coherent. The practices of seeing, reading, writing, and desiring are intimately intertwined in Aqa Husayn's patchwork of city knowledge. Before he could write his own anthology, he had to observe and read to understand the words and gestures of residents, the poetry they recited, their friendship rituals, and their ways of desiring the beauty of the city. In writing his anthology, however, Aqa Husayn actively engaged in inscribing himself into the urban agential sphere, displaying his mastery over a range of materials that awarded him status. He understood that to distinguish himself as a migrant, it was not enough to master religious knowledge, even though he held a respectable position in a seminary. He knew that as a migrant he needed to take part in the invitation to create and write the bounty of this metropolis, to perfect his urban skills, whether through the medium of letters, the occult power to see the future of residents, or the regulation of his physical activities, his bodily humors, and desires. To write was an act of agency, but it was also a subjective act of making the city his own, of participating in the aesthetics of Isfahan, that in dynamism exposed the many dimensions and even points of conflict of Aqa Husayn's authorial self.

Reassembling Muhammad Qasim's *Muraqqa'*

Muhammad Qasim (d. 1660) was a talented painter and portrait artist who felt unrecognized. He composed some poetry, one example of which is preserved in an anthology of contemporaneous poets collected and recorded in Isfahan by Muhammad Tahir Nasrabadi. Himself a poet from a suburb of Isfahan, Nasrabadi identifies and admires Muhammad Qasim as a master artist, praising the nobility of his character and his sense of humor. Although the painter did not extend much effort in the composition of poetry, Nasrabadi notes that Muhammad Qasim extemporaneously improvised the following revealing verses:

> Today, no one realizes my true measure
> Nobody knows about my bookbinding tape [*shiraza*]
> Just as the silkworm's remembered by his silk
> Only when I'm dead will they sing my praises[71]

Whether it belongs to the poetics of biography or to the artist's lament, Muhammad Qasim recorded his talent as a master painter for posterity. Perhaps the art market was saturated with Riza Abbasi originals and forgeries, and collectors did not distinguish works of art from their fake counterparts. Or perhaps it was his migrant status that made it difficult for him to infiltrate the market, because he had not been trained by the master painters of Isfahan (see Map 0.1). Muhammad Qasim complained that his art went unappreciated, but his portfolio is sizable enough to assume that he made a living from his craft. Despite the vagaries of Isfahan's economy of patronage, Muhammad Qasim declares in verse that he knows that the binding of the *muraqqa'* will preserve his works for future generations of collectors with a keen sense of the aesthetics of *adab*; they will recognize his true value.

Muhammad Qasim's portfolio of paintings serve as a model subject of study, for he had to make his living primarily through patronage, beyond the royal workshops. He painted hundreds of works for collectors, which included a female clientele.[72] Today Muhammad Qasim's oeuvre is dispersed around the world in museums, even though each individual composition was meant for a distinct household collection or a private patron. Here, I reassemble a selection of his paintings, just as would an eighteenth- or nineteenth-century resident of Isfahan who engaged in the habit of collecting a *muraqqa'*. My reading of Muhammad Qasim's paintings ponders what the artist's "collection" might signify. What do his various works specifically tell us about the households for which they were produced, the collectors themselves, and the social worlds in which they circulated? Muhammad Qasim's compositions, particularly his self-portraits, allow us to assemble the patchwork of his life and to interpret the range of his and his clients' curated choices. I read the themes of his paintings, as I read Aqa Husayn's literary anthology, to give texture to the range of ways that living in Isfahan was imagined and performed.

Between 1650 and 1655 Muhammad Qasim completed his *Bastinade* (Figure 2.3), picturing himself in nature, accompanied by his own workshop of students and equipped with the materials necessary to transmit his skills.[73] This signed and dated drawing captures the production and circulation of knowledge that binds communities of literacy together.[74] Knowledge and discipline spring forth from the graying master, who holds a stick with which he is about to strike the bare soles of one of his students. He is the extension of the book and inkwell that rest on a small wooden table in front of him. The master leans on a heavily stylized tree with large leaves (*barg*) that semantically and visually remind the viewer of leaves of paper (*barg*). Here the painter tells the natural history of how trees were transformed into sticks for transmitting knowledge from former masters and how collected leaves were bound into books like the one on the table. Significantly, the tip of the master's stick points to Muhammad Qasim's signature, as he slyly writes himself into a genealogy of master painters in this pedagogical scene.

The circulation of knowledge and discipline involves present and future in its pedagogical themes. Along with the master and the manuscript, students are drawn out as vital to transmission, as they too are brought into participation with the ritualized discipline of education. The fearful culprit's feet are tied to a rod as his two fellow students hold him. Balancing his weight with one hand on the ground while the other clasps the rod, the master is involved in a triangulation through the exchange of grimaces that connect the three peers as they cultivate a fellowship. The two students assisting the bastinade appear to hesitate in complying with their master's wishes. Muhammad Qasim distinguishes the two fellow students from each other in dress and in expression. The one wearing a cloud-designed cloak and a pencil around his belt appears concerned. He may be feeling empathy with the victim, perhaps wondering if his turn will be next. In contrast, his partner wears a distinctly plain white robe and seems to be enjoying the scene, taking pleasure in the anguish of his fellow brother as he awaits and anticipates pain. Behind this scene lurks the old white-bearded shaykh, gazing at the bastinade, twirling his rosary beads in contemplation. Are the men in white, masters and disciples, all complicit in this triangulated mise-en-scène of fear and pleasure?

Two younger students are crouched in the foreground. They feign total ignorance of the bastinade, yet they are clearly aware of the consequence of misbehavior and so intently show off their own obedience and industry. The younger of the two is

FIGURE 2.3 Muhammad Qasim, *Bastinade*, signed "the work of the lowly Muhammad Qasim, the year 114 [1014/1605–1606]." The date of composition, however, is most probably 1650–1655. Tinted drawing on paper (15.8 cm × 24.3 cm). Metropolitan Museum of Art, 11.84.14. Frederick C. Hewitt Fund, 1911.

diligently reading from a piece of paper, and the older one is busy burnishing his own sheet of paper. A distinguishing feature of Muhammad Qasim's drawing is the deliberate words written out in this latter student's notebook: "I speak love/eros [*'ishq*] and cry / I'm an ignorant child, / that's my first lesson." These words from the student's notebook elucidate the bastinade scene. They function as an explanatory gloss that identifies the "transgression" as speaking homoerotic love. The concept of carnal love and its relationship to a community of literacy is central to the pedagogy of punishment. *'Ishq*, as the caption reads, with its erotic overtones in this circle of friends, is literally at stake. From the very beginning, educating the rude child entailed the taming of homoerotic desire and passion, expressed both in word and affect; it required an etiquette of the body (*adab*). The student's moral character is literally to be inscribed on the soles of his feet. We are reminded of the new year's greetings that Aqa Husayn composed, likening the palms of children, beaten by the stick of the teacher, to a manuscript of knowledge.

The ritual disciplining of "seekers of knowledge" (*talib-i 'ilm*), as a method of initiation into fraternal communities, was a common representational trope in early modern Persianate visual texts. Although generally depicted as a pedagogical practice within mosque and seminary settings, such images render an explicit hierarchy between master and disciple, where "white- and black-bearded" teachers pass on their knowledge through bodily chastisements, the most common of which was the bastinade. Their pedagogical discipline depends on the complicity of empathetic beardless brothers who had themselves endured the same physical pain. Mir Findiriski (d. 1640), Aqa Husayn's teacher, records in poetry the memory of his lesson in a religious school, the *maktab*, in Isfahan.

> I'm one of the schoolboys,
> At class today, I learned how to cry
>
> O heart, you must work very hard
> 'Til you've learned your lesson by heart[75]

This humorous lament illuminates a shared *adab* of performing the discursive practice of the bastinade across the arts and sciences. Its poetics involve emotions, particularly the act of crying as the primary pedagogical tool of a child's education. The experience of pain, resulting in an outburst of tears, was a mnemonic tool used to beat the content of study into the student's body. That so many educated men in Isfahan performed the trope of the bastinade and communicated their pain through the medium of words and images produced a shared experience of boyhood, whether one was a philosopher or a painter, whether one had directly experienced the bastinade or not. Mir Findiriski plays on the word *ravan* as a double entendre to associate the *flow* of tears with the *mastering* of the lesson. The student's *fluency* (*ravan*) was an emotional record voiced by the heart; "O heart, make an effort to memorize your lesson [by heart]." In Galenic philosophy, tears were associated with bodily humors in need of purging to remove excess. Crying produced an awareness of the emotions of fear and pleasure, which were to be disciplined as they simultaneously created communities of learners who empathized, publicized, and collected memories of their childhood education. In the process of socialization, the *adab* of physical punishment was to beat submission into the student's body and memory. Male subjects experienced and circulated the bastinade as an image, whether they were painters in search of patrons, bureaucrats, or religious scholars. As disciples and students, they had to write and read to learn their lesson, to tame carnal love (*'ishq*) and homoerotic desire; they engaged in the *adab* of the bastinade to become cultured men in Isfahan. But, as we saw in Chapter 1, seeing, reading, writing, drawing, and collecting could also produce desire.

Both the palace mural portraying Shah Abbas I as the beloved cupbearer (see Figure 1.3) and Muhammad Qasim's drawing of the bastinade (Figure 2.3) mobilize the disciplinary stick to exhibit the technique with which novices are socialized into communities of men in Isfahan. Both images feature the initiation of an apprentice into a circle of masters, making hierarchies visible according to age and rank. Men with beards and mustaches bear the stick, the sword, the goblet, the book, the pen, and the rosary; they hold the instruments of power. A shared performance of *adab* marks their bodily comportment; in gesture and gaze they embody knowledge, authorizing its transmission and initiating smooth-chinned youth into the social order.[76] Asymmetries of standing between master and disciple intersect with symmetric associations between peers. Model affective ties, arranged according to ideals of *'ishq* and friendship, bound together men of all ages in configuring communities of learning. The didactic message of the bastinade, however, alerts the audience that *'ishq* must also be channeled, or contained, as it moved between sensual and spiritual planes. Desire must be governed by the *adab* of *'ishq* to safeguard the prescribed order. Inscribed in students' notebooks as a first lesson and beaten onto the palms of sworn brothers at court, *'ishq* is to be practiced according to established codes of behavior to ensure the apprentice's loyalty and obedience to both sacred king and master painter.

Along with the physical punishments that were meant to inculcate submission and mark students' bodies and memories, reading and writing are depicted in Muhammad Qasim's *Bastinade* as twin technologies through which the student is schooled into a whole new mode of comportment. The term *technology* conveys the transformative power of rendering passionate youth into well-crafted and mannered men. Muhammad Qasim interprets the bastinade, the stick that inscribes a process, as a mimetic device for unambiguously communicating the importance of the word. Here, even within a familiar iconic illustration, the word gives a recognizable scene its signification by disseminating the message. Muhammad Qasim's subtle characterization of symmetric and asymmetric relationships gives meaning to the memory of the bastinade; they animate communities of learning for us, communicating complicated emotional knots that bind youth to men through pain, pleasure, and humor.

Muhammad Qasim's *Bastinade* is a product of a shift in the practices of patronage outside courtly circles; it is an example of the dissemination of poetry, prose, and painting in early modern Isfahan. Although the religious sciences and the arts shared pedagogical tools and poetic tropes—such as the bastinade—in their teachings to inculcate discipline and inscribe knowledge on the bodies of students, the subjects and the objects produced to engrave this knowledge, remember it, and learn from it are distinct. Muhammad Qasim pens a drawing on a sheet of paper and Mir Findiriski writes a verse of poetry; Aqa Husayn composes a spring greeting in the form of a letter. None of these works were produced within the walls of state or religion or collected in institutional archives. *Sabaq*, the double entendre used by the painter Muhammad Qasim and the mystic scholar Mir Findiriski, signifies "the lesson," but it also designates "what came before." This double entendre communicates that teaching is accomplished through collections of prior knowledge—of anthologies, paintings, talismans, or precious stones—just as communities are built on sharing this prior repertoire of objects and images. Such spaces of recognition allowed for city knowledge to be curated, collected, and recorded outside the scrutiny of institutions, even as these spaces were themselves the products of the collective pedagogies and cognitive environments that animated *maydan* walls or the folio of an illuminated manuscript on public display in Isfahan. They were mediums through which the self unfolded, in dialogue with and distinct from the imperial imaginary.

Like many artists hoping to gain fame and employment, Muhammad Qasim moved at a young age to Isfahan from Tabriz, a former capital city and center of the arts (see Map 0.1). Two self-portraits by the artist bear no seal of ownership (Figures 2.4 and 2.5). Muhammad Qasim's representation of a young male beauty with a letter in hand communicates his standing. Clearly written out on a large sheet of paper so that it can be read, the letter is addressed to "the magnificent Khan." And he names himself as the one who addresses: "I, Muhammad Qasim Musavvir [the painter], who invoke a blessing upon you, am among your devoted servants" (Figure 2.4). He praises his sought-after patron and writes that he is a novice in comparison to those already in the service of the khan. Muhammad Qasim focuses his eyes on the letter as though he is reading it aloud, thus creating a patron and an audience with his form of address. He composes his letter of appeal, drawing in symbols that elicit a favorable response; displayed in the hands of a beautiful male youth, who stands in a spring meadow with clouds and bright blue skies in the background, this watercolored letter seeks an affirmative response: "I hope to be exalted by your acceptance of this letter and to be referred to for your service, the execution of which would be a great honor."

At every stage of his life, Muhammad Qasim would convey to his audience his position as an artist in search of employment. In the second self-portrait (Figure 2.5), the painter is mid-career, as indicated by the moustache and goatee he has now grown. Muhammad Qasim is looking up to an absent patron as he holds an anthology shaped as a *jung* (boat), the portable portfolio of an itinerant poet or painter. "Verily, Muhammad Qasim drew," as he advertises his skill to paint or draw a patron's desired compositions. He writes his name and profession on a loose sheet of paper while presenting his anthology of paintings bound in a *jung*, to perform versified words that acknowledge his perfection of crafting the bookbinding tape that will preserve his collected oeuvre for future collectors. Moreover, he places himself in nature and draws a singular tree to provide him with shade. The outstanding tree implicitly interprets his position as a sovereign artist drawing images for collectors in the city. Using the media of a letter and an anthology, the painter reveals the mechanics of his practice of patronage. Muhammad Qasim's self-portraits communicate the artist's

FIGURE 2.4 Muhammad Qasim, *Youth Holding a Letter*, 1635. Opaque watercolor on paper (33.5 cm × 11.5 cm). Gulistan Palace World Heritage Complex, Royal Library, Tehran, Album no. 1629.

FIGURE 2.5 Muhammad Qasim, *Seated Man With an Album*, signed "Verily, Muhammad Qasim drew it," 1640. Tinted drawing on paper (11 cm × 8.2 cm). British Museum, 1920-9-17-0278 (2). Trustees of the British Museum.

message through graphics framed in letters and in the folios of bound anthologies, recognizable artifacts of city life in the eyes of a cultured clientele.

Muhammad Qasim also sought patronage in other ways. He had applied for employment at the Safavi court shortly after he arrived in Isfahan, presenting Shah Abbas I with a portrait of the king and his cupbearer (Figure 2.6). The painting is one of two signed works by Muhammad Qasim that are also dated. He carefully notes the date of composition as Friday, March 12, 1627, two years before the death of the shah. Friday was a day off from work, a time when many artists drew spontaneous gifts for their friends. On this second Friday in March 1627, Muhammad Qasim drew the shah and his cupbearer in intimate embrace, gazes locked, although he maintains the asymmetry of stature evident in size, positioning, bodily gesture, and clothing. The shah's gaze possesses visual authority as he locks in his lover's eyes. The cupbearer grips the neck of the wine jug placed between the shah's thighs, an obvious image of intimate touching, while he offers Shah Abbas I a goblet. Their bodies are wrapped together as the shah leans on a tree trunk at the banks of a stream. With colorful emotions, Muhammad Qasim represents the *adab* of homoerotic love, creating an idealized moment of amorous exchange when the shah's tender touch clasps the wrist of his beloved. Typical roles of lover and beloved are discretely reversed, to honor the status of Shah Abbas I as sovereign cupbearer and passionate lover. Muhammad Qasim inscribed this drawing with his own poetry to spell out its symbolic meaning:

> May three lovely lips bring joy to your days:
> The lip of the friend
> And the lip of the goblet
> By the "lip" of the river![77]

The brimming lips of the beloved friend, the mouth of a fresh stream of water, and a goblet of wine are mystical signifiers of a life blessed with divine favor; all three symbols are double entendres that play on sexual innuendo. With word and image Muhammad Qasim calls to mind the stature of Shah Abbas I as the divinely guided master, just as

→ FIGURE 2.6 Muhammad Qasim, *Portrait of Shah Abbas and a Page*, signed by Muhammad Qasim and dated March 12, 1627. Tinted drawing with gold on paper (25.5 cm × 15 cm). Musée du Louvre, MAO 494.

he discreetly celebrates the shah's performance and promise of a homoerotic paradise in Isfahan. Muhammad Qasim's auspicious wishes that illuminate his portrait of the shah identify the drawing as a gift, a gesture that was also a plea for royal patronage. Whether or not this gift of the portrait of Shah Abbas I and his cupbearer won him favor in the royal atelier, it was archived in the palace library, as can be seen from the royal seal of ownership on the upper left side of the drawing.

During the reign of Shah Abbas I's grandson and successor, Shah Safi (r. 1629–1642), Muhammad Qasim produced several works for the household of his patron, including Qarachaqay Khan (d. 1625), an Armenian convert who was the shah's slave and later the governor of Mashhad, and Qarachaqay's son and his grandson.[78] Two years after Muhammad Qasim drew the portrait of Shah Abbas I and his cupbearer, the shah's death precipitated a crisis of sovereignty. Opposition, both in the provinces and at the royal court, threatened the Safavi imperial hold on power.[79] With his imperial vision and personal engagement, Shah Abbas I had been the pillar who had maintained the empire's and the capital city's cohesion. A new elite of Georgian and Armenian slave converts to Islam, whom Shah Abbas I had introduced to consolidate power within the dynastic family, controlled the court in the following decades.[80] Qarachaqay Khan was an Armenian from Erevan, captured as a slave, trained at court, and later manumitted for his loyal service to the shah. Muhammad Qasim painted for three generations of this elite military family, who, as governors of Mashhad, played a central role in protecting the eastern frontiers of the Safavi realms.[81] Muhammad Qasim's self-portrait (see Figure 2.4), cum letter, cum petition, may have been a gift to Qarachaqay Khan. In 1636 Muhammad Qasim completed an illustrated romance, Vahshi's *Farhad and Shirin*, for the library collection of Qarachaqay Khan's son; this is the same romance whose preface appears in the cleric Aqa Husayn's anthology. Muhammad Qasim drew four paintings to turn Vahshi's *Farhad and Shirin* into an illustrated romance. In addition, he contributed to the illustration program of another romance, Nizami's *Khamsa*, and painted forty-two illustrations for the epic *Shahnama*, which he completed twelve years later in 1648.[82]

Whether Muhammad Qasim lived in Mashhad for over a decade, sent his paintings to that city from Isfahan, or created his work in the governor's workshop for tracts of time is not clear. What is evident is that he composed single-page paintings and drawings for multiple patrons in Isfahan, even while he was in the service of Qarachaqay Khan's elite slave household.[83] That Muhammad Qasim was identified by contemporaneous biographers as an Isfahani and was buried in Isfahan is testimony to his urban association.[84] Even though Aqa Husayn Khwansari and Muhammad Qasim were buried in the same cemetery, their bodies were placed in distinct sacred zones that marked their religious proclivities and social affiliations. Muhammad Qasim migrated from Tabriz and worked in Mashhad, but he was buried in the city where he lived and painted. When he died, his body was interred in the Takht-i Fulad cemetery, on the grounds of the mausoleum of the Sufi saint Baba Rukn al-Din Shirazi (d. 1490). One of the oldest sacred burial sites in Isfahan, this sanctuary was a site of visitation for Sufis. Poets, calligraphers, painters, and religious scholars who venerated this saint in life were laid to rest by his side.[85] As Isfahan was transformed into an imperial capital, new members of the community, whether migrants or Christian slave converts to Shi'ism, were honored through their integration into collective tomb sites. Muhammad Qasim lay with his Sufi community of Baba Rukn al-Din's devotees. Aqa Husayn was buried alongside his teacher in the religious sciences. And Qarachaqay Khan rested in the vicinity of the holy shrine of the eighth Imam in Mashhad to signal his entry into the Shi'a faith. As a convert and a loyal servant to Shah Abbas I, he was buried alongside members of the Safavi royal family, blood descendants of the prophet Muhammad, his daughter Fatima, and his son-in-law Ali.

Given the importance of Isfahan to Muhammad Qasim's artistic portfolio, it is remarkable that none of his extant freestanding works depict the built environment; none of his paintings or drawings are set within the walls of the city or the household. Every single-page painting, whether of the bastinade, a gathering of female friends, a nude couple, or a scene of nighttime entertainment, is set in nature. Even though Muhammad Qasim breaks with pictorial conventions to create portraits that resemble his subjects, to paint male and female nude bodies, or to inscribe his work with a signature, there are no urban landscapes.[86] Instead, Muhammad Qasim paints cognitive and affective environments of homosociability set in an idealized background of Isfahan as garden. He figures a variety of models of intimacy and discipline in the mystic garden where erotic love and desire frame the themes of everyday sociability.

Muhammad Qasim's repertoire includes childhood memories beyond the classroom. He captures boys playing the game of bird nesting in nature (Figure 2.7). At first glance their game seems innocuous in its innocent mischief. Wrapped around

FIGURE 2.7 Muhammad Qasim, *Boys Bird Nesting*, no inscription, dated 1650–1655. Tinted drawing on paper (18.5 cm × 13 cm). British Museum, 1964-6-13-02. Trustees of the British Museum.

a tree, at the center of the painting, a boy stands on the palm of his friend's hands that lift him toward the bird's nest. He holds a bird in one hand and extends the other along the tree, reaching for the nest that is cradled in its branches. While the boy on his left directs him to reach the nest and the prized egg, at the foot of the tree another boy grasps a bird and, with his right hand, points his finger to his lips, a visual expression of the idiom *angusht bi dahan*, signaling his bewilderment. He is absorbed in thought, perhaps wondering about the game of bird nesting and its meaning. Two boys are fighting over a captured bird, and another is unable to break up the scuffle; in despair he solicits the help of an older man, perhaps their guardian or a passerby, who is contemplating the scene.

The older man leans on his stick and extends his left hand toward the boy in a dithering gesture of inaction, as though to say, "Such is the way of boys." It is the perspective of the elderly man that Muhammad Qasim draws in his image. The older male spectator is engaged in the ritual of boy gazing that is his visual prerogative. *Boys Bird Nesting* recalls the *Bastinade* as a disciplinary counterpoint. Muhammad Qasim memorializes the confusion, competition, and aggression of boys at play moving and looking in all directions. A fourth friend ignores the commotion as he crawls along the ground in an effort to ambush a bird. Muhammad Qasim brings to life the pleasure and excitement, the chaos and perplexity, of the experience of boyhood. Once again, the painter engages in the production of urban knowledge, creating a masculine memory of boyhood that differs from the didactic lesson of the pedagogy of discipline. *Boys Bird Nesting* depicts the range of behaviors of boys at play, their competitive hostility, and their power dynamics—all acts that must be disciplined by the rules of male homosociality in Isfahan.

These are the urban rituals of *adab* that patrons commissioned Muhammad Qasim to paint. His detailed rendering and twist on old tropes disclose an observing eye, a witty mindfulness of the ideal. Even when Muhammad Qasim paints himself in an act of soliciting patronage, he paints himself as a beautiful male youth or a desiring old man. When women appear in scenes of men feasting, they are inscribed as entertainers, touching their tambourines with their fingers and allowing for male viewers to both enjoy female-female sex and mimic the male prerogative of foreplay. Female spaces of friendship are framed in separate homoerotic compositions, which I discuss in Chapter 5. Muhammad Qasim's portfolio is dominated by male subjects. Although he painted for a female clientele, women were not his primary consumers.

The incitement to engage in the culture of *adab* is a gendered invitation, first and foremost meant for male participants in the public life of Isfahan.

Women appear in Aqa Husayn Khwansari's anthology as subjects of divinatory outcomes or as objects of pleasure in a Galenic sexual economy. And, like Muhammad Qasim, Aqa Husayn similarly does not speak about the built environment of Isfahan in explicit terms, though he evokes its cityscape implicitly through the mirrored image of the garden and through the map of Istanbul. Of course, Aqa Husayn's status as a religious scholar was also quite different from Muhammad Qasim, the artist; subjects such as divination and timekeeping were peculiar to the cleric's professional milieu. Nevertheless, it is through the idioms of love and the *adab* of sociability that both men mark their urbanity, familiar with the rituals, protocols, and words with which to perform their status and write themselves into their idealized city. We do not know if the two knew each other; perhaps they may have only heard of each other's reputation. What their anthologies make clear, at least, is that if they had encountered each other, they would certainly have known how to comport themselves, what to say, and how to hold their bodies in their interaction, governed by complementary understandings of *adab*.

Both cleric and painter also deploy similar urban media of communication—paper, the letter, and the anthology—to convey their aspirations and desires, but each makes use of these media to transmit the knowledge relations they inhabit and perform. Aqa Husayn composed his spring greetings to friends in prose to flaunt his compositional skills, yet he draws on the rhetoric and the poetics of love and eros to configure his social relations. Both authors studied the romance of *Farhad and Shirin* but collected it in different ways: Aqa Husayn curated segments that he includes in his anthology, and Muhammad Qasim painted four vignettes for an illustrated manuscript of the romance. Even as they read and interpreted the benefits and detriments of this worldly love that haunted Farhad and Shirin in different ways, these were among the popular texts in Isfahan that helped shape their urban and sexual selves. Aqa Husayn and Muhammad Qasim were conscious of the conflicting practices of spiritual and carnal love as they constructed the terms of their composition. A shared phenomenology inspired their verbal and visual productions as they saw, read, compared, wrote, and desired their subjective urban reality. These two migrants draw their refined and erotic selves through the idiom of love to negotiate, memorialize, and participate in the imagined city of paradise.

Finally, even as Aqa Husayn curated his own anthology while Muhammad Qasim catered his paintings to the tastes of his clientele, each interpreted the idiom of mystic love to depict a diversity of erotic desires. When cleric and painter represent themselves, they do so as objects of love; Aqa Husayn writes himself as a male youth composing the beauty of spring, figured as a female bride, and Muhammad Qasim poses as a beautiful male youth seeking his gendered patrons. The erotic desires these two migrants to Isfahan communicate move between male and female subjects. Male homoeroticism is ubiquitous in the depictions of Muhammad Qasim examined in this chapter, whereas, for the cleric, carnal tensions lie in regulating his desire for women. Friendship, however, is a practice that even the cleric represents in terms of love for men, and it is here that the lines between homo- and heteroerotic desire are mobile and unstable. *'Ishq*, with its sexual overtones in circles of male friends, is salient for both painter and cleric, expressed in word and affect. Love requires an etiquette of the body (*adab*), (re)assembled here by different media, to discipline a range of sexual behavior through the communal rules of male homosociality in Isfahan.

CHAPTER 3

Disturbing the City

> As Isfahan turned brilliantly into the image of the world [*naqsh-i jahan*]
> Witness a world [*'alami*] of people who wander there in travel
> I'jaz Herati (visited Isfahan shortly after 1650)[1]

The City Disturber

Muhammad Tahir Nasrabadi, who collected an anthology of seventeenth-century poets living in Isfahan, was offended by I'jaz Herati's foray into the literary tradition of the *shahrashub*, literally "city disturbance."[2] He writes that, when the poet I'jaz traveled from Herat to Isfahan, "in the guise of praise for Isfahan, he made some jokes about the city. This humble one's [Nasrabadi] provincial intolerance [*ta'assub-i rusta'igari*] was inflamed. I wrote a couple of paragraphs in response to him."[3] News about their exchange circulated in Isfahan among Nasrabadi's friends and the community of literati, until finally I'jaz Herati apologized for having insulted Nasrabadi. That did not, however, hinder the circulation of his city disturbance, which was widely recorded in household anthologies.[4]

The *shahrashub* became the preferred mode of writing cities in the early modern Persianate world, offering a detailed walking tour of the urban spaces and spectacles that were not to be missed—especially opportunities for catching the sight of lovely young men. Through an alternative reading of Isfahan, seventeenth-century authors of the *shahrashub* in particular sought to rectify the anxieties fueled by a new moral order that cast male homoerotic practices as vice.[5] The *shahrashub* was the medium through which sexual desire and sedition were folded into the celebration of male urban beauties in Isfahan. As I'jaz Herati's words indicate, he saw Isfahan as "the image of the world," a copy of perfection that enticed travelers to witness and partake in its wonders. Irony and metaphor, the rhetorical figure of excess, were intended to be playful, but the effect of the city disturber was mixed; evidently it was a sensitive matter to write about Isfahan as a city of male homoerotic delight.[6] Nasrabadi had taken I'jaz Herati's new iteration of the *shahrashub* to heart. Slighted by the casting of Isfahan as a site of erotic wonder, Nasrabadi reveals his insecurity toward the author, a poet born and trained in Herat, the fifteenth-century cultural capital of the arts and sciences. Isfahan was fashioning itself as a rival to Herat. Still, even as a "crude" subject, Nasrabadi considered his city with pride, as something to be protected and defended. It was not that Nasrabadi was a moralist; in fact, many of the poets he introduced in his biography "fell in love" with male youths. It would seem from his collection of poets that male homoerotic practices where the norm among Isfahan's literati. Even the patron-king, Shah Abbas I, entered Nasrabadi's anthology as a client who frequented the Qahvakhana-yi Arab coffeehouse because he was smitten with a Georgian beauty who worked there. Yet when an outsider such as I'jaz Herati publicly sexualized the beauty of his city through the figure of the male youth, specifically by writing men—as lovers of younger men—so brazenly into the urban landscape, Isfahan's honor was at stake.

In the *shahrashub* writing about a place and writing in a space converge. My reading of the *shahrashub*s on Isfahan indicates that, although the imperial project built around the *maydan* fostered graphic legibility, as described in Chapter 1, it also helped to generate new urban imaginations and reinvigorate preexisting literary forms in less predictable ways (Map 1.1). Seventeenth-century authors transform the *shahrashub*—expanding it beyond a catalog of beautiful young men in the bazaar—to narrate in verse and prose an affective picture of Isfahan; they encapsulate the urban experience into a discrete speech act that addresses all male residents, inviting them to encounter erotic desire in the city.[7] The sensitivity around the production of the *shahrashub* that exposed homoerotic urban practices was precisely its rhetorical power. Moving out of the homoerotic space of the bazaar, the established purview of the *shahrashub*, these guides take the reader on a tour of the entire urban landscape. Isfahan's built environment becomes a site to write guidebooks on the best urban locales and neighborhoods where male beauties populate coffeehouses, bathhouses, the central square, and garden promenades. As authors name their favorite coffeehouse owners to be visited, recommending the most beautiful male servers who might prepare this stimulating beverage, they inscribe these desirous, transient encounters in a more durable fashion on the cityscape and on the page. The *shahrashub* opens a space for visualizing, reading, and writing desire; like the familiar haunts of the city, it was also a site to revisit, as authors would often later revise their compositions to foreground new details. Beyond its role as an aural text, the seventeenth-century *shahrashub* was thus a visual object meant to be experienced on the page, through the medium of the gaze, which it also trained in particular ways.[8]

As we have seen, the image of Isfahan gave material form to a different range of urban artifacts. Yet whereas Aqa Husayn Khwansari's anthology was gathered and preserved in his library, largely for his family to read and experience on paper, the *shahrashub* communicates directly with the residents of Isfahan through an alternative form of address and process of performing the *adab* of urbanity. Not only does the beloved enter the consciousness of the city disturber through the gaze of the lover, but Isfahan's built environment, the city itself, is envisioned through the *shahrashub*. The effect produced new forms of sociality: from the materiality of their paper to the emotional resonance of reading, the experiences of the city disturbance inspired men and also shaped urban rituals and habits. The knowledge of how to see and act in a coffeehouse or of beginning the day with a morning smoke at the hookah shop in the bazaar collectively created male communities bound together in urban spaces through various rituals of masculinity.

Mobilizing a new form of immanent authority built on the vitality of embodied experiences, the *shahrashub* is a literary experiment, a contestation that activates eros to reimagine the city of Isfahan, the very symbol of transcendence. *Shahrashub* is derived from *ashub*, which signifies sedition, and *shahr* (urban). In the medieval urban poetics of the *shahrashub*, the bazaar was the voice of dissonance, a public voice that distinguished it from courtly circles and their patronized poetic genres. Although scholars are still engaged in a debate about the distinct characteristics of the *shahrashub*, in its earliest iteration the bazaar featured as an alternative social order. We can observe this in the work of Masʿud Saʿd (d. 1121), who utilizes the *qiʿta*, or short poem, to highlight the confessional and physical diversity of male youth working in the bazaar. Punning on male body parts and goods sold by young artisans, Masʿud Saʿd uses irony to figure male beauty and desire as central to the economy of the bazaar.[9] From its nascent articulation, the *shahrashub* was already about sexual desire. The medieval poetess Mahsati Ganjavi (twelfth century) chose a different poetic form, the quatrain (*ruba'i*), to give voice to her city disturbance.¹⁰ Writing on the western frontiers of the Islamic world, Mahsati was a contemporary of Mas'ud Sa'd, though the two probably never met, because he was living on the eastern edges in Lahore. She too drew on the poetics of eros and irony to write about young men at work in the bazaar. Mahsati composed for the Seljuk court of Sultan Sanjar (r. 1097–1118) in the city of Ganja in modern-day Azerbaijan. Breaking with courtly poetic forms of romance (*masnavi*), she singled out the marketplace as her subject of composition. Inserting herself into a male homosocial sphere, she turned male beauty into a metaphor for sedition. Mahsati helped shape the *shahrashub* because she too made the bazaar the object of her poetry. The bazaar as a site of disrupting order underlies the act of writing a *shahrashub*, whether for Mahsati, who mobilized it as a form of resistance against gender segregation, or for Mas'ud Sa'd, who sought to break the silence around male homoerotic desire. Both poets mobilized the bazaar, male youth, metaphor, and irony as characteristic terms of disruption to break from the hegemony of courtly panegyrics or romance and to speak publicly about erotic desire.¹¹

By the early modern period, the *shahrashub* had been canonized as a male homoerotic mode of poetic expression, providing the occasion to write about the beauty of the male body in its youthful perfection. The city disturber—both as a literary form and as an urban guide—deployed artisanal tools of production to distinguish the physical attributes of apprentice craftsmen, who were cast as ideal beauties. The apprentice who embodied the craft became the figure of desire through whom goods and services were mediated. The traffic of eros between client and artisan fashioned the aesthetics of male desire, a masculine pleasure of trade and commerce that was cultivated and refined in the city disturbance. Moreover, the tools and commodities they produced had acquired sexual connotations that circulated in the city. By the time I'jaz Herati wrote his *shahrashub* in mid-seventeenth-century Isfahan, the groundwork had been laid for him to deploy the form to offer an alternative reading of the city; his writing encapsulates the experience of traveling to Isfahan twice during its imperial renovation before he finally left Herat and its legacy of creativity behind. Certainly, Shah Abbas I's epigraphic and architectural program shaped this experience: I'jaz Herati's narrative of Isfahan begins with its gardens in the district of Dardash and Juybara before gravitating toward the *maydan*, the image of the world, the Naqsh-i Jahan, where travelers suffered the pains of love and lost themselves in its beauty.

Much as I'jaz Herati infuses the *shahrashub* with metaphors of male beauty, other writers likewise blended the core ethos of the *shahrashub* into an urban guidebook. To explore the ways in which writers recast the experience of Isfahan as the scene of homoerotic writing, I turn to two authors who used fashionable urban media to communicate and translate their city disturbance: Mir Rukn al-Din, who wrote a friendship letter to his beloved, Aqa Mansur, who in turn wrote a popular conduct manual in response. As we saw in Chapter 2, friendship letters were an instrument of *adab* literacy and social discourse. Distinct from diplomatic and chancellery epistles (*sultaniyyat*), this form of correspondence was also regularly collected in household anthologies. Scribes, authors, and owners of anthologies categorize them as a distinct genre: *rasa'il-i ikhvaniyyat*, or "fraternal" letters.[12] Manuals of model friendship letters, preserved along with personal examples of letters exchanged between friends, were thus anthologized by residents of Isfahan such as Aqa Husayn Khwansari, in part to help collectors master the form. Moreover, specialized manuals instilled writing techniques and established rules and conventions of communication. Their content conformed with the ethics and protocols that governed sworn friendships in the context of craft and mystical communities; their language was indistinguishable from the expression of love deployed in *ghazal* poetry. Friendship letters were a medium by which residents learned how to maintain social relations; hence they reflect not only idealized bonds but also anxieties around the vicissitudes of friendship. Model letters typically contain requests to meet with a friend, chides of negligence, or forgiveness for disloyal behavior. Yet the authors' epistolary voice is singular in its keen awareness of the physical absence of the friend, his face and his body.

It is in this context of *adab* that Mir Rukn al-Din uses the friendship letter to write the longing for a face-to-face encounter with his beloved, Mir Muhammad Mansur, better known as Aqa Mansur Semnani (see Map 0.1). But in the process of writing to his beloved, he complains about the shortcoming of the letter as a mode of communication. It fails to materialize the absence of the friend; in fact, his letter is an incitement to see, to feel, and to touch Aqa Mansur.[13] Mir Rukn al-Din's letter sparked a response that provides us with a dialogue about the ethics of friendship that circulated more widely across anthologies and households in Isfahan and therefore serves as the central focus of this chapter.

In writing his response to his friend, Aqa Mansur does not reply with a letter. Curiously, he uses the didactic form of a conduct manual (*dastur al-'amal*) not only to address his beloved friend, Mir Rukn al-Din, but also to direct his words to all male beloveds residing in Isfahan. As a religious dignitary, the Shaykh al-Islam of the city of Semnan, 400 miles north of Isfahan, Aqa Mansur was familiar with the practice of publishing conduct manuals. It is thus revealing that his manual applies humor to mock the disciplinary manuals of state and religion. Aqa Mansur uses the form of the manual to instruct his audience on the *adab* of disturbing the city, guiding the longing hearts of his readers to anticipate the promise of Isfahan: the gifts of paradise, the most prized award being the encounter with the beloved. His manual is a sensory travelogue of the city of Isfahan, where the male audience is educated in the erotic performance of urbanity. For Aqa Mansur, whose pen name was The Lover (*'ashiq*), *adab* literacy allowed him to apply the power of language in a critique of this imperial project, making use of the very technologies of state power to undo and question authority.

Shah Abbas I's Isfahan was modeled on the male homoerotic promise of paradise in the Quran, offering a counterpoint to Aqa Mansur's city disturber, which imagined the city itself as the spectacle of wondrous sights of pleasure for the fulfillment of licit desire. In other words, Aqa Mansur modeled Shah Abbas I's imaginary in earnest. There was no longer any need to anticipate heavenly delights; in Isfahan, that experience could be had in the here and the now. To stroll through Isfahan was a healing experience, a remedy for suffering souls who longed to see their beloved. Drawing on the mystical journey away from home as a way to encounter the divine, Aqa Mansur offers the city of Isfahan as a site of pilgrimage; rather than travel to the Ka'ba in Mecca or visit the shrines of Sufi saints and Shi'a Imams, he invites pilgrims to lose themselves in the presence of the beloved in Isfahan. The mystical quest for divine union is translated onto the entire experience of the city, and the spiritual is deployed to attain the physical and tangible beauty of the city and its beloveds. Indeed, Aqa Mansur turns Isfahan into an alternative Ka'ba. Moving beyond Abbas I's imperial imaginary that inscribed the Friday Prayer Mosque as the second Ka'ba, he extends the metaphor from a figure of speech to the virtual enactment of pilgrimage to the city of God. Walking through Isfahan is likened to a spiritual migration (*muhajirat*) in which one seeks oneness with God through the figure of the male youth.

The Friendship Letter

Mir Rukn al-Din addresses his letter to "the one thanks to whom I am happy, my life [*jan*], Aqa Mansur."[14] Not only does he name his beloved, but he also describes the emotional bonds that tie them together. Aqa Mansur was like a brother (*baradar*), equal to life (*bi jan barabar*), a true friend and companion (*dust-i sadiq va yar*); he was the desired one for Mir Rukn al-Din's heart (*mahbub al-qulub*), the very soul of life itself (*jan-i 'umri*).

The language that Mir Rukn al-Din uses to address his beloved situates him in a practice of friendship, or the cultivated display of emotions and affect, performed in a letter. It was common practice between friends in early modern Isfahan to exchange vows of brotherhood (*sigha-yi ukhuvvat*) and vows of sisterhood (*sigha-yi khwahar khwandagi*). Anthologies preserve a paper trail of certificates of sworn friendships, evidence of the legal status attributed to unions between two brothers and two sisters.[15] Pledges of solidarity were penned to certify loyalty in this world and even in the afterlife, where one friend was to ensure the entry of the other into paradise. Drawing on verses from the Quran, these certificates proclaim friendship to be a social institution characterized by ethical obligation. A bond with religious overtones, sworn friendships were a form of voluntary kinship that augmented those social networks that were formed through blood and marriage ties. Friendships served the social channel of advancement in politics and commerce, broadening the family network. As such, they sometimes enhanced and sometimes rivaled or even directly competed with matrimony and blood kinship. Recorded and collected in anthologies, friendship vows are the materials that formalize amical collectives within larger social entities, be they fraternities, neighborhoods, the city, or the state.

In the absence of his beloved, Mir Rukn al-Din uses the medium of a friendship letter to communicate his love. He breaks with prior protocols by explicitly naming his beloved and making public his secret, which he knows may well be collected and copied in household anthologies. Speaking of a misunderstanding (*kudurat*) that had caused distance between the two friends, Mir Rukn al-Din composed his "letter of longing" (*tangnama*) to reveal his secret love for Aqa Mansur. Mir Rukn al-Din's letter, along with his beloved's response, allows us to explore one of the most challenging questions framing histories of friendship: how to properly historicize the different valences of intimacy that bound together friends living in previous centuries.

It is in the state of separation, a mystical stage of longing and anticipation for a visit from his beloved, that Mir Rukn al-Din composes this letter. "You departed and vision [*bina'i*] fled my teary eyes. It is time for the light of sight [*nazar*] to return."[16] Mir Rukn al-Din's beloved has deprived him of sight. Sight is the modality through which the poetics of the *shahrashub* educates the reader or collector about the experience of Isfahan. The construction of this sensual knowledge, which trains readers to gaze on the city through the lens of male desire, unfolds in complex ways. In his letter, Mir Rukn al-Din reaches for his pen to draw the image (*nigar*) of his long-lost friend. Memory serves to picture his face, even as the beloved has physically withdrawn from his eyes. However, it is especially the sight (*nazar*) of other male beauties that ignites his desire to meet with his beloved; it is sight that inscribes the cityscape with the image, the pictured memory, of his personal desire. The complex interplay between sensual temptation and disciplining the carnal body brings to sight the presence and absence of the figure of the beloved friend.

With the pain of separation and longing foremost in his mind, Mir Rukn al-Din asks in frustration, "How can the nail, on the tip of the tongue of the pen, undo this knot from the thought of sorrow?"[17] The tip of the pen, like the pointed fingernail, is scripted as the extension of the tongue, a vessel that translates pain into speech and circulates it on paper. Tactility is written into the letter, whose subtle indentations invite the reader to imagine another body: the fingers of Mir Rukn al-Din manipulating the sharp tip of the pen as he draws his tongue to speak from the heart. Put simply, his entire body is written into the letter. Yet for Mir Rukn al-Din, the letter is also an inadequate medium of conveying absence. The intensity of his emotions cannot fit into words, no matter how refined by *adab*: "If I were to write a hundred letters, one hundred times more, I am in anticipation. I do not know how to measure words and weigh meanings; I am so excited about seeing you, my soothing soul." Through these references, Mir Rukn al-Din guides the reader's attention to the act of producing a letter, from the dimensions of its paper to the syllables that poets count to create rhyme and meaning—an act presumably meant to alleviate suffering, though here one that only heightens the degree of his anticipation. He even envisions fate to be written on a piece of paper, where God has sketched out the separation between these two men: "Since the designer of faith [God] drew this physical separation onto the pages of my state, this broken-winged one has not taken a soothing breath on the mirror of my imagination."[18]

In the letter Mir Rukn al-Din also draws on the memory of past encounters to envision the shape a future meeting might take. "When I remember the conversations built around deceit that surrounded you in the assembly of alleged loyal lovers, you come to my mind and a flood of tears flow through my head," he laments.[19] And so, by explicitly drawing attention to the art of letter writing, Mir Rukn al-Din reveals himself as Aqa Mansur's true friend. Despite its shortcomings, the letter provides the space in which the etiquette of friendship and the declaration of his loyalty is performed in the hope for a future reunion: "All this talk of letters and paper will not fix my affair [*kar*]; until I see you, my heart will not be the same."[20]

Other senses gradually come to the fore. Mir Rukn al-Din's state of anticipation is particularly sharpened through the olfactory sense, which is tied to memory and emotion in the limbic region of the brain. In a revealing manner, olfaction orients him in the direction of his unseen beloved.

> How pleasing it is that you, my friend, are my companion [*yar-i rafiq*]
> You are like the wind that blows through the friend's garden
> May we be companions [*rafiq*] strolling through the city
> May we be companions strolling through its streets and bazaars[21]

Significantly, this orientation points toward the city. The breeze of past intercourse (*ulfat*) fills his imagination (*tasavvur*) with smells of the garden of friendship. With every breeze that blows in Isfahan he longs for the scent of his beloved's clothes, to catch a whiff of his beloved in the desired letter (*maktub-i marghub*). The physical encounter, however, is repetitively delayed. A day without his beloved feels like one hundred years. "Without him," he complains, "every day seems like a lifetime, and each hour a year."[22] His sense of time has been altered; as he waits in separation, he lives in the past. Mir Rukn al-Din is surprised by his own behavior. For a heart like his own that was drawn to male gazing, he no longer experiences the feverish shivers that used to overwhelm him when he witnessed male beauties in the coffeehouse. And so, Mir Rukn al-Din calls his beloved to join him in Isfahan, the city where Joseph-like shopkeepers abound, the city where tulip-faced beauties throng the streets in the spring. Until that blissful reunion, he notes, the act of strolling through a flower garden or of gazing at beautiful male youths under the newly constructed Hasanabad Bridge (built in 1650) only serves to inflame the sorrows of separation anew.[23] Notably, unlike the Parisian flâneur, for Mir Rukn al-Din exploring the city of Isfahan is a social experience that cannot be fulfilled alone.[24] The spectator's gaze is part of the urban practice of friendship that fosters social bonding, making public the vows of brotherhood.

For the lover, walking in the city of Isfahan is a cure for the longing heart, yet for Mir Rukn al-Din it is for naught. He misses his kind companion (*musahib*). It is with him that he wishes to be joined in companionate spectatorship.

A hundred chapters of letters forbidden in the code of love [*shar'i mahabbat*], why do you not write to me? In the *Abode of Sorrow*, in the anticipation of spiritual union, a letter is better than one hundred treasures.[25]

Although Mir Rukn al-Din complains about the limitations of a letter, in the absence of his beloved the disembodied letter acts as a suggestive sign. Having voiced his love and loyalty in writing, he anticipates a response. Mir Rukn al-Din ends with an enticement that may hasten the awaited letter or, even better, the encounter: "Let me leave our secrets to utter when we meet."[26] The reader, like the addressee, is left intrigued by the secret that cannot be written: What is concealed and what will be revealed when these two men finally meet? The sharing of secrets, overtly and covertly, is a practice that can make or break friendships; eros is configured out of silence as well as out of speech. As this letter implies, the ethics that govern loyalty between friends demands that their secret remain hidden—but with the knowledge that all will be divulged in the fullness of time, whether to deepen trust between friends or to forge new friendships.

The Conduct Manual

Just as elements of the *shahrashub* tradition can migrate across different literary forms, so too can a friendship letter be answered, directly or indirectly, in many ways. In this case, Mir Rukn al-Din's friendship letter inspired a response by Aqa Mansur in the form of a creative reading of the *shahrashub*. To answer a letter with a how-to manual on masculine urbanity, which Aqa Mansur frames as a handbook on *adab*, might strike modern readers as an odd evasion. After all, such a response cannot explicitly address his beloved friend's particular complaints. What it attempted, however, was to offer Mir Rukn al-Din a more enduring cure for his longing: an education for the senses, especially for his sight. In his own words, Aqa Mansur specifies the purpose and audience of his manual, as a "guide for afflicted [*dardmand*] lovers," in what essentially is a refined rejection of his friend's love.[27] Of course, Aqa Mansur's response was yet another delay of Mir Rukn al-Din's request to meet with him. In place of meeting, Aqa Mansur invites Mir Rukn al-Din to discover male homosocial desire in the city of Isfahan, empowering his love-struckness in a collective experience of male urban bonding. The utility of this manual clearly resonated with collectors in Isfahan; Aqa Mansur's city disturbance is copied in numerous household anthologies; however, Mir Rukn al-Din's accompanying letter is usually more conspicuously absent.[28] Widely disseminated as an essay in praise of Isfahan, sometimes without even crediting Aqa Mansur as the author, the manual's circulation indicates a reading of his city disturbance as a generic manual on the beauty of Isfahan for the love-struck. Habits of collecting transformed the dialogue between two friends into a single combined speech act; these curatorial choices recontextualized the communicative life between a letter and a manual to privilege Aqa Mansur's address to both residents and visitors—those who desired to learn and experience Isfahan—whether through reading or encountering the city itself.

Isfahan is both the city where Aqa Mansur composes his manual and the site through which he represents a masculine space for beloved friends to learn about urban rules of sexual behavior and the *adab* of love. Forlorn men are invited to travel, observe, and discover a cityscape of masculine erotic pleasures. Aqa Mansur's guidebook recursively configures the rituals of urbane masculinity to fashion a spectatorship of refined male gazers. His knowledge of sexuality is conceptualized and woven together in mixed prose and verse to picture Isfahan's homosocial scene on paper. The choice of a conduct manual on love also disturbs the city of Isfahan through its irony, because it draws on the authority typically invested in a didactic manual but does so to expose the hypocrisy of court and mosque in the policing of "proper" public displays of masculinity. Put differently, Aqa Mansur subverts the didactic agency of a manual into a city disturbance to fracture the order intended by formal conduct manuals, painting an alternative practice of masculinity in his wake. Irony serves Aqa Mansur's play on the promise of pleasure and abundance in postapocalyptic, paradisal Isfahan. The courtly culture of leisure designed around gardens and tree-lined boulevards enables Aqa Mansur to expose the duplicity of celebrating homo-eros at court at a time when, by the midcentury, such expressions of love were being banned in the streets. His city disturbance is not about taming masculinity to fashion a cultured courtier but rather to cultivate male sensuality in public spaces as part of the urbane display of pleasure and erotic desire. I argue that these contested and authoritative acts remake the city of Isfahan into an earthly, homoerotic domain.

Imperial imaginations of social order—the aesthetic and ethical visions broadcast by court and mosque through the dissemination of manuals and monumental decrees carved in stone—helped to open up the city of Isfahan as a space for its inhabitants' critical investigation. Aqa Mansur's participation in and fascination with street life exhibits his disparaging attitude toward the official ordering of life in the city. Of course, in the face of everyday social practices, control could only ever be provisional. Although the Naqsh-i Jahan square is central to Aqa Mansur's production of the city, his is not a linear experience of the architectural project of empire that organized movement between the city's two lungs, the marketplace and the mosque, on opposite corners of the *maydan* (see Figure 0.2). Aqa Mansur therefore begins his tour at a small tobacco stall (*timcha*) on the square and then moves the reader through a labyrinth of homoerotic commerce, the bazaar and coffeehouses, where an exchange of desires for goods and money occurs. Only toward the end of his manual does he curate the public performance (*ma'rika*) of a wrestling match staged in the central square. Aqa Mansur also disrupts the noontime movement of artisans, craftsmen, and shoppers from the bazaar toward the Friday Prayer Mosque by taking a detour in the medieval quarter, drawing the old Friday Prayer Mosque and the Harun-i Vilayat quarter into his project. In Aqa Mansur's city manual, the spectacle of Isfahan is itself disorganized, mixing together older and newer spaces and forms of sociability. His wanderings reorient imperial readings of the city, which, though not fully standardized, were reflected through monumental epigraphic writing and by other didactic writings produced by clerics.

Aqa Mansur conveys a density of signs in his *shahrashub* in which familiar codes are contested and reinterpreted. At the time of Aqa Mansur's writing, the imperial idiom had not been standardized; it was not yet available to all as was a loaf of bread, a piece of halva, or a cup of coffee. The categories of collective life—of city, neighborhood, and sex—were in the process of being transformed, and so Aqa Mansur's spectacle of Isfahan presents a variation on the reading of Isfahan's habitus.[29] A consciousness of change is unraveling the social fabric of the city, and Aqa Mansur uses the *shahrashub* to visualize that process.

Isfahan's previous image as the symbol of paradise (*nishan-i bihisht*) is reconfigured by Aqa Mansur as male homoerotic spectacle as he draws on the common Sufi practice of gazing (*nazar*) to envisage the hidden meanings of Isfahan as an allegory for paradise. The etymology of the Persian noun *nazar* derives from the Arabic root n.z.r, "to view," "to eye," "to look," "to gaze," or "to glance," but also "to watch," "to observe," "to notice," "to contemplate," or "to consider." The poetic recording of the spectacle of Isfahan on paper drew on all these senses of *nazar*, cultivating insight, consideration, and discernment in the reader's eye. Similar to the etymology of the word *spectacle* (derived from the Latin *spectaculum*, or "a public show," and *spectare*, "to view," "to behold," or "to watch"), *nazar* was an instrument used by Aqa Mansur with the assistance of sight as a mediating eye.[30] Yet the contemplative practice of *nazar* also did more, in part by igniting carnal desire as the viewer/beloved was drawn to the viewed/lover. The practice of gazing was central to Aqa Mansur's education of the senses of male residents. Urbanity and the figure of the beloved became signs for sociability, and desire rendered a new kind of masculine culture visible. The built environment and the spectacular events patronized by the court in the Naqsh-i Jahan square served Aqa Mansur as a mediator between the eye and the affective senses of the spectator already associated with gazing and erotic desire through the ubiquitous culture of Sufism.

The manual also deploys metaphors that draw from the technology of writing and the environment to help visualize Isfahan. Aqa Mansur is the scribe (*katib*) who turns the trees of the tree-lined boulevard, the Chahar Bagh, into reed pens through reflection. Writing requires tools but also necessitates a contemplative engagement with the urban environment. Aqa Mansur's composition of his *shahrashub* provides him with an occasion to translate his surroundings onto a sheet of paper, engaging the organic matter in Isfahan's ecosystem to capture the fabric of the city. For instance, the author-scribe uses a reed pen plucked from the Zayanda, or "life-giving," River, to draw the central square. The *maydan* is described as the surface of a page on which the scribe uses his reed pen together with water to write. His reference to paper, which is liquid until it dries and solidifies, reflects his understanding of the mechanics of its production. To author his poetic imagery of the city, Aqa Mansur even likens the art of papermaking to the process of drawing water toward the square to irrigate trees. In drawing attention to the production of city-/papermaking, he gradually signals that he—the author—will inscribe his own reading on Isfahan's built environment. Moreover, this reading will often be at odds with the imperial project.

Writing about the emotions of longing presents Aqa Mansur with a greater challenge. How is he to turn sentiments into the materiality of words on paper? The tools of writing, he declares, are wanting. Aqa Mansur, the scribe who, by his extended hand, narrated the Age of Separation, faces an impossible task. Years of writing, he says, will not suffice for this endeavor. Words, paper, ink, and time are incapable of encapsulating the intensity of his emotions. Much like the constraints that Mir Rukn al-Din voices in his letter, Aqa Mansur evokes the space of a sheet of paper to communicate the material limits of this medium for writing passion. Just as it is impossible to capture the movement of horses racing across the *maydan*, Aqa Mansur says, he is unable to convey his grief.

At the start of his manual, Aqa Mansur breaks with the mystical temporality of divine union to write the city as a site for the lonely to experience physical love and desire. He disrupts the play on Sufi conventions of longing by declaring to his readers that he intends to leave the state of separation behind. Not only do paper and words restrict him, but so too does the ideal of unrequited love. Aqa Mansur positions himself as a spiritual prisoner (*zindani*) in the "Abode of Misfortune" (*bayt al-akhzan*).[31] His language of mourning uses the poetics of mystical love poetry (*ghazal*). As a lover—the meaning of *'ashiq*, his pen name—Aqa Mansur states that he is trapped by the conventions of love, where both lover and beloved must remain in the state of separation and melancholy. He is in the Abode of Misfortune because of the absence of his beloved, but his eagerness (*mushtaq*) to meet and experience his lover (*'ashiq*) is untenable. He does not know with what tongue to articulate the intensity (*shiddat*) of his pain. How is he to represent his state, and how is he to bring into utterance (*zaban*) and materialize his emotions? The literary device of rhetorical questioning allows him to break with practice. "In what manner am I to illustrate [*sharh*] and depict the reasons for leaving the Abode of Misfortune, leaving behind this feeling of longing and separation to migrate [*muhajirat*] to Isfahan?"[32] Here, the reader expects a return to the melancholic refrain. After all, Mir Rukn al-Din had written about his agonizing strolls through the Chahar Bagh gardens, where the garden is a metaphor for union with the beloved. In mystical love poetry, the garden is a place where longing for the beloved is rendered even more painful by the knowledge that true spiritual union can only be fulfilled in the garden of paradise. But in a cathartic act, Aqa Mansur translates his longing into earthly, embodied union, turning away from the traditional garden to reflect on the fulfillment of union and pleasure in the city. Although the garden remains as a trace in his city disturbance, it signifies the idyllic past.

Once Aqa Mansur voices his complaints about the state of separation from his beloved and his anticipation for reunion in Isfahan, it is the pen of articulation that composes his city manual (*dastur al-'amal*) to guide the forlorn toward union with the male beloved. With pen, ink, and paper, he folds his vision into the form of a manual, which takes the reader into the didactic language of disciplinary discourses of state and religion. The manual, addressed to the residents of Isfahan, provides Aqa Mansur with an ironic authoritative voice.

> In no manner may they [the residents] violate. . . . They must act according to this order [*dastur*]. . . . The desire of this heart [the author] is such that a passionate [*dagh*] order be written about the healing qualities of every chapter/gate [*bab*] of Isfahan.[33]

Traveling through Isfahan becomes a universal command and a remedy for the suffering heart. As the pun on *bab* makes clear, such travel can be read and experienced as reading a book, as the sightseer walks from one city gate to another, as though flipping through chapters. "Since time is not sufficient, let them be content with this model manual [*numuzaj*]. . . . Since the nature of speech is thus [limited], it [the manual] will have to suffice."[34]

Aqa Mansur's tour of Isfahan begins at dawn on the eastern corner of the central square. As the sun rises, the dexterous master-craftsman (God) lifts the morning gate of the eastern stall, warming the entire marketplace and filling the mirrors at the mirror seller's stall with light. For Aqa Mansur, the bazaar symbolizes the shining mirror, a mystical metaphor for the reflection of the self that divine beauty—here embodied by the urban environment—makes visible. The surface of the mirror is a space of reflection much like the sheet of paper on which the author writes. An interface between viewer and subject activates desire and sight to affect insight and union. Traveling through the bazaar becomes a spiritual journey of self-fashioning, where the exchange of male desire and commerce is written as a facet of the economy of piety. Aqa Mansur calls out to the residents of Isfahan, "Wear your pilgrim's garb and begin the journey!"[35]

To experience Isfahan in all its beauty was an ethical duty that had its own set of rituals and rules. Aqa Mansur guides his reader to the best coffeehouses, tobacco stalls, bakers, halva makers, and, of course, the most stunning male beauties of the city, naming them all as he lays out a prescribed order of performing the rites of masculinity in the city. The first two stops on his city tour set the tone of the manual's transgression. To pay a first morning visit to the tobacco stall is a must.[36] To heighten the feeling of intoxication, it is in the small bazaar (*timcha*) of the tobacco vender where morning pleasure is to be sought: "At the sweet delightful stall of the tobacco vender, a puff of tobacco hits the tumult of intoxication due to separation with the beloved. If your heart desires to unite with the beautiful ones, do not miss the stall of that angel-faced beauty. Thanks to his face your sense of separation will further be pronounced!"[37]

In the bazaar the confessional lines drawn by the imperial project, which entailed constructing separate quarters for Armenians, Jews, Zoroastrians, and Tabrizis, break down. Here, disparate groups mingle in the erotic trade and commerce of the marketplace. After an early morning smoke, the traveler must pay a visit to the stall of the infidel Armenian boys (*dukkan-i kafir bachchagan-i Armani*): "Their look will conquer your heart with the art of magic, their friendship is the enemy of life [*jan*]."[38] Although Aqa Mansur's heart turns to dust on account of an Armenian idol, he shares a piece of advice: "Whenever you place your foot in the circle of love [*dayira-yi mahabbat*], you must forget shame, name, fidelity, and Islam. Once you embark on love, be like a mirror and take on the color of the other. Acquaint yourself with the 72 religious sects [*millat*]:[39] at times be a Christian, at others a devout Muslim [*parsi*], a Sufi, or a wondering dervish [*rind*]. Choose from every creed, for once you enter the *religion of love* [*dawlat-i 'ishq*] [my emphasis] you will benefit from love's fortune in the hereafter."[40] With these words of advice, Aqa Mansur declares, "Enter the Grand Bazaar, the Qaysariyya, with the intention of buying the beauty of Joseph!"[41]

Strolling through the bazaar, Aqa Mansur begins to educate his male readership in the everyday aesthetics of commerce to distinguish the value of commodities through the cultivation of the senses. He instructs the traveler in the Grand Bazaar to first take in his setting: "Let them observe their surroundings, left and right ... so as to pass through the bazaar of melancholy [*sawda'*]."[42] Even as the senses are to recognize and appreciate the delights of the bazaar, Aqa Mansur's recurring refrain paradoxically warns the reader not to fall for pretty male youths: "Do not make public the secret of the beloved, the very place where you will be wounded. Stay away from it!" Drawing on the similar tensions that sexual desire and its discipline elicit, Aqa Mansur enjoins his male audience to feel desire in the body to stimulate the pleasures of urban commerce rather than to effect abstention. For Aqa Mansur, the tension between desire and abstention is what sharpens perception, even though that desire is not acted on; it is the secret that needs to be delayed, at least for the moment. He directs the traveler to observe all the beauties of Isfahan, whose sights, textures, and tastes stimulate these pleasures. For example, the jeweler has adorned his stall with emeralds, rubies, and pearls that embody the physical attributes of his apprentice, whose "eyes, lips, complexion, forehead, and teeth are onyx, emeralds, rubies, and pearls." Consumption of goods and services on sale in the marketplace involves the education of the senses. To drink a cup of *thaqlab*, which is sweeter than the syrup of sugar candy and blackberries, introduces the palate of the male lover to the flavor of sweetness. "There is no getting close to union by the stall of the sherbet seller!" our guide to the city advises.[43] "Drink however much you are capable of. With the excuse of drinking sherbet you will sweeten the palate of your heart [and] drink from the sight [*did*] that is the wine of union with the beloved." From the spectacle of overflowing wine cups, drink was to trigger sight and activate the senses in tandem: "With every breadth mix the gaze [*nazara*] of a gulp of *thaqlab* with the sherbet of meeting [*didar*] the friend."[44]

To further arouse the palate, Aqa Mansur guides the reader from the Qaysariyya bazaar toward the caravansary of merchants hailing from the southern city of Yazd and the northern city of Kashan.[45] This road leads the traveler to the small bazaar of Mulla Abdullah, who will sweeten the sense of separation with halva. Aqa Mansur's map of Isfahan animates streets and buildings with names of venders and their choice goods on sale. He even conjures up the paper with which sweets are wrapped in. Here the ephemeral love letter ends up being reused as wrapping paper for halva! "No matter what, the reed pen of the sugar cane and the letter written on paper [*nama-yi kaghaz*] will turn into halva," he assures readers.[46] Paper was recycled for multiple purposes. Often lamenting the disposal of letters addressed to beloveds, poets whine that their letters were not worth collecting as tokens of love. Instead, they are used to wrap halva and sugar cones or to make kites for children to fly. The transitory nature of love letters perhaps offers a clue as to why Aqa Mansur writes a manual, as though hoping it will not meet the fate of the discarded letter, cast aside by an inattentive lover and recycled as wrapping paper.[47] Still, he must have kept Mir Rukn al-Din's letter, because it was copied as a model letter by several anthologists, though not widely circulated in Isfahan's household anthologies.

From the taste of sugar that is likened to speech, flavorful for the lover's palate, Aqa Mansur likewise trains his reader to cultivate an appreciation for coffee. Coffee imported from Yemen in the sixteenth century had provided occasion for friends in Isfahan to socialize at home as well as in the public space of coffeehouses.[48] In household anthologies, we commonly find model friendship letters, written in simple

Persian, that invite a friend over to savor coffee (*chisht*) and conversation (*suhbat*) in the morning.⁴⁹ And coffeehouses were quite the craze; men from different walks of life frequented them in both the early morning and the evening. Jean Baptiste Chardin, the French jeweler who resided in Isfahan during the midcentury, speaks of coffeehouses as numbering among the most beautiful buildings in Isfahan. With high ceilings and a central fountain, customers sat on platforms along the walls "à la manière orientale."⁵⁰ These were spaces for entertainment and pleasure, where residents could tune into the latest news and gossip, hear poets recite their compositions, and listen to storytellers perform epic romances, such as the *Shahnama*. Mullas and dervishes gave speeches and moral lessons while customers sipped coffee and smoked their hookahs, chatting and playing chess. For Aqa Mansur, the coffeehouse was a place to render the spirit of the friend joyous. He directs the reader toward his choice of the best coffeehouse in town: that of Khwaja Ali, located at the entry of the Qaysariyya bazaar, which he calls the "idol house [*butkhana*] of the coffeehouse maker [*qahvakhana saz*], the home of the lewd [*rindan*]."⁵¹ There, drinking coffee was accompanied by the sight of male beauties: "Spend a couple of hours watching that *picture gallery* and experience the melancholy of that flower garden. . . . What great companionship [*suhbat*] it [the coffeehouse] is in reality!"⁵² The reader imagines Khwaja Ali's coffeehouse as an art gallery where the customer can observe a spectacular staff, a "place where beauties are on display [*jilvagah*]."⁵³ Aqa Mansur's reference to a picture gallery is a poetic gesture that evokes Mani (277 CE), the founder of Manichaeism, who figures in Persianate poetry as the master painter because of his illustrated book, the *Ardahang*, composed to accompany his cosmological teachings.⁵⁴

Homoerotic desire configured Isfahan's social and moral fabric, inscribing masculinity and its desires onto the walls of the city and painting beautiful figures on sheets of paper collected in households. The "distribution of the visible" drew the viewer's empathy in the process of cultivating homo-eros in private and public spaces of the city.⁵⁵ "From the image [*'aks*] of the face of that singular [*yigana*] beloved [*yar*], the picture gallery [*nigaristan*] of China was turned into a coffeehouse."⁵⁶ Modeling the visual arts, Aqa Mansur associates each male attendant with spring flowers, from the narcissus to jasmine to daffodils. Each floral scent and color enhances the senses of the viewer. Collectively they display a vivid array of blossoms in the spectacle garden (*bagh-i tamasha*) of the coffeehouse. They give pleasure (*lazzat*) to the palate (*kam*) of desire. "In playfulness, bantering, and coquetry, one lovelier than the other, well-built and tall, each one ready to be desired. Everywhere two eyes, looking like foreigners [*farangi*] with colorful hair . . . in every corner a group of beauties gathered, inebriated, dancing and stamping their feet . . . all those angel-like bodies with narrow waistlines, these beauties are heart stealers."[57] The art of boy gazing was a ritual of male bonding in Khwaja Ali's coffeehouse. In private, bureaucrats, artisans, and craftsmen collected portraits of coy male youth as mimetic tools that nurtured their taste for male beauty (Figures 3.1 and 3.2). Hundreds of such portraits were commissioned in Isfahan during the seventeenth century.[58] Today they are housed in museums and libraries throughout the world. Some had been commissioned individually, and some were later collected in anthologies. Aqa Mansur's description of coffeehouses and the practice of male gazing links this ritual with the production and collection of the portraits of youths, who posed holding a cup of coffee, a jug of wine, or a flower. These were the works of art, the material objects, the gestures, the gazes, and the poses that men had to embody—and recognize as symbols of erotic delight—to act out their urbanity.

From the gallery of male youth on display in the coffeehouse, Aqa Mansur takes his audience through the shoemaker's bazaar and into the palace complex off the central square. The traveler is guided toward the Gate of Felicity to visit a pavilion known as the Talar-i Tavila, "the envy of the picture gallery of China and the *Ardahang* of Mani."[59] Although Aqa Mansur may have witnessed this royal audience hall firsthand in his capacity as a religious dignitary, residents did not have access to the palace precincts reserved for the royal household, courtiers, governors, and ambassadors. Aqa Mansur's city disturber invites the male public to imagine the interior walls of the pavilion through a corresponding aesthetics he draws between the beautiful serving staff at the coffeehouse and the representation of male figures on the palace walls. In the same vein, he continues to instruct the eye of the observer: "Gaze at the encounter between lovers, color upon color, the imagination is enlivened. Colorful enchanting faces drawn by magic, cold stares knot the viewer's heart in madness through their exchange of coy glances."[60] Directing the reader's gaze, Aqa Mansur appeals to the graphic sensibility of Isfahan's residents and invites the spectator to interact with the figures on the wall. The magic of the image lies in its power of animation, which stimulates an exchange between the audience and the painted object. He trains his audience to imagine and see how drawings and wall paintings are the extension of the hand of the artist, whose passion embodies every physical detail, infusing sexual desire into the figure he draws, much like Mir Rukn al-Din

FIGURE 3.1 An exemplary sample of a seventeenth-century portrait of a male beloved. A boy with a narcissus attached to his belt is serving coffee. This painting, *Kneeling Youth with a Tray of Coffee*, is signed by Riza Abbasi and dated 1618. Gulistan Palace World Heritage Complex, the Royal Library, Tehran, Album no. 1663, *Muraqqaʿ-i Gulshan*.

asks to be seen in the composition of his letter. To help his audience master the art of gazing, Aqa Mansur directs them toward the lane of the engravers (*hakkakan*). Aqa Mansur instructs his readers to look at the signature of the engraver, which denotes more than just the artist's name. Deploying a mnemonic device, the signature is to act as an aid, recalling the emotions that went into the craftsmen's making of his beloved object.[61] The two are so entangled that, in Aqa Mansur's phrasing, the engraver and the beloved become indistinguishable.

> The engraver [*hakkak*] whose wheel is bound to his love
> O God, may no harm reach the tip of his eyelash
> The engraver's diamond recognizes the beloved's pain
> And carves his coquetry onto the tip of his eyelash[62]

Aqa Mansur teaches his reader how to appreciate a wall painting by experiencing it, by visualizing and feeling the touch of the craftsman who engaged his entire body to shape the figure of the beloved. To draw love, the artist had to have felt pain; Aqa Mansur makes this association legible to his audience. Tools, such as the diamond pen of the engraver, are metaphors used to sharpen the point that translated heartaches into the material image itself. The reader of this manual was to remember the symbol, to fill his mind with the affective emotions that embody material objects. The image on the wall incites an emotional reaction through the medium of color and stones, where gestures and gazes are ciphers for male desire. By way of curating these images of Isfahan, Aqa Mansur instructs his reader in the *adab* of masculinity, into *his* "religion of love." Male friendships are fostered around habits of viewing and collecting images, to be read, discussed, and performed in the bazaars and coffeehouses of Isfahan. Aqa Mansur's interpretation of the wall painting and the craft of the engraver further a body of knowledge on love and erotic desire, creating the memory of Isfahan shared by a male readership. A literary aesthetic of a new kind of affective experience of friendship particularizes Aqa Mansur's poetics of friendship, where the Aristotelian concept of *takhyil*, or image evocation, is mobilized to fashion urbanity.[63]

← FIGURE 3.2 Another fine example of a seventeenth-century portrait of a male beloved. This painting is signed by Muʿin Musavvir and displays the Europeanized object of desire, depicted with a Western hat, to mark him as other. Muʿin Musavvir, *A European Youth with Hat and Dog*, 1687. Ink, opaque watercolor, and gold on paper (6⅞ in. × 3⅝ in.). Portland Art Museum, Portland, Oregon. Gift of Dr. and Mrs. Edwin Binney III, 70.27.13.

The art of masculine *adab* involved the ritual of boy gazing; it required an aesthetic performance to skillfully engage with friends in public displays of love and sexual desire. To develop a taste for male youth, men had to be aware of the protocols of gazing, which were circumscribed by the taboos associated with the practice. Repentance was part of the public act of piety and the mosque was the space for such reckonings.[64] Aqa Mansur voices his guilt for the first time as his reader is called to prayer: "With the bloodied sight of the beloved and a heart concerned with Judgment [*dil afkar bi qaza nigaran*]," he begins to weep at Ali's gate (*dar*) of the Friday Prayer Mosque. He takes the traveler toward the mosque only to experience one last temptation before he finally repents. At the entry of the mosque, he suggests lingering at the perfume seller's stall that belongs to Hajji Tahir 'Attar *dildar*, the possessor of hearts. As his name suggests, men in Isfahan were drawn to this perfumer; many even suffered broken hearts from seeking his skills. Aqa Mansur wonders if Hajji Tahir's "coquetry, his amorous gestures [*'ishva, ghamza va kirishma*], and his lip-staining grape sherbet and cider will help remedy the sickness of longing, separation, and anticipation?"[65] According to the city disturber, Hajji Tahir had a reputation for his ability to heal nearly every pain, thanks to his knowledge of Ibn Sina's *Canon of Healing* (*Qanun-i Shifa*).[66] But the "lip of desire fell on an appropriate time, the noon prayer!" The call to prayer marked the daily rhythm of piety and commerce, and on Friday at noon it sounded the hour for repentance.

At this auspicious hour, the muezzin with his sweet and raised voice called (*azan*) beloved friends to the mosque. His voice was awe-inspiring, projecting throughout the square and resonating in the dome of the Friday Prayer Mosque, where the Shi'a call to prayer echoed the name of Imam Ali. Isfahan's soundscape amplified the Muslim message that Allah is great, calling to witness Muhammad as his prophet and Ali as his successor, the Friend of God (*Vali Allah*), and inviting resident lovers of Ali to open their hearts and fulfill their desires in the mosque. In pursuit of his divine mediation, worshippers entered the mosque embraced by his divine protection, for as lovers of Ali they shared his secret.

> O lover, as you arrive at the door of the secret Ka'ba
> Ask from it anything you may need
>
> From there, by the door [*dar*] of the Ka'ba, the door of purity,
> You will be taken to pray in paradise[67]

The Friday Prayer Mosque signified the secret Ka'ba for Shi'a believers in Isfahan, creating community around the shared knowledge engraved on the interior walls of the mosque. Just like the Ka'ba in Mecca, the Friday Prayer Mosque in Isfahan represented the abode of God; as the epigraphy recalls, entering Ali's gate was to enter the knowledge of God. Aqa Mansur disturbs this imperial secret. He speaks of all kinds of people, rich and poor, who are present in the mosque. They have memorized the word of God and are together engaged in worship.[68] On the throne of the pulpit (*minbar*) sits Mulla Muhsin, who resembles Moses on Mt. Sinai. The association drawn between the Friday prayer leader, Mulla Muhsin Fayz Kashani (in 1656), and Moses also suggests that the mulla played a role similar to Moses in the Quran—that is, as the guide for believers to the true religion and arbiter on the Day of Judgment.[69] The court-appointed Friday prayer leader, Mulla Muhsin, is thus cast as the Moses of Isfahan. But Aqa Mansur disapproves of Mulla Muhsin's scrutiny, perched, with a judging gaze, on top of the pulpit, where he polices piety below.

Aqa Mansur directs the reader instead to don a pilgrim's garb and seek refuge in the sacred sanctuaries of the medieval city, where residents are free from state surveillance. The rhythmic play between temptation and abstention and the movement between the new and old quarters of the city continue to mark his pedagogy of love and desire. The traveler is advised to enter the medieval city by way of the bazaar, perhaps feeling the temptation to commit an unlawful act with the flowered beauties on display along the path. Yet this is not the time for indulgences; as the manual has been at pains to make clear, the protocols of gazing require time, even if only for a moment to glance longingly at male beauties or to savor the smoke of their hookahs and drink coffee in their attendance. Now the objective is different: The gazer/disturber has to resist this labyrinth of distractions as he makes his way through the alleys of the bazaar into the medieval city to pray at the mosque of Harun-i Vilayat, the Sultan of the Dominion of Guidance.[70] "Visit this shrine which is the Ka'ba of hope [*Ka'ba-yi amal*] and the prayer niche [*qibla*] of good fortune [*iqbal-i mustamidan*]," Aqa Mansur commands.[71] It is here in this sanctuary of Aaron, the brother of Moses, associated with Ali in Shi'a discourse, that the pilgrim must repent (*tawba*) for these acts of gazing and desiring and then seek guidance, worship, and prayer.

Aqa Mansur considers the sanctity of mosques with deeper roots in the medieval city of Isfahan as more authoritative than the Friday Prayer Mosque commissioned by Shah Abbas I in the new city. The old Friday Prayer Mosque, the "Ka'ba of protecting angles,"[72] encapsulates the history of Muslim settlement in the city. With its origins in the migration of Arab tribes (Taym) in the eighth century, the mosque experienced several transformations in the eleventh and thirteenth centuries, when each new ruler (the Seljuks and Ilkhanids) marked the shrine with their architectural imprint. Aqa Mansur describes the built environment of this medieval mosque as the rival of another city, but that city is not Mecca. Instead its beauty is the zeal (*ghayrat*) and honor of the holy city of Jerusalem (*bayt al-muqaddas*). Playing on the primacy of Jerusalem in Abrahamic sacred geographies and the novelty of Mecca, this medieval Friday prayer mosque is an amulet filled with religious benefit. From its physical attributes to its ancient waterworks, blessed (*sayyid*) descendants of Ali and Fatima labor and worship there; the entire mosque complex is characterized as the manifestation of divine favor. It is this history and the network of holy descendants of Ali that have consecrated it with a sacred aura. In Aqa Mansur's religion of love the reader must pray and repent in the two sanctuaries (Ka'ba) of the medieval city.

Beyond these alternative Ka'bas that ground the sacred topography of Isfahan, Aqa Mansur leads the believer toward yet another space of worship, the Sufi cloister of Malik (*khaniqa-yi Malik*). Here, in master Malik's circle of Sufis, the believer is to practice the language and rituals of Aqa Mansur's religion of love. The pursuit of mystic love is experiential; neither acts of licit or illicit behavior scrutinized in the royal mosque, under the judging gaze of the Friday prayer leader, nor declarations of repentance are in order. By the mid-seventeenth century, when Aqa Mansur was writing his city disturber, the public defamation of Sufi piety and practice was openly debated on the streets of Isfahan. Aqa Mansur maintains that only mystics are capable of attaining the ultimate stage of divine love, filled with an emotional cognition of God embodied in the figure of the master. Devoting his life to God, master Malik had made God his Friend (*dust*): "The religion of the Sufi is the religion of the heart that is sacrificed on the path of the Friend."[73] To enter master Malik's cloister was to enter the "circle of pure Sufis with singular beliefs."[74] He is the peerless dervish, complete in intellect (*'aql-i kamil*). There in the space of master Malik's circle, "sons of pure masters [*bani arbab-i safa*]" have assembled in ritual worship. Sufis, according to Aqa Mansur, are the "bachelors' of desire [*hava*]," celibates who spend their days and nights "weeping at the door of the beloved. Their state was the translation of hidden love."[75] The language of love that Aqa Mansur deploys in his *shahrashub* is recognizable in the mystic circle (*halqa*) of the master Malik. A true Sufi opens his heart to the pain of longing. Experiencing love has little to do with the rational intellect or the paradigmatic rules of the sharia, for the lover has to move beyond himself; madness and bewilderment are the condition to be practiced in the presence of master Malik or the presence of the absent beloved.[76] Love and longing, as Aqa Mansur experiences them, are felt through ritual lamentation and weeping, a state of being that communicates a deeper, more genuine inner love (*batin*).

Aqa Mansur draws the contours of his concept of love from mystic love and friendship. What particularizes his practice of love, however, is its performance beyond the frame of religious institutions, whether a mosque or a Sufi cloister. Although the believer has to experience mystic love, Aqa Mansur's masculine ideal boy gazer is far from being celibate, even though he has to discipline his body to enact desire publicly. Aqa Mansur translates the aesthetics of mystic love into the material temporality of the urban fabric of Isfahan as allegory, for this paradise allows Aqa Mansur to disrupt eschatology. Spiritual and carnal desire are joined in the temporality of the urban environment where heaven and earth merge. In this way, Aqa Mansur maps the pilgrim's route through familiar spaces of worship in the old and new quarters of the city only to attain ecstasy in full public view. The pilgrimage to Isfahan reaches its temporal climax as the reader enters the Naqsh-i Jahan square, the final enactment of love in the *maydan*, which resembles the plain of resurrection. Tellingly, this ecstatic moment also doubles as a lesson in sight.

> Once you arrive at the Naqsh-i Jahan Square, take a moment to absorb the entirety of the space so that it will come into view. Watch [*tamasha*] the tumult [*shur u ghawgha*] on the page of the square [*safha-yi maydan*]. Surrounding you, the multitude of people congregate like the heavenly sphere filled with stars and planets, which has the qualities of the end of time. With the sound of drums and the blowing of the trumpet, the joyous clamor of people in the *maydan* resembles the field of resurrection. In every corner a performance [*ma'rika*], and in every place assemblies of men come into view.[77]

Aqa Mansur refers to the square using the first-person possessive pronoun: *my maydan* (see Map 1.1). The gazer/disturber is to find a niche amid the crowds of people that populate the *maydan*, as he directs his gaze toward the best wrestling troupe in town, the troupe of Baba Qasim, the long-bearded beloved. "Find an appropriate corner, a place where you can see all the beauties walking in with elegant and well-proportioned bodies and pomp like lions, they will gratify the space of sight for those with longing thoughts [*mardum-i khiyal tang*]."[78]

> Once that coquettish sweetheart enters into the Square,
> with his flaming face and long braids
>
> Consciousness [*hush*] and ability disappears among the crowd,
> whosoever gazes [*nigah*] upon his face.
>
> Consciousness and patience distance itself from his heart,
> he bedazzles the heart with his coyness and his colorful style.
>
> His mannerism is like a peacock,
> his black hair like two wings.
>
> His name is Aqa Husayn Ali,
> his skirt is sealed shut.[79]

Aqa Mansur transports the ritual practice of communal weeping from the Sufi cloister onto the theatrical stage of Isfahan. Patience and restraint can no longer be sustained in this final phase of the ritual of boy gazing. "Whoever stands upright at the performance [*ma'rika*]," he wryly observes, "is a lost cause." Aqa Mansur disturbs the city as he calls lovers to lose themselves in ecstatic union. Here, amid the crowds of the Naqsh-i Jahan square, the *adab* of masculinity requires the male audience watching the wrestling match to look on Aqa Husayn Ali and faint from his beautiful face. The beloved wrestler taunts and teases: "His eyelashes have the force of the arm of love; he holds the power to pierce open the gazer's heart." The Naqsh-i Jahan is a place of encounter, a successful architectural production of a public space where people congregate to lose and find themselves. But it is not the shah who commands authority as the beloved, but Aqa Husayn Ali and his lovely face, his long legs, and his artful coquetry. It is Aqa Husayn Ali who will throw the pilgrim to the ground. If Aqa Mansur's reader has embodied the mannerism of love and eros, he too will break with imperial conventions and lose all sense of self in the presence of Aqa Husayn Ali. Then he too will become a city disturber.

Aqa Mansur takes his readers to the last stop on his tour of Isfahan at the New Street, where men are at work selling the raw material for the making of paper. It is no coincidence that Aqa Mansur ends his manual at the rag sellers' street; it is on account of their labor, and the gathering of rags from the city, that city disturbers have the paper to write their dissent. There on the rag sellers' street Aqa Mansur ends his education of the senses with a rebuke to readers, critiquing those who falsely accuse these men of sodomy (*livat*). "If you want a lover who will be a companion," he admonishes, "a lover with whom you will be able to gain complete enlightenment through conversation/intercourse [*suhbat*], go to the New Street [*kucha-yi naw*], where the peacock-like rag sellers reside; drunk with desire they await intercourse [*sukhan*]."[80] Playing on the meaning of the word *intercourse*, Aqa Mansur evokes both the *adab* of speech (*sukhan*) and the *adab* of desire (*sukhan*). The flamboyant mannerism (*atvar-i na-mulayim*) of sellers of rags, according to Aqa Mansur, had given them a bad reputation in Isfahan: "Being accused of sodomy, they have been thrown into the abyss of infamy and disgrace."[81] Once again, he draws on irony to subvert the social order, for, in reality, he claims that many among these rag sellers are pious: "There is an old beloved [*yar*] in the New Street, where the heart-breaking moon-faced white beauties reside."[82] The playful banter between the old and the new, between Jerusalem and Mecca, takes on ironic twists with the encounter of an old lover on the New Street. The so-called sodomite is a double entendre; for those who have fallen prey to the project of Sufi defamation, the rag seller is an abject figure, but in Aqa Mansur's project of urban love, he is the object of desire to be pursued by the city disturber. Aqa Mansur praises the beauty of the rag seller; his speech is pleasant, and he is the very image of a budding daffodil, an image that takes the reader back to the portrait gallery of the coffeehouse and the wall painting of the royal audience hall. As Aqa Mansur moves the reader to imagine the body of the beloved, he begins to disrobe this figure on the page, first pulling his belt loose, removing garments all the way to his belly button, before interrupting this activity. "I restrain myself from the tip of my pen upon the tulip-like page because according to the law [sharia] of *adab*, it is forbidden to write about these hidden secrets [*raz-i nihan*] and to unveil them [*parda gusha*] in public."[83] Aqa Mansur negotiates the dynamic between secrecy and disclosure in a sly way: By pointing his pen to the rag seller's belly button, he implicitly invites readers to visualize the rest, that which he cannot commit to the page.

The experience of Isfahan produced by Aqa Mansur, written on paper and collected in household anthologies, disturbs imperial imaginations of community and social order. These forms of knowledge both impinge on and are configured in relationship to the moment between making public and making secret. In writing the city of Isfahan, Aqa Mansur translates the form of the *shahrashub* to capture the city, reimagining the collective experience through his subjective images of

Isfahan's beauties, which he assembles to be read as a guidebook. Much like the anthologist, the processes of subject formation are connected to the dialectic between the exteriority of imperial institutions and discourses and the interiority of household collections. The observer-participant dynamic, evidenced by the culture of male gazing, focuses on the flamboyant and theatrical figure of the male youth to create a visual sense of self-consciously masculine acts. The double figure of the male youth as both desire and disorder, feared by court and mosque, is studied by male residents, who perform their masculinity to forge their network of friends and enemies. Such acts exemplify the city disturber's active participation in and fascination with street life, even while displaying a critical attitude toward the discipline being imposed on life in the city.

Aqa Mansur turns to a narration of the city—and movement through it—as the antidote to his suffering, breaking with the ideal state of Sufi love. His conduct manual animates the city as the writerly response to this longing malaise. Like I'jaz Herati, he therefore sees Isfahan as a copy of beauty and draws its image in the figure of a beautiful male youth. The city and travel through it become *defined* by the experience of homoerotic love; to cope with abstention and separation from the beloved, a plethora of beautiful urban objects are necessary to see, smell, and taste. Making the city the space of masculine desire, Aqa Mansur aestheticizes the built and lived environment in a manner both similar to and divergent from the conventional mystical garden scene, as the location of the vicissitudes of love. Assuming the agency of sight, he claims the power to see, to read, and desire through a higher visual perspective that in Sufi poetics is reserved for God, the Sufi master, and, in the context of the imperial project, for the Safavi shah. Aqa Mansur ultimately challenges sovereignty by using mixed prose and poetry to produce an alternative visual authority; he thus opens the competition for sovereignty to all male residents of Isfahan. Out of his guidebook, an entire economy of coy gestures and sexual innuendos circulate to test, taunt, take pleasure, and fashion masculine urbanity in the city, thereby disturbing the imperial politics of seeing and desiring inscribed on the walls of the Forty Pillars Palace, where love is directed toward the beloved Shah Abbas I (see Figure 1.3). Aqa Mansur's city disturber offers a way to read the city beyond idealization and metaphor, as the mystic language of erotic love and friendship is mobilized to forge and sustain actual bonds between beloved friends.[84]

CHAPTER 4

Cultivating and Disciplining Friendship Letters

Every letter from the true friend [*yar-i jani*]
is for the living, a blissful-letter [*tarabnama*]
Every letter in the friend's [*yar*] voice
is a divine talisman, a body amulet[1]

                        Nasira Hamadani (d. 1620)

Loving Letters to the Friend

Men and women in seventeenth-century Isfahan translated mystic tropes and conventions into profane and mundane contexts, described their male and female beloveds, revealed their personal identities, and situated themselves in Isfahan's public spaces and private gatherings. Letters were the state-of-the art medium in Isfahan. Correspondence between men reveals a masculine culture of friendship and competition where mystical love, written in the poetic form of the *ghazal*, permeates the folios of anthologies as the most common expression of intimacy.[2] In the sixteenth century the *ghazal*, once the medium for voicing divine love, was grounded in human objects of desire to describe real encounters between human lovers. No longer confined to literary circles at court, salons, or pleasure gardens of the elite, *ghazal*s evolved as part of the quotidian language of communication; they emerged as the dominant paradigm for sociability adapted into the friendship letter. Like amulets, the iconic letter guarded and protected the body of the friend from enemies or social harm. In a letter addressed to his friends in Shiraz, the religious scholar and literati Nasira Hamadani wrote that if the speaking letter (*natiq*) was from a "true" (*jani*) friend, it was a gift of life (see Map 0.1). Letter writing was a joy (*tarabnama*) and an art, where erudition and eloquence were to be flaunted and deployed to incite even more deft responses.[3] Letters themselves were a loving endeavor. To perform the aesthetics of *adab*, one needed to develop skills for engaging in letter writing, the medium of choice for alliances as well as conquests and defeats on the battlefields of love. Artisans, craftsmen, bureaucrats, and religious scholars composed letters of love, proclaiming their passion, boasting their seductions, and revealing anxieties over the betrayal of their beloveds.

The sharing, circulation, copying, and collecting of friendship letters educated the anthologist on the *adab* of friendship and on the language and media for communicating with friends, processes that fashioned urban subjects and household anthologies alike.[4] To enter the politics of friendship, friends were taught how to perform its poetics. Love letters between men collected in household anthologies archive the sensibilities and debates over codes of friendship; shaped by male subjects and amical collectives, these amorous letters animate Isfahan's social circles. In household anthologies, the letter, or *nama*, can be seen undergoing a transformation into the modern letter form, that is, as a discrete prose genre that began with an addressee, included a verse or two that set the tone of the letter's intent, and concluded with the sender's signature.[5] The proliferation of manuals and form letters collected in household anthologies are a testimony to the popularity of letters as the medium of everyday communication. Friendship letters surface as a distinct type of correspondence, written, copied, collected, and transmitted over several generations in Isfahan. Seventeenth-century scribes, authors, and owners of anthologies classified this epistolary genre as *rasa'il-i ikhvaniyyat*, or "fraternal" letters. As model letters of friendship, they performed a set of conventions and protocols resembling the practices that governed sworn friendships between male members of craft circles and mystical communities who were "married" in spirit and had become "brothers" to one another. Earlier expressions of male friendship in the sixteenth century, once verbalized through the *ghazal*, were outsourced to the prose form of fraternal letters by the seventeenth century. They retained features of the *ghazal*, particularly by drawing on the figure of the absent friend, which was already central to mystical tropes of longing for and separation from the beloved. These letters also deployed the emotions of yearning, as well as the *ghazal*'s language of amorous love, widely used and circulated among friends, to render palpable a new mode of virtual conversation. As the letter became an alternative vehicle for the *ghazal*'s lament, it acted as an affirmation during a physical separation.

The adabizing culture of friendship produced new modes of communication among men and women in Isfahan. To be urbane, residents had to learn the techniques and competing modes of a flourishing *adab* of letter writing. A well-established practice since medieval times, letter writing was used by bureaucrats, who composed letters for the chancellery (*rasa'il-i sultani* or *divani*), and by poets and scholars, who participated in the habit of literary exchange through letters (*rasa'il-i ikhvaniyyat*).[6] In Isfahan, letter writing became an urban fashion. Face-to-face performances of *ghazal* love were enhanced by the epistolary practice of friendship letters. The proliferation of the *adab* of letter writing situates reading and writing as social practices in the urban context of seventeenth-century Isfahan. Friendship letters were a new site of writing; their communication was a largely oral affair, direct or through intermediaries, but always in the presence of people, who witnessed facial and bodily expressions, glances, mannerisms, and actions. To render the practice of letter writing more perceptible, epistolary culture relied on the image to succeed. And although model friendship letters used the conventional language of mystical union, they did not make explicit the erotic emotions that had characterized the *ghazal*s of the realist school, nor did they require such skill and deftness in composition from their authors. Indeed, friendship letters achieved a level of standardization whose purpose was to create a new habit of communication, disciplining eros among a broad spectrum of the population.

Letters were the cultivated medium of exchange through which the social institution of friendship was performed; they were messengers who stirred ties of affection among men and women.[7] Nasira Hamadani tells us in the epigraph of this chapter that letters are blissful when voiced by a true friend; when well written by a master like himself, they are among the most prized collectibles assembled in Isfahan's household anthologies. Letters written by such luminaries as Nasira Hamadani,[8] Sa'ib Tabrizi, Mir Ilahi, and Mirza Ali Akbar were collected together with model letters in anthologies; reading them together allows us to see how each letter possessed its individual and personal styles, where the author drew on the *adab* of epistolarity to write his experience of friendship. For collectors they served as models for the writing of affective selves. As Nasira informs his friends from Shiraz, he takes his "pen in hand and cracks open the ink to get close to his own heart."[9] Focusing specifically on love letters exchanged between men, I read these epistles as speech acts that communicate the voices of friends through a range of emotions that blur the lines between desiring and loving. Mindful of the epistemological challenges faced by historians of friendship, I read the verbal sentiments expressed in friendship letters as sincere (*jani*), spiritual (*ruhani*), or physical (*jismani*) in order to historicize friendship in an age when sodomy (*livat*) came to be associated with the heresy of Sufism and friends were cognizant of contemporary modes of reading and debating homoerotic love. To write love effectively was to practice the *adab* of urbanity. And love was the mystic's idealized state translated into urban friendships, where the friend declared his love not only for God but also for his beloved. True to the form of the *adab* of friendship, connoisseurs enacted love and affection in verse and prose. Drawing on the mystical language of *ghazal* love poetry, the friendship letter became a powerful medium; it could protect one just as it could render one vulnerable. Such letters conveyed homoerotic messages that fused love with desire and friendship, thus exposing the friend to a variety of readings of his relationship. The modalities of *ghazal* love poetry deployed in friendship letters recount the erotic bonds between friends that pervaded Isfahan's social fabric. Circulating widely in household anthologies, personal letters exchanged between men render the not-so-transparent homoerotic code legible on paper, implicating both writers and their friends in a web of shifting alliances. At times, letter writers preferred to write anonymously or to sign with only their pen names; the semantics of their letters conveyed changes in the affective experience of friendship.

Anthologies weave the practice of writing to re-collect the textures of friendship. They stage the discursive habits that produced and mediated affectionate relationships between men, as the letters map out an emotional topography of the city. As products of the *adab* of collecting, these vows of brotherhood and model friendship letters were gathered together with *ghazal* poetry and essays on love (*'ishq*) and friendship to assemble household anthologies. The anthologists collected personal letters to and from friends; some were copied along with facsimiles of letters exchanged between famous poets, painters, or scholars, such as Nasira, to memorialize friendships. Vows solemnized sworn friendships, and form letters educated the collector in the language of engagement and the rituals of sustaining relations with friends. These objects of amity reproduced in households connected the residents of Isfahan to a shared *adab* of friendship, sentiments, ethics, and behaviors that fashioned, disrupted, and reconfigured bonds across multiple networks of alliances. Residents from all walks of life wrote to each other, just as they socialized in coffeehouses, in the central square, and in Isfahan's homes and bazaars. Letters bring the city to life and also link households and their residents to friends across the Safavi dominions and beyond, into Mughal India and the Ottoman world.

Many residents had migrated to the city from other urban and rural centers in the Persianate world. For these newcomers, letters kept them connected with friends and family abroad. Some, like the poet laureate of Isfahan, Sa'ib Tabrizi (d. 1676), corresponded with friends in Mughal India, because he had spent the early years of his career in Kabul (1625–1632). There he had befriended his patron, the governor of Kabul, Mirza Ahsanullah Zahir Khan (see Map 0.1). Once Sa'ib returned to Isfahan, the two corresponded and maintained their close friendship through letters. In response to a letter Sa'ib had received from Zahir Khan complaining that he had not heard from him, Sa'ib replies with an opening *ghazal*: "Were I to forget the very thought of you, O intimate [*anis*] heart of the grief-stricken, who would I remember? The bird of life [*jan*] is imprisoned in my body's cage; only when it flies to you will it be freed." The opening *ghazal* sets the tone of the letter, in which Sa'ib apologizes for his silence and assures his friend that he had neither forgotten him nor been delayed in responding by the pleasures of life and the demands of work: "I have drunk wine with you, and without you when do I drink? I will drink the blood of my liver, if I drink without you." Sa'ib explains that it was only the abundance of letters he had received that postponed his writing; his days were spent reading letters, leaving him no time to write back![10] Not every resident of Isfahan received as many letters as did the famous poet Sa'ib, but his response can be read as a caricature of the times, capturing the writing craze that the *adab* of friendship had triggered.

The proverbial emotion communicated in friendship letters is, of course, the longing to encounter one's friend. Yet these affective exchanges are also bundled with myriad other material wishes and desires. Letters are cognizant of the necessity for everyday accoutrements, such as yogurt, wine, prayer beads, eyeglasses, ink, and paper, providing us with an appreciation for the commodities in circulation and in demand. For instance, the literati Tughra Tabrizi writes to his merchant friend, Amina, that he is in search of good quality paper to record his most recent literary composition, *The Sermon on Speech* (*Khutba al-Bayan*).[11] Tughra had traveled between northern India and Isfahan, where he probably had first met Amina.[12] According to Tughra, the best paper was produced in Multan and was therefore hard to come by in Isfahan. Even fine paper from China, Samarqand, and Kashmir was a rare commodity. He asks his merchant friend, whom he refers to as a "trusted spirit" and the "throne of commerce" (*ruh al-amin va 'arsh-i tijarat*), to help him acquire refined paper while in Hindustan. Amina must have traded in Indian goods, paper being among the commodities he purchased and later sold in Isfahan. But Tughra also asks his friend to inquire about the location of a paper shop owner in Isfahan by the name of Mir Ali. "Every time I knock on the door of his shop, it is always closed," he explains, hoping that Amina might learn why Mir Ali is never around. We do not know whether Amina sold Mir Ali paper from India; whatever their connections may have been, it is clear that the circulation of paper mediated relationships in many ways, allowing friends to communicate about the things and practices that shaped Isfahan's habitus.

Letters to friends locate hospitality as a virtuous practice; to invite and receive friends at home was to cultivate friendships.[13] Invitations to a morning cup of coffee, to eat specialty foods such as sheep trotters (*kala pacha*), soup (*ash*), and vegetable frittata (*kuku*) for lunch at the friend's house, or to attend the wedding of a friend's daughter or son were all part of the economy of entertaining companions.[14] Similarly, letters of invitation deployed *ghazal* tropes of longing for the friend—such as remembering their faces, or anticipating their arrival—as they called them to partake in collective activities prepared by a host around food and coffee. It is the "desiring heart of the friend" who begs for conversation and companionship (*suhbat*), treasuring pleasurable moments spent in the company of the affectionate friend; the heart signals the position of the sender and his hopes for the future of friendship.[15] In fact, friends often visited each other at their residences in Isfahan, aided in part by the exchange of these letters. From the poet Mir Ilahi's letter to his friend Mir Munir, we get a sense of visitation practices and the speed with which letters circulated in Isfahan. In his letter of invitation, Mir Ilahi regrets having missed Mir Munir's impromptu visit. When he returns, he finds a note that Mir Munir had left and responds immediately to invite his friend back that very same day. Mir Ilahi relates that, when he read the note, he did not recognize the identity of his visitor, for Mir Munir had not signed his name: "Because your pen name [*takhallus*] was not inscribed in your note, at first I did not recognize you. But once I glanced [*nazar*] at your verse, it became clear to me [that it was you], and this verse came to my mind: For an ill-fated one whose bright heart brings good omens [*shugun*], without the candle, the morning of fortune is but a moonless night." Only when he read the verse inscribed in the visitor's note did he recognize his friend's identity. And what a coincidence it was, writes Mir Ilahi, for he had been reading Mir Munir's poetry that very day. The host evokes the practice of *shugun*, the blessing of the sight of a pure soul, and immediately sends out his letter of invitation to Mir Munir, relaying his excitement

("Words cannot express my anticipation of your companionship [*ishtiyaq-i suhbat*]") and inscribing his signature as Mir Ilahi, your "loyal, devoted [*mukhlis*] friend [*yar*]."¹⁶ The anonymity of the guest and the recognition of his voice were part of the test of friendship; it very well may have been a calculated trial for the impromptu visitor to assess the *adab* of his host, including his familiarity with Mir Munir's poetry and his desire to host the friend in the privacy of his home.

Friendship letters throw light on the mechanisms of social disruption and the trials of sociability in Isfahan's urban spaces. The charms and agonies of being in love were at the core of the politics and poetics that friends valued and recounted in their letters. Nasira Hamadani, the author of the *ghazal* at the start of this chapter, plainly lays out the *adab* of love and of being in love in the letter he wrote to his friends in Shiraz. There he addresses his spiritual friends (*dustan-i ma'navi*), residents of the pure dust of Shiraz (*khak-i pak-i Shiraz*). He speaks of letters filled with love poems (*shi'r-ha-yi 'ashiqana*), a practice of letter writing that literally fashioned individuals (*mardum sakhta*). In his opening *ghazal* Nasira boasts about how he had performed the path of *adab*, sustaining the rituals and the habits of urbanity. "I am in love [*'ashiqam*]. In every street, I have stared at the lips [of male youth] on the rooftops . . . in every cloister I have a master, in every wine-bar a devotee. There is not one seminary where I have not taught students about the book of speech [*sukhan*]. My heart is cut in hundreds of pieces, with a hundred drawings [of male youth] on each piece. For every cut on my breast, on every patch, I have a spectator [*nazara*]. What shall I do? And what shall I write, and to whom?"¹⁷ Nasira lays out a genealogy of literati, whom he models as he takes his "pen in hand and cracks open the ink to get close to his own heart."¹⁸ He writes his speaking letter (*natiq*), greeting his spiritual friends so that his desire may become apparent.

> O friends of sweet conversation,
> who in pleasure have won my heart
>
> You have not remembered me even with a single letter,
> so that I may take pleasure in that fortunate writing [*bayaz*].¹⁹

Nasira frames his letter, addressed to his spiritual friends, as a precious gift. His address is didactic: "Value this famous letter and copy it in the collection of your sight. My eyes anticipate the very desired letter to be turned into a response to mine.

Let the letter of union [*visal*] arrive—soon is too late, may it be sooner." Indeed, many copies of Nasira's letter to his friends in Shiraz were duplicated in multiple anthologies, for a beautiful letter to a friend was to be copied, especially when written by a master of speech (*sukhan*). Valued by collectors as an object of *adab*, Nasira's chiding letter thus not only lays out his love-struck state in skillfully chosen words but also alludes to the conquests he has made *through* this same mastery of speech. His letter is therefore generative: It invites his friends to engage him in dialogue, by composing more letters, *and* to copy his letter as a model love letter to friends.[20] In this way, it encapsulates the *adab* of letter writing.

The addresser occupies different positions and articulates unique tonalities of love, depending on his relationship with the addressee. In a letter that Nasira writes to his friend Husayn Kashi, he takes a different tone, disclosing how the *ghazal* was reiterated to voice the emotional and social turmoil love could produce. Nasira had moved with his father from his hometown of Hamadan to Isfahan, where he studied with such religious luminaries as Mir Damad (d. 1632). In Isfahan Nasira also earned a reputation as a witty conversationalist, known for his skills in mathematics, poetry, and prose; consequently, he became a prized guest for such hosts as Shaykh Baha'i (d. 1621), who invited Nasira to his gatherings, guaranteeing an entertaining assembly (*majlis-i namaki*).[21] Nasira's charisma is also on display in his letter to the mystic Husayn Kashi, a classic among collectors (Figure 4.1). He vividly depicts a range of affective experiences, from the pleasure of a chance encounter in Isfahan's coffeehouses to the waves of enchantment, giddiness, and even disillusionment that accompany new love. Isfahan's cityscape becomes the index of his emotional life, staging his experience with Husayn Kashi, his beloved, on its streets. Nasira begins this letter of pain (*dardnama*) with the convention of an introductory *ghazal*: "Even if the pen of the page of desire writes a thousand times, it inscribes a thousand pardons for [its] shortcomings in the margins." Nasira exposes his "hidden pain," which he makes public by writing a letter to his beloved friend, whom he refers to as Khalil, the Quranic Abraham, the true friend of God (*Khalil Allah*).[22] And, of course, the setting of the letter is the beautiful city of Isfahan, where his beloved resides.

> Truly, I swear to God that if the coffeehouse does not lighten your eyes in the morning, your sight shall be darkened and the adorner of the bride will shave off the braids of the male youth [*mughbachcha*]. Neither the seminary will be

FIGURE 4.1 Nasira Hamadani's (d. 1620) letter to Husayn Kashi copied in Majlis Library, MS 3455, fol. 125v.

illuminated nor will its students gain insight into the kettle of knowledge of the coffeehouse. And the mosque, thanks to its purity of essence and gaze, will wash its sight so clean that even the muezzin will sing the praise of the coffeehouse with his songs. Look at my state, this humble Nasir [his pen name means "the helper" or "the friend"], moved by the anticipation of welcoming Husayn Kashi! From the mosque to the wine bar, the seminary to the coffeehouse, I searched for you. [There is] no trace of you, O possessor of intimate assemblies [*sahib-i khalvat*]. Yes, [in] those days when we were *single-hearted* [my emphasis], when we consoled each other like children [*tifl-i tasalli*], what a rare gem was the complicity of our conversations. But today, how is it that you [Husayn-i Kashi] are two-hearted [*du dila*]? I am lost in love [*'ishq*]; I do not know who I am. Upon whose feet shall I fall and beg to reach you? Between you and me, a distance of a hundred deserts—every step I take I fall on fire.[23]

Passion for a newfound lover had the power to unsettle affective bonds; even such friends as Nasira and Husayn Kashi were tied by oaths of "single-hearted" friendship, the trope of one soul in two bodies. Such is the fear of love between men: that a male object of desire could come between two friends who competed in a culture of masculinity that both prescribed loyalty and yet promoted conquest on the battlefield of love (*ma'rika-yi jihad-i akbar*). Nasira's declaration of love to Husayn Kashi relates their experience of friendship to the spaces in Isfahan where they had loved and, together, gazed and conversed about beautiful male youths in coffeehouses. The two men experienced the cult of friendship by praying in mosques, visiting wine bars and coffeehouses, and debating the beauty of the iconic figures of male youth, from whose hands they drank coffee. By associating emotions with the built environment, or fusing an affective and urban landscape, this articulation of male friendship became constitutive of Isfahan's masculine habitus, akin to the tradition of city disturbance (*shahrashub*).

It is this model of friendship that connects two lovers of beauty; they are lovers not because they are alike but rather because they appreciate the value of each other's tastes and practices. Husayn Kashi was known for his mystic piety, but he is said to have had devotees from the mosque to the wine bar.[24] Even though he had a cloister in Isfahan, the coffeehouse was his hangout; there, in the company of male youth (*javanan*), he engaged in the game of love (*'ishq bazi*). His contemporary biographer, Muhammad Tahir Nasrabadi, tells us that Husayn Kashi did not sleep a single night without the "companionship of pain," making sure to note that his was an aesthetic appreciation of the figure of the male youth and that "never did [Husayn Kashi] sully [*aluda*] himself with the crime of sodomy [*fasad*]."[25] Nasira and Husayn Kashi's spiritual friendship was based on a shared experience of love and pain; this dynamic of erotic love and its denial is what engendered their single-heartedness—a trust built on masculine pleasures, the aches of boy gazing, and intimate conversations, all of which were predicated on feeling eros and appreciating the aesthetics of Isfahan's urban delights.[26] Hence Nasira describes the vow of single-hearted friendship as the genuine love of children; a love built on shared emotions that ensured intimate familiarity and dependability.

The emotional grammar of love had its own set of rules and vocabulary when written out in letters, but not all love letters adhered to these, particularly when the letter writer was known for an affair that had become public. In a letter identified by the collector as a correspondence between Mirza Ali Akbar and Zahid Khan, the impulse to transgress spiritual or platonic friendship is disclosed. Copied in an anonymous anthology, this letter is titled "Mirza Ali Akbar's Letter to Zahid Khan." Although the addresser writes neither his name nor pen name and although he does not disclose his beloved's name in the body of the letter, the collector must have known about Mirza Ali Akbar and Zahid Khan's love affair and took the trouble to record their names himself. The anonymity of the letter writer illuminates the anxiety felt around the exposure of male homoerotic love in Isfahan, even though rumors had clearly already publicized this particular affair. We know little about either man today; Mirza Ali Akbar's identity is obscure, and though Ali Akbar was a common first name, it does not appear in contemporary biographies of poets or scholars. The only sign of the addressee's status is the fact that he was a *mirza*; that is, he was part of the notable group of the prophet Mohammad's *sayyid* descendants. As we study the language of this letter, we recognize his profession as a man of letters who deploys metaphors of the library, calligraphy, and bookmaking and bookbinding to describe the event of his beloved's betrayal. As for his beloved, Zahid Khan, he most probably was a Turkman tribal leader, as the title khan suggests.

The body of Mirza Ali Akbar's letter exposes the tenor of his transgression. The reader is transported into the euphoria of Mirza Ali Akbar and Zahid Khan's affair as it navigates romance, deceit, rivalry, accusations, and forgiveness. Each phase of their love story is marked with a *ghazal*, which made full use of the range of the rhetorical *gharaz*, or "intentions," of the genre, such as praise, complaint, reproach, advice, and self-reflection.[27] Mirza Ali Akbar's letter moves away from the spiritual conventions of romantic love that celebrated the beauty of the beloved, exemplified by Nasira's letter to Husayn Kashi. Instead, as a lover who loses himself in the experience of eros, Mirza Ali Akbar indulges his carnal pleasures and passionate attractions. He addresses his letter to "the mount Sinai of lovers, the beauty of the water of animals thirsty for union, the lamp of reflection [*fikrat-i hal*], and the candle of the assembly of paradise-dwellers," casting Zahid Khan as his "sweet-smelling jasmine." His friend's beauty, he writes, is a rare find: "It is the blessing of spiritual anticipation that entreats hidden states to be voiced [*bayani*] and manifested [*izhar*] in writing." Although Mirza Ali Akbar is aware that his "exposition is unholy [and] secrets are the enemy of the heart of those in love, they must be written in words on the pages of deer skin. Love's sigh of pain must be tied to the wing of the [carrier] pigeon. . . . It must be transmitted to the desired heart [*matlub-i jani*]. May the response record amorous glances onto the page of shame, word by word, line by line, and be returned with your seal of loyalty."[28]

Mirza Ali Akbar refers to his friendship letter as a speaking letter (*natiq*), almost as though it too were a friend, a trusted intercessor, in a relationship that has fallen on difficult times. He complains that he has no choice but to voice his bewilderment. Evoking his longing and separation (*firaq*), he is baffled by rumors that Zahid Khan has taken up company with inappropriate (*na-munasib*) friends (*yaran*), squandering his time with their sweet talk (*chaplusi*). Yet Mirza Ali Akbar heaps his accusations at the feet of his trusted friends, marshaling a particularly material language to do so: "How could friends, with whom I have left you in safe keeping [*amanat*], steal you from me! The manuscript, which embodies the knowledge [*matlaʿ*] of beauty [*jamal*], written on Chinese silk paper, should not fall into the hands of illiterate practitioners of the rational sciences [*ʿulum-i nazari*]. They do not have the depth nor the discernment [*diqqat*] of the enchanted gaze that looks at [the master] Ibn Muqla's calligraphy, preserved in an elegant [*naz*] library. [The manuscript] should not fall into the hands of someone who will tear its pages apart from the manuscript.[29] Laughing with no shame, nor respecting the binding that has tied the precious volume together, they [the friends] take it [the book of calligraphy] into the assembly and separate it from its core."[30]

In this moment of rage, Mirza Ali Akbar records his resentment and brings out accusations against his friends. Disclosing his love for Zahid Khan, he divulges a secret that *adab* required him to conceal. But his friends' betrayal of the most valued trust of custodianship (*amanat*) was a shameless act of insincerity that provoked Mirza Ali Akbar's revelation. He desires to reunite with his beloved in body (*jismani*) and spirit (*ruhani*). He cannot control his passion for Zahid Khan, who has shared himself with other men. His humiliation lies not only in the revelation of obsessive love but also in his beloved being flaunted openly by deceitful friends in a public gathering. Everyone in Isfahan could see that he, Mirza Ali Akbar, had been betrayed by his circle of friends. This public deception has rendered him vulnerable to his former friends, now his enemies, a state that triggers the revelation of his physical desire. He calls his friends robbers, uncultivated men who tear apart a precious volume of calligraphy and showcase it in a public assembly. Struck by the malady of love, he writes that his physician (*hakim*) has prescribed him herbs and syrups, but his only remedy is the sweetness of Zahid Khan, his singular cure, whose eyes, nose, and mouth he likens to sweet beets adorned with pistachio nuts. Mirza Ali Akbar forgives his beloved and ends his letter in anticipation of devouring him when they meet.

The expression of male homoerotic love, preserved in contemporaneous correspondences, coincided with polemics against Sufi practices of boy gazing. Sexual discipline generated erotic speech in the body of the letter, which, among other objects, celebrated love affairs between men in Isfahan.[31] Mirza Ali Akbar's revelatory letter was subject to rumors and deliberations because it inverted the social order. Not only was he publicly betrayed by his friends, but also, in his reversing of roles, he upset the asymmetries of power between cultured men and their beloved youths. Moreover, Mirza Ali Akbar's unambiguous melding of sincere, spiritual, and physical love broke with the *adab* and ethics of urbanity. Although Nasira's love letters to Husayn Kashi and his friends in Shiraz displayed a shared language of affection, Mirza Ali Akbar openly declared his sexual desire, inscribing it on the surface of a sheet of paper, which was then copied and collected in multiple anthologies. It was Mirza Ali Akbar's physical desire for Zahid Khan, to devour the sweetness of his beloved, that was his revealed secret, resisting the cultivated display of masculine emotions bound by affective and bodily discipline.

Learning to Write to the Friend

To discipline affective ties between men, the friendship letter was codified as it moved beyond the walls of the palace and elite households to connect networks of urban friends. By the middle of the seventeenth century, epistolary manuals such as the *Munsha'at-i Sulaymani* (Epistles of Sulayman) came to classify form letters in simple Persian, thereby disciplining both language and affect.[32] Assembled in anthologies, these didactic manuals taught forms of polite communication between biological and surrogate family members and friends, systematizing the social etiquette of addresser and addressee. By order of Shah Sulayman (r. 1666–1692), the *Munsha'at-i Sulaymani* was composed by a collective of scribes (*kuttab*) for the Safavi household and courtiers as well as for the middle strata of refined residents of the city (*avasit al-'avvam*), such as calligraphers, painters, artisans, and merchants. A third category, classified as "other people" (*sayir al-nas*), signaled an intended audience defined by its interest in cultivating social ties through the *adab* of letter writing. The *Munsha'at-i Sulaymani* thus addressed a broad audience, creating a letter-writing culture that was to be shared by the elite, artists, merchants, and even grocers and barbers. Gendered titles of proper address are clearly delineated and outline the hierarchical relations of courtly, elite, merchant, and artisanal households. Sex, age, and occupation index the power differentials of Isfahan's epistolary culture, as a variety of model letters demarcate the stations of addresser and addressee according to their positions in the household, at court, and in society at large.

Because manuals of epistolary *adab* illustrate the ideal social order in Isfahan, they provide a view of a vertical network of ties that connected inhabitants of Isfahan through the valorized practice of letter writing. The *Munsha'at-i Sulaymani* therefore instructs letter writers of different social, sex, and age standings. The body and language of each form letter differed according to sets of hierarchies involving addressers and addressees. Moreover, consumers of the epistolary genre were understood to possess different degrees of literacy. The manual considers the possibility that the addressee may not know how to write (*agar khatt nadarad*); these addressers are instructed to copy key sentences from the model letter and include their personal seals to configure a discrete composition. Clearly, the *Munsha'at-i Sulaymani* acknowledges that reading and writing (*khatt*) are not always conjoined technologies. A catalog of seals identifying the addresser was available to wives, younger brothers, or sisters who did not know how to write; they could address their husbands, older brothers, sisters, aunts, and uncles using these seals as their signatures. In the correspondence copied by the unlettered, what would normally be articulated through idioms of deference to more powerful addressees finds expression in a simple, partial signature, emblematic of the compounded status of the addresser's subordination—younger in age, in social position, and in the ability to write.

Reflecting anxieties around the vicissitudes of friendships in early modern Isfahan, model letters contained requests to meet with friends, chided friends for their neglect, and offered forgiveness for disloyal behavior.[33] Corresponding to the range of intentions of *ghazal* poetics, these rhetorical motifs were translated into moods and acts that classified friendship letters in different categories. For example, the *Munsha'at-i Sulaymani* catalogs model letters that begin with the category of requests to meet (*mulaqat*) the friend. Similarly, a series of model letters of appeal, each using distinct narrative techniques, converge around the face (*ruy*) of the friend. "Seeing" the friend's face and "dreaming" of a face-to-face reunion are discrete images evoked and sent in a letter to highlight the friend's anticipation.[34] When model letters requesting a meeting with a friend received their intended response in the form of a letter, they confirmed the reciprocity of friendships. The physical meeting could once again be delayed. Waiting was a temporal mode of idealized love and gazing in Sufi practice, for attraction and inaction heightened desire for the true beloved, God. Hence the manual user needed to be aware of the temporalities of knowing how and when to respond. The letter from the friend was to alleviate doubt temporarily, placing a momentary pause on the suspense of the "meeting of two spirits." In this process the body of the letter was transformed into the beloved friend's face, which could trigger the actual encounter.

The *adab* of writing and seeing are central to the processes of turning the absent and missing body, the face-to-face encounter, into the disembodied letter. Form letters taught the etiquette of proper speech and discourse, but they also educated the letter writer in the ways that words conjured images that allowed for the reproduction of intimate encounters on paper. Model letters textualized and texturized gazes. They mobilized the familiar poetic language of the *ghazal* to invoke the beloved, calling to mind, for example, the absent one's braids, their arrow-shaped eyebrows, or their black facial mole. The practice of writing to a friend and of drawing and seeing the friend, key to the graphic culture of the day, were visual aids that facilitated the conjuring of the beloved. Memory was inscribed; whether written or painted, it scripted the encounter on the page to recognize and anticipate the friend. As one model letter affirms, "The practice of friendship requires that occasionally true loyalty arrive in the form of a letter that is written with veracity and in reality represents the spiritual encounter and the actual physical meeting."[35] Seeing the letter and reading and reflecting on the words written on the page converged to cultivate an awareness of time, which nurtured friendships; as though a gift, the letter was a material bond of affection that the addressee could wear like a scarf, caressing it to feel the friend's closeness and loyalty.[36] The friendship letter was an instrument for picturing and sensing the absent friend as present. Still, even as the language of the letter valorized sight (*mushahada*), gazing at the handwritten page (*sahifa*) did not supplant the actual encounter, which was the most treasured desire explicitly written into the content of model letters. But embodying a writerly tone and posture prepared the writer for the performance of the face-to-face encounter. Memories of past meetings were to be recalled, maintaining the anticipation of reunion; they were to be written as declarations of loyalty in the body of the letter: "Never was there a moment when I did not remember the noble and kind friend."[37]

Dissatisfaction in the form of complaint letters (*shikayat*) follows the category of requests for a meeting (*mulaqat*), another trope adopted from the *ghazal* and incorporated into friendship letters.[38] Complaints about friends who neglect their letter-writing duties make up this grievance category, for such lack of care saddens the heart of expectant friends. The addresser is instructed to voice his disappointment in the friend. Despite all the addresser's attempts at communicating through letters, writing his desire, and sending "picture letters" (*nigarinnama*), the true friend (*jani*) had failed to reciprocate. The exchange of friendship letters is a transaction, and if the addressee does not respond, then the desired message confirming their alliance, or the "memory of their encounter," is deficient. The manual therefore reproaches readers "who fail to remember the friend with a letter," calling it an unmannered act that "is surely a sign of the lack of urbanity [*gustakhi*]; it is insincerity, I say, to boot."[39]

The letter from the friend is a memento, an object that materializes the beloved on the "page of union."[40] It is transformative, as it "ease[s] the pain of the friend's heart" and turns sadness into joy. But for the letter to have a physical and curative effect, both sender and receiver have to engage in the exchange. The *adab* of writing lays the groundwork for the labor of visualizing, moving from the act of letter production to one of letter *perception*, drawing on the paper and ink's texture, color, and form, a process that activates the images and sentiments voiced on the page.

The arrival of the physical letter moves the friend beyond the state of reflection and into actual experience: "Reading it [the letter] is as though you were present and I were engaged in conversation with you," one model letter reads.[41] The *adab* of writing friendship letters stimulates consciousness as a site of witnessing. In another model letter responding to complaints from a friend, the addressee is instructed to write.

> Despite the depth of sincerity and the purity of belief in our friendship, you have laid accusations of carelessness and thoughtlessness on me, and called it a sign of my negligence. If, as you were writing the letter, you would have turned to your noble conscience, without a doubt you would not have permitted yourself to make such a statement about me, the just witness [*shahid-i 'adil*].[42]

The friend and the self are inseparable allies, reliant on each other in the process of transcendence, self-expression, and social realization. The manual revealingly correlates the material of a letter, termed the page of imagination (*safha-yi khiyal*), with a mirror, the smooth material surface that reflects the believer's soul, a ubiquitous metaphor in Sufi poetics. The friend who acts as his brother's witness before God is thus like the mirror, or the page that calls for introspection. It is in friendships, through the reciprocal attempt to challenge the spiritual growth of the friend, that the lofty ideal of human perfection is attained.

Friendship letters are material objects generated by the practice of sworn friendships, vows of brotherhood (*sigha-yi ukhuvvat*) and of sisterhood (*sigha-yi khwahar khwandagi*). Anthologies preserve a paper trail documenting these sworn friendships, evidence of the religious status attributed to unions between two brothers or two sisters.[43] Pledges of solidarity are penned to certify loyalty in this world and even in the afterlife, where one friend ensures the other's entry into paradise. These single-hearted friendships take on the duties that parents fulfilled toward their children or that saints and Imams fulfilled toward their devout believers. Drawing on verses from the Quran, these certificates proclaim friendship to be a social institution characterized by ethical obligations. The culture of epistolarity in Isfahan allows the historian entry into the social dynamic of sexual knowledge and affect, where speech, gestures, and gazes are written into the friendship letter and where the oral and the written are fused to shape alternative modes of expression.

In epistolary manuals, paper is turned into the site of writing as an act of witnessing, a process of mirroring the self in the composition of the letter to the friend.

Such imaginings were meant to associate the letter with face-to-face interactions and familiarize the manual user with the new medium of the letter, a technology that would facilitate self-recognition. Like the face of the male youth, the friendship letter mediated the practice of gazing, drawing on the image to locate the power of the letter. Form letters educated the writer about his or her voice and posture in the narrative of composition. As a technique, the student was instructed to conjure a dialogue, for the letter was identified as a form of conversation that transpired in the absence of the friend.

Instructions on composition were part of the education of the friend; friends were required to familiarize themselves with the interpersonal dynamics of a letter-writing style that begged a response. The addresser, in his role as the friend, was to engage in the habit of writing a plea letter with the full knowledge that complaining was a rhetorical stance. And the addressee recognized that he had to solicit his friend's forgiveness, as he too understood that his participation in the traffic of accusations would result in a pardon—that is, if he wrote back and deployed the proper language and affect in his response, as noted in the following model letter: "Since the purpose of official complaints are in any case part of the custom and habit of the day, and the tongue of speech is followed by the pen of the tongue to write it as an addict would, do give solace to this yearning heart."[44]

Traces of the complex contemporaneous meanings of intimacy are found in form letters, whose location I place at the intersection of the histories of friendship, letter writing, and collecting. Epistolary representations in model letters were stylized performances of emotions, meant to act as ciphers for particular kinds of erotic desire that were regulated by new adabizing codes of conduct. Although the form and content of fraternal letters confirm the strong impression that friendships in early modern Isfahan were highly conventionalized and routinized, it is worth recalling that such templates were, by design, preliminary; the model could not account for the full range of human behavior. Nonetheless, convention and routine were important ways of experiencing and scripting affect. In fact, these scripted forms of *adab* were agentive, insofar as they were embodied and performed by the letter writer. Epistolary manuals taught one how to write a letter for the reader to conjure his lover, as though the addressee's face and voice were recorded by the addresser. These were usage manuals for an audience in the process of adapting to a new technology; they promoted the *adab* of the letter as a form of social media.

Moreover, by positioning letters as integral to social relationships and community making, these manuals provided the rhetorical and interpretative tools for grasping the letter's communicative power.

Reading Letters from the Friend

Personal letters exchanged between friends also archive the practice of requesting portraits of beloveds to be drawn by artists. Painters gifted their works to friends, dating the occasion and even identifying the location as the friend's house, where gatherings often took place on Thursday evenings or Fridays.[45] Nasira Hamadani, in a letter to the famous painter Riza Abbasi, recounts a dream he had the night before in which handsome Hindustani beauties hosted him with great care and generosity. The dream made him long for Isfahan. Nasira voices his lament for Isfahan's splendor and his desire to gaze at its beauties. When he woke up, he immediately wrote this letter to his painter friend, whom he names, asking him to draw and send him a memento of Isfahan's beauty. He writes of his certainty (*yaqin*) that with

> the life-giving human image drawn by Riza Isfahani [Abbasi] . . . I will lose consciousness. My erotic desire [*havas*] for the beloved's stature and body curves will throw me to the ground, as though [the beloved's] shadow. At the sight of his taunting eyebrows, resembling a prayer-niche [*mihrab*] hollowed in my chest, I will fall for that heartthrob [*dilbari*]; his coy gestures [*'ishvagari*] and his face will take the breath out of me. Perhaps you will produce such a portrait [*surat*] for me, a face [*surat*] that no eye has seen? The meaning [*ma'na*] of this image [*surat*] will come into view [*numayan*]. . . . I will open the doors of eternal paradise, if I attain the [divine] meaning of this image. O cream of the workshop of image-makers [*karkhana-yi surat*], O offspring of the family of the prophet . . . send me a gift so that I shame those who deny the power of your portrait [*surat*].[46]

Nasira's letter makes it difficult for the painter Riza Abbasi to deny his friend's request. He flatters the artist who had once participated in the shaping Isfahan's beauty, adorning the walls and domes of the central square with his calligraphy. Longing for Isfahan's splendor, Nasira calls on Riza Abbasi's honor, claiming that his acquaintances in Hyderabad think that theirs are the most beautiful female and male beauties. Interestingly, it is the power of Riza Abbasi's craft, which can materialize beauty, that Nasira emphasizes, begging to "let me show them how your paintings encapsulate the beauty of Isfahan." Nasira lays out the cognitive labor that portraits perform, bringing an image to life, in all its sensuality; the power of the master image maker is to incite passion. He probably composed this letter while on a trip to India. Drawing on the mystical language of transcendence, he legitimizes his distant yearning for a portrait of Isfahan's male beauty, which he associates with the city and a medium of attaining a spiritual state of union; thus Nasira evokes Shah Abbas I's Isfahan as the image of the world, the perfection of beauty itself.

Other letter writers made similar requests. For instance, in a letter to the painter Mu'in Musavvir, Mulla Rawnaqi asks for a portrait of his male beloved. Referring to the painter as the "adorner of assemblies of images [*surat*] and the supplier of color to the assemblies of meaning [*ma'ani*]," Mulla Rawnaqi inhabits the rhetorical position of a submissive supplicant, describing himself as "this weak and humble one, whose being has been maddened by the desire to acquire a portrait of my beloved." Similarly, Mulla Rawnaqi also hopes to collapse the distance between himself and his beloved through the medium of the portrait. "Since I have been deprived of his sight," he explains, "if, through the incitement [*tahrik*] of your pen [*qalam*], you can draw a mirror image of the beauty of my beloved on a sheet of paper, with your assistance I will indeed fill my deprivation [*mahrumi*] with the pleasure of union."[47]

Whereas iconic representations of male youth were commonplace drawings that circulated in Isfahan on sheets of paper, some were personalized. In the margins of one portrait of a male youth, Mu'in Musavvir writes that it was executed "on Friday, the 20th of the holy month of Ramadan in the year AH 1047 [February 5, 1638]" (Figure 4.2). Along with the date, the painter records that this "watercolor [was painted] in the blessed home [*dawlatkhana*] of my dearest ['*aziza*] Shafi'a." Mu'in adds his signature to the portrait of his friend's beloved, "drawn by Mu'ina [*raqamahu*]." He paints Shafi'a's beloved in his home on the penultimate Friday of the fasting month of Ramadan. Calling attention to the viewer's gaze, the beloved's facial hair, his arrow-shaped eyebrows, and the distant look in his eyes, he highlights the verbal and visual topoi of the beauty of the beloved. Here, on this page the beloved is realized, historicized, and identified. As we have seen, friends often visited each other at one another's homes; in this case Mu'in Musavvir and Shafi'a were probably waiting for the sun to set so that they could break their fast together. Composed to mark an intimate occasion, these singular paintings

FIGURE 4.2 Muʿin Musavvir's drawing for his friend Shafiʿa, dated 1638 and signed Muʿina. Freer Gallery of Art, Smithsonian Institution, Washington, D.C., F1953.57. Charles Lang Freer Endowment.

collected in household anthologies preserve a gradual turn to naturalism. Together with the friendship letters that circulated in and out of Isfahan, such drawings archive everyday life. Muʿin's drawing of Shafiʿa's beloved tells us something about passing time on empty stomachs, appreciating the beauty of a male youth, even on a Friday during the holy month of Ramadan.

One folio collected in a sixteenth-century album signed by the calligrapher Mir Ali exhibits the relationship between writing mystical love poetry on a page, the materiality of paper, and the context in which poetry is to be exchanged between two men (Figure 4.3). The book of love poetry, compiled in the form of a *jung* or *safina* ("boat" in Chinese and Arabic, respectively), is often sized so that the traveler could tuck it in his belt comfortably. The painting depicts a male figure holding a book of poetry that initiates intimacy with his companion. The hand gesture of the male on the left signals his receiving the gifted book from his friend. It is not until we read the poem by the medieval poet Hafiz in the top right-hand side of the image that the meaning of the exchange becomes clear: "Two clever friends, drinking from the aged jug of friendship— / A delightful moment, a book, and a secluded grassy spot." It is in a secluded space, complete with the accoutrements of mystical union, that the ritual performance of friendship was to be experienced in the sixteenth century. A garden in full bloom, a book of poetry, a jug and cup of wine—these were the sites and objects for fast friends to experience the pleasures of intimacy and conversation (*suhbat*).

Iconic representations of two friends exchanging poetry in intimate garden spaces visualize the masculine etiquette of love and friendship. This technique of love draws on the intermediary of a book of poetry, performances of thematic illustrations that are plentiful in the sixteenth century. Produced by imperial and elite circles, such illustrations convey the proper *adab* of love, relations between age-old friends, as the painting portrays equals, even though one friend initiates the talk of love by gesturing and giving the book of *ghazal* poetry. This private moment of exchange between friends did not threaten to disrupt the social order. However, by the seventeenth century, these visual celebrations of friendship between two men exchanging poetry on a grassy spot disappear. Instead, as we have seen, single male figures, either framed simply as male objects of desire or posed with a book, a page of poetry, or a letter, are most commonly commissioned or gifted. When two men are depicted, it is in the context of Sufi gazing, where a pious older man with a beard gazes and resists his desire for a beardless male youth (see Figure 0.5). What do we make of this curious shift? We know that affective bonds between men came under close surveillance and regulation in seventeenth-century Isfahan. But what of the mannerisms, the body language and gestures, that came to circumscribe epistolary practices of male friendship?

→ FIGURE 4.3 *Muraqqaʿ* of calligraphy by Mir Ali, dated 1540–1550. Institute of Oriental Manuscripts, Russian Academy of Sciences, St. Petersburg, 1958.70, no. C-860, fol. 466.

Art historians have associated this painting with a stylistic innovation by Afzal Husayni, who worked in Isfahan (Figure 4.4). The topoi of including the image of the beloved on a cushion or wine bottle had been introduced a decade earlier by the famous painter Riza Abbasi.[48] Given the adabizing project I have outlined, the popularity of depicting a single friend reading a poem or a letter, at times accompanied by the image of his beloved on the cushion (under a rubric of friends in conversation, as depicted in sixteenth-century works of art), speaks of social transformations in the practice of friendship. By the mid-seventeenth century, the acts of reading, of conversing with the beloved friend in his absence, and of reciting poetry aloud were understood as ciphers for intimacy in such paintings. The disciplinary project of *adab* here affected an entire manner of comportment, rendering passionate friends into well-crafted men. Indicative of a broader phenomenon, the recognition of beauty, so central to the hermeneutics of *ghazal* poetry, fostered self-reflection in the context of a graphic culture that aestheticized love and beauty. Whether partaking in boy gazing or in the act of composing a letter or a portrait on a piece of paper, Afzal Husayni paints the friendship letter as a mirror to reflect on as a technique of self-fashioning.

In thinking about curating the self in terms of the lines of force between collecting, self-creation, and friendship, we should also consider the model of the self, current among painters, poets, and collectors in Isfahan. Teaching and remembering were achieved by filling one's mind with objects; these processes took place through familiarity with what had come before. In other words, teaching was carried out through collections (*majmu'a*s, *muraqqa'*s, *divan*s, *safina*s), model letters, and manuals, just as communities were built on the sharing of an image repertoire. In this context, Afzal Husayni fashioned a new kind of affective and aesthetic experience of friendship, where the Aristotelian concept of *takhyil*, or image evocation, was mobilized to particularize his poetics of friendship (see Figure 4.4).[49] The male figure in the cushion holds a handkerchief, a symbol of the absent, lamenting beloved. Tactility is painted into the image as the beloved touches the lover's belt, who in turn caresses the letter on his lap with his fingers, his gaze, and, in fact, his entire body. The poetics of love and mimesis that a century earlier were to be communicated through face-to-face encounters, between two friends on a secluded grassy spot, are now practiced in the *adab* of letter writing. The absence of the friend is inscribed through the medium of paper; the image evokes an emotional reaction

FIGURE 4.4 *Youth with an Album*, by Afzal Husayni, Isfahan, dated 1620–1630. Opaque watercolor and gold on paper. Victoria & Albert Museum, London, IS 133:30/A-1964.

where gestures and gazes are drawn in as codes for forbidden desires. We do not know who commissioned this portrait by Afzal Husayni; perhaps it was a friend who simply asked him to draw a male beloved. Yet it is also possible, at this initial phase of writing friendship letters, that such images were sent *with* letters as mimetic devices, simultaneously filling the beloved's absence and acting as pedagogical tools for the *adab* of letter writing.

I began this chapter on the *adab* of letter writing, didacticism, and collecting and then turned to personal letters to friends, epistolary manuals, and portraits whose graphic surfaces faded into objects, rituals, and practices. My readings of these verbal and visual texts therefore treat the *adab* of friendship as the epicenter of a praxis of assembly, one that not only draws certain kinds of people together but also connects people *through* objects and *to* objects. Isfahan's early modernity, then, can be understood as a history not only of the changing nature of the state and its control of literacy but also of the changing nature of the literate and prosaic self. Existing at the seams of materiality, literacy, and visuality, the lineaments of the self that are fashioned by the history of male friendship come into view; men knew when, where, and what to draw from a refined grammar of sociability to reinscribe the poetics of amity and participate in the cult of friendship.

The variety of models of friendship categorized in epistolary manuals and private letters affiliate verbal sentiments of sincere (*jani*), spiritual (*ruhani*), or physical (*jismani*) emotions with an array of associations that are literally embodied. Occupying different forms of address, the friend draws on a vocabulary of mystic love to formulate the syntax of affective male relations. Terms of friendships embedded in words and images take on the form of life; they inhabit the friend as he engages in "sweet conversation" and "the game of love." As I have argued in this chapter, reading friendship involves seeing the friend and the self as inseparable, reliant on each other in the process of writing, desiring, and social realization. References to the paper on which the letter is composed as "the page of imagination" evoke the mirror, the smooth material surface that reflects the believer's soul. Friendship letters turn paper into the site of writing as an act of witnessing, a process of mirroring the self that addresses the absent friend; the addressee inhabits the body of the friend and the self to realize the ideal of single-hearted friendships. Such imaginings of the letter and the image enhanced face-to-face conversations and produced presence through the new medium of the letter and the portrait, technologies that facilitated the writing of urban and erotic selves.

Cognizant of contemporary modes of reading and debating homoerotic love, friends deployed mystic tropes and conventions to express a range of love and affection in everyday forms of sociality. By the middle of the seventeenth century, the dynamic of erotic love and its denial, so central to the conventions of Sufi love, was mobilized by the Safavi court to discipline male-male desire, which was perceived as a threat to rule and the maintenance of stability in Isfahan. But the dynamics of soliciting and disciplining also reproduced sexual love. Even as friendship letters were being standardized along with the regulation of carnal pleasures and passionate attractions, the temptation to resist this process could also be overpowering. As we have seen in the case of Mirza Ali Akbar, despite the social urge to discipline or the shame of revealing desire by its name, he still announced his unholy love for his desired heart (*matlub-i jani*), making public his desire to reunite with his beloved in body (*jismani*) and spirit (*ruhani*). Mirza Ali Akbar refused to follow the *adab* of male friendship, and anthologists who collected his private letter valued his irreverence and treasured the display of his erotic self, even as homo-eros, male and boy love, was to remain the secret many knew and practiced.

CHAPTER 5

Family Archives and Female Spaces of Intimacy

The Anthology as Archive

> O God, protect this writing from being dispersed
> ... On the date 16th of Jamadi al-avval, in the
> year 1109 [November 30, 1697],
> this anthology was begun.[1]

God has indeed protected the anthology that archives the history of the Urdubadi family. Beginning with the date—November 30, 1697—written distinctly in the preface, the curated contents trace material collected during the seventeenth century, when members of that family first began their employment at the imperial court in Isfahan. Much like an archive, the anthology selects, records, and organizes the activities and literary works of the Urdubadi family. And as a family archive of bureaucrats and literati, it assembles distinct objects that were written, read, and studied by male and female kin. To learn the epistolary practices of chancellery correspondences, those holding bureaucratic posts used manuals on composition and copies of diplomatic letters. Poems composed by family members—including by one remarkable widow—are gathered together with endowment deeds and diplomatic letters that register collective household ownership; professional and personal property figure as part of a larger corpus from which this anthology was bound into a manuscript, ensuring the preservation of material recorded on single sheets of paper. And like other archives, the Urdubadi anthology marks time, divulging traces from past moments of collecting and disclosing the logic of its own assembly. As a codex, the Urdubadi anthology traveled. Beyond facilitating movement through the discoursing city in ways we have already seen, this anthology journeyed away from Isfahan to the city of Urdubad, the family's ancestral home in northwestern Iran. The 1697 preface introduces Muhammad Muʻin Urdubadi as patron and author of the anthology, who together with his anonymous scribe drew from documents, letters, poems, and essays collected in the Urdubadi family library. As an archive, the anthology enables us to recognize both family and city of its collection.

In this chapter I read the anthology as a family archive to argue that anthologies preserve communal processes that produced the spatiality of social life, a habitat where family *adab* was lived and kinship ties were negotiated. Just as friendship letters and city disturbances index emotional encounters between friends that give meaning to the topography of the city, the household anthology assembles practices and objects that define kinship; it furnishes and configures family space.

We enter the social world of the Urdubadi household, contextualizing the anthology that fashions its particular history, to hear the words of one family member: an unnamed widow who writes her own extraordinary self-narrative (see Map 0.1). Her versified travelogue (*masnavi*) begins as she leaves Isfahan and her family behind, a distance that incites the expression of an emotional and gendered sensibility. The Urdubadi widow's story, written in the first person, relates female spaces of intimacy to the institution of sisterhood. Moreover, her *masnavi*, situated in the context of other curated Urdubadi household objects, illuminates the heterosocial spaces that characterize this family. This is but one household, a literate environment that cannot be generalized as typical of Isfahan's households, but it offers a model of how both prominent and anonymous household anthologies in all their heterogeneity can be interpreted.

As we have seen, household anthologies were nothing like the better-known single-subject anthologies of poetry, epistles, medicine, or philosophy. Although they share an affinity with classic encyclopedic compendiums composed in the medieval and early modern urban centers of Baghdad, Cairo, and Istanbul, seventeenth-century household anthologies assembled all the knowledge necessary for being urbane and literate in Isfahan; the city grounded their content and scope.[2] Interpreting the anthology as a household production allows us to read it as a family archive, through which we enter the Urdubadi household and learn about their cultural practices and modes of communicating social relations. In recent scholarship, family archives in the form of a manuscript have been posited as sites for more broadly rethinking archives in the premodern Islamicate world.[3] In the context of Isfahan, household anthologies provide a particularly rich ground for theorizing and reassessing premodern archival mechanisms and spaces. Generated and then collected and assembled in the interior spaces of the house, such anthologies were also objects fashioned with the precise purpose of traversing the spaces *between* households—as letters, paintings, and gifts—bringing the city and its many forms of urbane dialogue into focus.

Although the range of material and the variety of compositions deployed in anthologies showcase the heterogeneous interests and character of households in Isfahan, these collections also have many commonalities. For instance, many shared city objects populate the household anthologies of both the religious scholar Aqa Husayn Khwansari and the bureaucrat Muhammad Muʻin Urdubadi. Both anthologies curate similar texts, from standard requests for paper, wine, and eyeglasses, to generic communication forms that model letter writing and practices such as friendship. In addition, both the Khwansari and Urdubadi household anthologies share the feature of a table of contents and a similar organization and distribution of material on the page. Still, each anthology is its own individual creation. Similar to what one finds in state archives, the acts of writing, collecting, and selecting texts for inclusion in these anthologies also reveal a politics of curation, or a need to represent the desired image of the family for posterity. Archival engagements with household anthologies bring into view the professional and intimate lives of families, even as they were a site where Isfahan's communal media connected households. Although the Urdubadi family knew of Aqa Husayn Khwansari and preserved a preface he composed in their anthology, familial and professional networks distinguish each household. Insofar as the Khwansari anthology records books of divination that divulge Aqa Husayn's engagement with the occult in Isfahan, it particularizes his *adab* of urbanity. In contrast, the profession of the Urdubadi household, which focused on producing bureaucrats and literati, was to write and represent the ruling Safavi household. Diplomatic letters were collected alongside personal letters, poetry, and family endowment deeds. Most conspicuously, among the assembled writings collected in the Urdubadi anthology, a versified travelogue written by an unnamed female member of the family illustrates the purchase of reading anthologies as family archives. The widow's husband is named as Mirza Khalil, who was the *raqam nivis*, or chief secretary, at the court of Shah Sulayman (r. 1666–1692); he was also involved in the production of the epistolary manual, the *Munsha'at-i Sulaymani*, that educated residents of Isfahan in the craft of letter writing.[4] This widow's voice, collected amid the mostly male authors of the collection, further particularizes the Urdubadi anthology; it allows us to move across gender lines to hear the ways in which one woman deploys the mystical language of love to speak about kinship, friendship, and Isfahan.

Inscribing the Family

The earliest authorial or scribal record in the anthology dates to 1075/1664, where, on folio 800, the scribe records a history of Iran written by his patron, Muhammad Mu'in. Thirty-three years before the production of this voluminous anthology, Muhammad Mu'in had made use of his family archives to narrate a history, just as a court historiographer would have done, having access to copies of chancellery documents that his grandfathers had penned and kept for their personal records.[5] In the process of collecting traces from the past, the patron interprets the archive and records it in his household anthology. Indeed, these seventeenth-century Isfahani family archives have a peculiar feature: They are both spaces of self-selection and reflection. Interpretative practices of archiving households relied on habits of curation and preservation. Whether performed by selecting documents to narrate a history or in the history of collecting sources for the Urdubadi family library itself, these are acts of interpretation. Materials from earlier days of household members working in the bureaucracy are dispersed throughout. Although not all of them are dated, their content divulges a longer history of collecting. A politics of preservation shapes the history of the Urdubadi family, in which fragments from the household library that never made it into this anthology are lost to the future.

The Urdubadi anthology is also marked by an event: the Afghan invasion of Isfahan in 1722 CE. The original *majmu'a* was then taken to Urdubad during the family's flight to escape the demise of the Safavi dynasty and the siege of Isfahan. In Urdubad the anthology was subsequently unbound and reassembled to include the next chapters of the family's history during the eighteenth and nineteenth centuries. Traces of this flight are visible in red-inked numerals added to correct the original

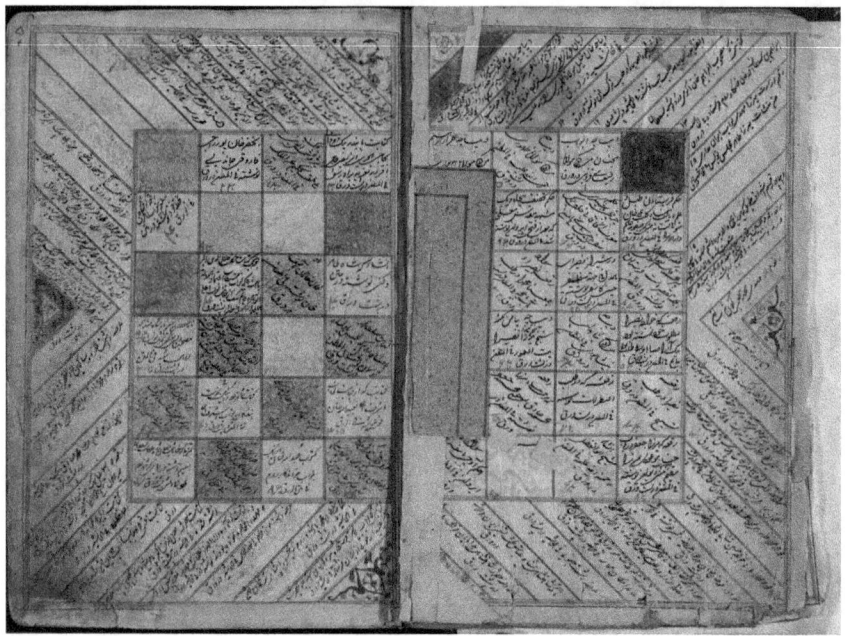

FIGURE 5.1 Urdubadi *majmu'a*, table of contents. Tehran University Library, MS 2591, fols. 4r and 5v.

table of contents, with new paginations written into the order of material collected in Isfahan in 1697 (Figure 5.1). The table of contents is a creative feature; only a few such lists have appeared in my survey.[6] The last date appears not at the end of the anthology but on folio 742, recorded in 1842 CE (AH 1263).[7] Clearly this anthology went through several stages of collecting, dismantling, and rebinding over a period of nearly two centuries.[8] Room is made for family members' future work and activities through the use of blank spaces, even as some past sections are blacked out; the anthology-as-archive anticipates erasures, restructuring and leaving lacunae for future inscriptions (Figures 5.2 and 5.3).

Official chancellery letters and decrees written by the father, Hatim Beg, a grand vizier (1591–1610), and by his son, Mirza Talib Khan, a royal secretary (*majlis nivis*)[9] (1629–1634) in the service of Shah Abbas I and his grandson, Shah Safi (r. 1629–1642), are collected alongside form letters requesting (*talab*) an astrolabe, sheets of paper, a pot of ink, a jug of wine, prayer beads, and a pair of eyeglasses. Standard requests for such objects surface in many household anthologies as urban accessories of the

Family Archives and Female Spaces of Intimacy   169

FIGURE 5.2 Urdubadi *majmu'a*, showing a blacked-out area. Tehran University Library, MS 2591, fols. 742v and 743r.

literate, whether they are bureaucrats, clerics, artists, or merchants. What distinguishes the Urdubadi household collection is that letters requesting everyday accessories are assembled together with Hatim Beg's and Mirza Talib Khan's collected copies (*savad*) of diplomatic letters from the sixteenth century. Included in their household archives are letters sent by Safavi shahs to Mughal, Uzbek, and Ottoman rulers. Father and son must have used these letters to fashion their own. Although these two "men of the pen" were the most prominent members of the Urdubadi family, they were both dead in 1697 when the preface was written. Moreover, Mirza Talib Khan had been disgraced in 1634 while holding the post of grand vizier. He was assassinated by Saru Taqi, who not only took over his position as vizier (1634–1645) but also confiscated Mirza Talib Khan's home, a house that Hatim Beg began building in Isfahan's Hasanabad District and that his son completed. Hatim Beg and Mirza Talib Khan were the first two generations of Urdubadis to move to the capital city and build their residence in Isfahan. Theirs, we are told, was one of the most beautiful residences. Even though we do not know where in Isfahan the Urdubadis

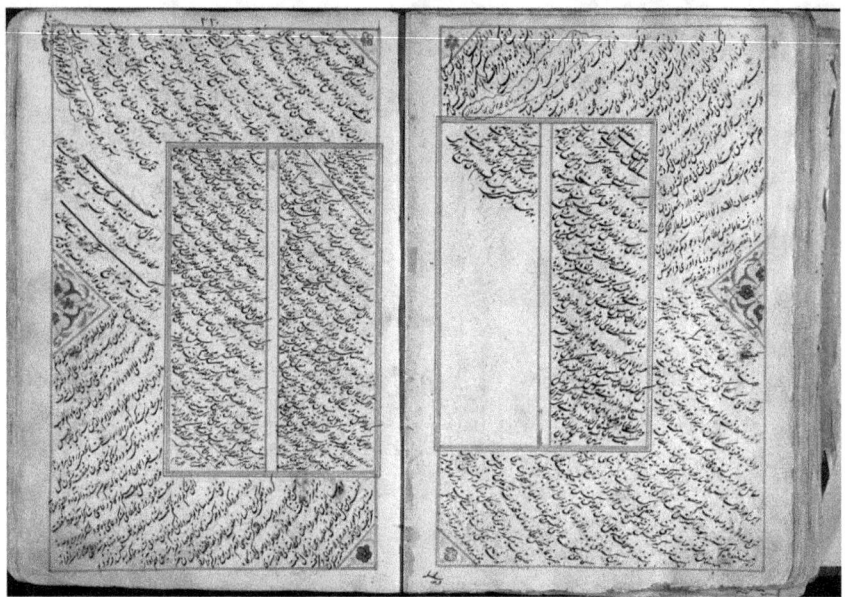

FIGURE 5.3 Urdubadi *majmuʿa*, showing a blank space left for future inscriptions. Tehran University Library, MS 2591, fols. 329v and 330r.

moved to when they left the Hasanabad District, nor what the library that housed their family letters and poetry looked like, we do know that their archive moved with them, furnishing their urban habitat and augmenting the family's story in a different way than did other relocated objects, such as a pair of glasses or an astrolabe. The Urdubadi anthology survives as urban artifact; by opening the home's interior spaces, it supplants architecture, which did not endure the vicissitudes of time.[10]

In this family archive from the second half of the seventeenth century, much of the material relates to the chancellery profession. Assembled during Muhammad Muʿin's lifetime, such documents display his habits of collecting and writing. In the case of the Urdubadi household, what one wrote as a professional court secretary was considered the intellectual property of the family; lines demarcating work and family, even for a functionary of the imperial court, were considered permeable. Because Safavi "state" archives have not survived the trials of time, this family archive provides important clues to what would have been included in notarial and imperial archives.

Ten years after the Afghan siege of Isfahan (1722), the family had resettled in Urdubad and the anthology was restructured. In its new iteration, the 1697 preface was preserved and the body of the anthology was reconfigured. Different hands, scribes, and authors left their traces on the anthology, which was then rebound, breaking with the material's original ordering. On folio 326 there is a telling inscription: "This page was written by the hand of Qasim Tabrizi, who, during his travels in 1732 CE [AH 1148], inscribed the copy of the anthology [*bayaz*] belonging to Muhammad Mu'in Urdubadi, who was the owner of the *bayaz* he wrote."[11] How are we to understand the term *bayaz* here? The word in manuscript terminology is typically applied to mean a "fair copy"? *Bayaz* appears in the 1697 table of contents, a usage most commonly deployed as the *dibacha-yi bayaz*, the preface to an anthology of compositions or epistles, like that of the religious scholar Aqa Husayn Khwansari.[12] As a technical term, *bayaz* is used in the Urdubadi anthology to refer to a copy of a collection of works, be they letters, compositions, or miscellanea, assembled together in a codex. In Urdubad, once the 1697 anthology was reassembled, expanded, and rebound, the original was transformed into its copy. Losing the status of an original because it was reorganized, it was only to be reinstated as a copy. Yet rather than a preoccupation with literal replication, the copy still endorsed authorship. This is precisely what is significant about the anthologizing practice of Muhammad Mu'in, who curated the Urdubadi archives and bound them into a manuscript. As new chapters of Urdubadi lives and objects of collection were assembled into the original, Muhammad Mu'in's authorial status prevailed along with that of his family for posterity.[13] The simultaneous practice of the archival function that is both originary and replicative illuminates the procedures of self-fashioning as innovative acts that reproduce the habits of collecting.[14]

The Urdubadi family continued producing writings by bureaucrats and poets until the end of the seventeenth century, as attested by the many samples of letters and verse they authored, by their collections of sayings, by a famous anthology of poets titled the *Tuhfat-i Sami*, and by the poems of Sa'ib Tabrizi (d. 1676), the contemporary poet laureate living in Isfahan.[15] In addition to poetry and epistle (*munsha'at*) collections penned by subsequent Urdubadi royal secretaries of Shah Safi and his son Abbas II (r. 1642–1666), the anthology also contains a selection of prefaces written by famous masters of the word. To be a literate bureaucrat, one had to know not only how to compose a diplomatic letter or a letter to a friend but also how to write a preface, or *dibacha*, for a collection. The *dibacha* was an established mode of introducing a literary work and was most commonly composed for historical chronicles. But by the seventeenth century in the Persianate world, histories of art and collections of compositions in poetry and prose all made use of prefacing, each drawing on distinct genealogies of masters in their craft to create prefaces that provided authoritative context. *Dibacha*s follow conventions; they traditionally open with praise for God and his creation, then laud the prophet Muhammad, and finally transition into sites where authors and/or patrons are named. It is in the preface that we learn about the patron's religious proclivities through telling details, such as whether the prophet's family is praised, whether Ali's name is explicitly inscribed, or whether prayers and blessings are devoted to his progeny. The *dibacha* is a place where histories of patron and author converge, where the author creates his genealogy, for instance, of historians, poets, or painters, alongside works that have inspired him to inscribe himself, along with his patron. Inside the contours of convention, an author or patron's particular social and cultural features are braided together, writing themselves into the rich fabric of the *dibacha* (literally "brocade" in Persian).

The City of God and the Masters of the Word

> To adorn an anthology [*majmuʻa*] is an ancient secret inscribed in the name of God. Its preface [*dibacha*] befits no other than the skilled masters of word and speech [*sukhan*], embellishers of the book of artistry and talent.

These words compose the first sentences of the Urdubadi anthology (Figure 5.4). The "name of God" marks the opening of the preface, as he embodies the secret of the *majmuʻa*'s beauty. Relating this anthology to the act of God's creation, the preface is to be crafted by masters of word and speech (*sukhan*); they are the ones who possess the graphic skills for deciphering the semiotics of the secret. Knowledge is materialized in writing and drawing, with color and ink, where figures of speech illuminate the folios of the book of arts assembled in this *majmuʻa*. Moving from God to family, the preface situates a genealogy of masters of the pen, which inscribes the Urdubadi legacy, its lineage, and its status in Isfahan. Visually and verbally, the preface communicates the sociology of the household in which it was produced, from the professional occupation of its patrons to the family's public engagement with the city. Distinct not only for its use of ornament and color to associate itself with the cosmos, the preface publicizes the idiom of a graphic culture that brings word and image together to engage with the visual aesthetics cultivated in the city of Isfahan. Intimately linked to one another, reading and writing become reversible acts, and in this anthology they are urban practices. Texts circulating in the city are mapped onto the preface diagonally, exhibiting a kind of literacy that imagines the streets, the squares, and circles of the city in the body of a page. More than 800 folios containing more than 180 entries are bound together with brown goatskin covers, each embossed with matching golden medallions at their centers.[16] The worn-out leather spine of the binding suggests routine use; time and again, this anthology has been held, touched, and read. Between the front and back covers, several thicker sheets of paper have been added to the original, evidence of the anthology's rebinding. As we turn to the first page, our gaze is drawn to the circles filled with writing on colored paper, guiding the reader's eye to the poetry that frames the two spheres. In bold verse and large *riqaʿ* script, typically used for the writing of chancellery documents, these words enclose the preface:

> If you begin, "in the name of God," as your crown-title
> Names of beloveds will accompany you at the head of the tablet of acts [*lawh-i kar-ha*]
>
> Till the end of time, you will paint the secret [*sirr*] of the written word [*khatt*]
> Dust [*khak*] is your crown of honor

The ekphrastic frame poetry underscores the meaning of the page and the significance of the act of writing. Associated with the preserved tablet (*lawh-i mahfuz*), referred to in the Quran (85:22) as the primordial text where the record of events was inscribed before creation, the anthology is imagined as an archive of divine knowledge collected in a book on the history of the universe.[17] Naming God is itself a sign associated with the symbolic crown that acts not only as the title of the universal book of history but also as the inspiration for earthly friends, prophets, and saints to join in the creative endeavor. Much like an archive, writing in the Urdubadi anthology is a collective pursuit containing traces of the past; everything from God's name to the tablet, from carefully chosen words to design and color, are the hidden secrets of the anthology settled with the dust of labor and time.

Articulated in terms of the name of God, the Urdubadi family history communicates intimacy with the divine. The experience of the city is imagined as

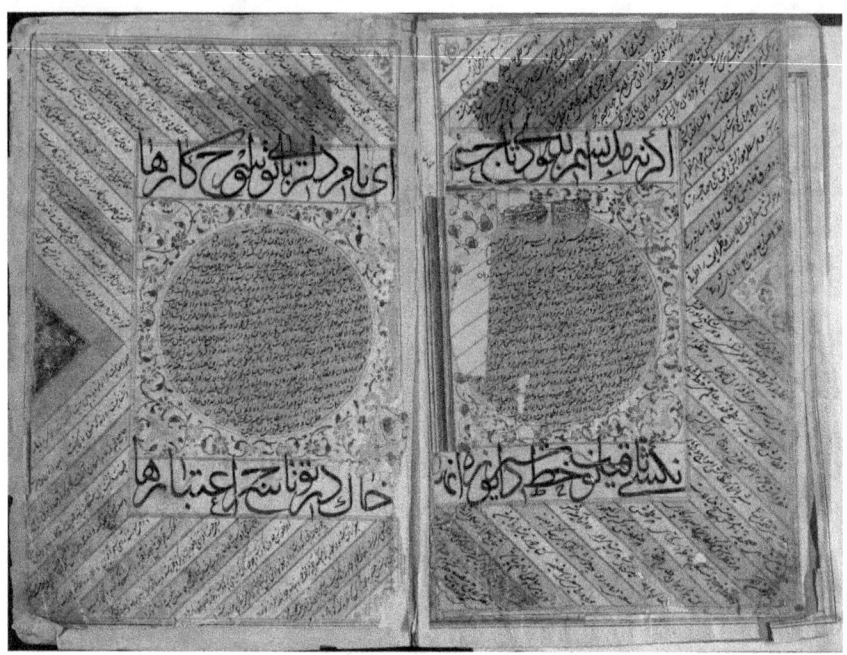

FIGURE 5.4 Urdubadi *majmuʻa*, *Dibacha* (preface). Tehran University Library, MS 2591, fols. 1r and 2v.

the experience of God, documented not only through inscriptions on architecture and in the urban space but also in the technology of the preface and the anthology. Enclosed in two corresponding discs that symbolize the two realms of the cosmos, the preface-filled circles are illuminated with brocades of flowers; they echo the literal meaning of *dibacha* as embellishment. Together, divine and human creation mirror a page framed by diagonal lines (*jadval*) along the margins of the actual folio (see Figure 5.4). As the scribe/patron begins to introduce the selection of materials assembled in this anthology, he draws on urban metaphors from the diagonal grid of streets and squares and intersections; the preface's mise-en-page is aligned with the urban environment. Laid out flatly on the folio, the preface constructs a multidimensional space where design, color, and script connect the content of the anthology to urban spaces and cosmic spheres. As we will see, particular idioms are at play, bringing cosmos, family, and city to bear on one another.

The preface helps situate how divine creation is impressed in writing, how the tools of a graphic culture—the pen, the page, paint, and ink—are marshaled for the task of relating city practices of anthologizing with pious acts of creation. These contingent worlds are imagined as joined by means of writing, as a creative medium, and through practices of collecting. From the very first circle of the heavenly sphere, the relationship between anthology and divine secrets is reinforced. Here, masters of word and illuminators of image are cast as meticulous discerners of meaning who write the pages of the universe onto the folios of anthologies of arts and crafts. Masters of speech, for example, paint the foundation of virtuosity and finesse (*nuktadani*); they are literate men (*savadkhwanan*) who can read meaning into the "garden of creation." For the flower to find its image or form and adorn God's signature, it must be written. Although the best kind of speech is in God's praise, without the composition of the word his cosmos would not take shape, form, or meaning. The interdependence of the divine act of creation and its communication through words, signs, and symbols fills the space of the first circle of the preface. Eulogies to God in verse and prose are curated and reassembled to align with the page of the "anthology of wisdom and perception" (*majmuʿa-yi danish u binish*). In other words, the author/scribe of the *majumʿa* materializes the act of creation, "painting the secrets of the written word" in the anthology. Material configurations, representations, and reproductions make visible the secrets of creation.

Moving from the first sphere of the preface, where devotion and blessings are addressed to God, to that sphere's closing verse (*maqtaʿ*), the author/scribe praises the prophet Muhammad and his family as the pillars of politics (*millat*) and religion (*din*); religion binds the folios of revelation into a single codex: "Once religion spread from him [Muhammad], Ali bound together its folios." The last verse scripted in the first circle is intentionally broken into interconnecting hemistiches; they link the two cosmic spheres into a single universe. "Muhammad, whose infidels empower his mission," guides readers across to the second sphere, which concludes "with the anthology [*divan*] of the two worlds, he is the chosen one." Muhammad and his prophetic role in this world bridge the two spheres, ending creation (*maqtaʿ*) and beginning prophesy (*matlaʿ*).

The patron's name and his eulogy fill the rest of the writing in the second sphere. Muhammad Muʿin ibn Hajj Muhammad Khan is praised as the patron, thanks to whom this *majmuʿa* has flourished and bloomed. He is the adorner of the newlyweds, resembling the stunning peacock's feathers; he is the gardener of paradise, whose thirst for truth and certainty mark him as the inspiration for this anthology: "Though the water of life bestows eternity, its companion is writing." Most significantly, the scribe associates his patron with Khizr, the invisible spiritual guide who leads Alexander to the eternal water of life; according to the scribe, his patron Muhammad Mu'in has arrived at the eye of the stream of immortality. But even though the water of life gifts eternity, the scribe inserts himself into the production of the anthology. Immortality can only be accompanied by writing; patron and scribe are thus conjoined in the practice of anthologizing.

Features of Isfahan's graphic culture, its beauty, wisdom, image, and script, are linked to the practice of friendship and collecting, for the anthology is imagined as a space of gathering, where an assembly of friends (*majma'-i yaran*) from the past is convened. Here, in the second sphere, the author/scribe scripts his own genealogy, moving diachronically from the prophet Mani, whose multimedia revelation was an illustration of ideal beauty, to master painters such as Bihzad (d. 1535); these are virtuosi of the image, friends whose craft has illuminated this anthology. As for experts of the word, every folio of the anthology draws together the uniqueness of poetic modes, from quatrains (*ruba'i*) that are testimony to ruby speech to *qasida*s that connect writing with allegory and parable. According to Muhammad Mu'in's scribe, the anthology incites, just as it assembles, various compositions by friends who have captivated their audiences with the sweetness of Layli and Majnun's romance. Like the lover's confection (*masnavi*), other works have marked memories with the melancholic tastes associated with the story of Khusraw and Shirin. Quatrains, *ghazal*s, and bawdy jokes (*hazl*) all furnish familiar poetic modes. They offer captivating stories and enchanting characters with whom the audience empathizes and laments, literary figures who form the charmed circles of friends gathered together in the Urdubadi *majmu'a*.

In the margins, beginning with the name of God, an opening sentence draws on another Arabic term to designate the anthology. It is a boat (*safina*), which enables travel just as its contents stimulate affect and performance: "What kind of anthology [*safina*] is this in which every hemistich generates travel through the stirring [*jush*] sea of meaning?" Like the boat that navigates the seas, linking land to water, the anthology steers movement from a literary imagination of the cosmos to that of the social imaginary. Poetic modes such as quatrains are aligned with streets and pillars of buildings; every line (*khatt*), every binding (*shiraza*), every page (*safha*), every dot (*nuqta*), and every square (*zilʿ*) are materialized through the medium of the cityscape. By bringing order to the density of the assembled material, the anthology authorizes the reading of the graphic infrastructure of the preface as the city.

Illustrating Female Friendships

Thanks to the creative innovation of the table of contents, I found the story of a female member of the Urdubadi household. Her writings are made visible by the road map designed by the scribe for navigating the anthology. On folio 5v, the scribe introduces a poem penned by a woman as she was traveling from Isfahan to Urdubad and Mecca; the mobility of this recording literally renders spontaneous movement and writing in motion, through the metaphor of the boat (*safina*). This metaphor carries its author not only through space but also, in a sense, through the broader context of the anthology. The anthologizing practices of writing and reading enabled the household's women and men to become masters of the word. As a place to collect thoughts, to draw on the patchwork of disciplinary and generic samples and deploy narrative parallels and borrowings, the anthology fostered the exercise of one's own compositional agency. Moreover, the city as an experience of God provided a site to imagine, if not also to practice, the way in which human intimacy with God also opened space—imaginatively, affectively, and materially—for intimacy with humans.

To situate the specificity of her textual record, let us step outside the Urdubadi family archive to put the visual archive into conversation with the verbal and sharpen our focus on the gendering of Isfahan's habitus. As figural and literal sites of household intimacy and urban sociability, the *majmuʿa* and *muraqqaʿ* produced multiple affective registers through which friendships developed in the city of Isfahan. For instance, Muhammad Qasim's portfolio, discussed in Chapter 2, captures some of these tensions that mark female friendships in seventeenth-century Isfahan. Although his dispersed paintings and drawings emphasize male sociability and the common motifs of male homoerotic love and desire, his portfolio is distinctive for its portrayal of women in their everyday urban practices. Other early modern painters working in Isfahan depicted female subjects, but these were mostly stock figures, arrayed for the education of the senses, to teach male and female audiences how to see and mimetically inscribe their gendered mannerisms. Muhammad Qasim, on the other hand, drew young and elderly women in conversation: women carrying infants, on horseback, smoking a water pipe, or playing the tambourine. These scenes of women busy with quotidian activities suggest that Muhammad Qasim painted for a female clientele (Figure 5.5 and 5.6). For example, in Figure 5.5 we see the image of a melancholic woman. She has let herself go. Distraught and disrobed, her torso is exposed. She contemplates her beloved as she smokes her hookah. By her side stands a jug of wine depicting a drawn image of a female beloved. Much like Afzal Husayni's drawing of the male beloved on a pillow, this is a visual device used by painters to signal the absent beloved. In this female-oriented painting, Muhammad Qasim captures the state of separation so critical to the Sufi practice of love.

The poetry that contextualizes Muhammad Qasim's painting, though added some time after its completion, provides an interpretative frame for this image of melancholia.

> The memory of your neck impressed [*furuʿ*] on me,
> like rays of the sun that cannot be stored

> One hundred odes in praise [*madh*] of you
> Each written on the backs and bottoms of a hundred pages [*jarida*]

> Having written a book of poetry, read not to a soul
> Weave another world [*dunya*] out of your disposition [*tabʿ*]

> I took another path from that loyal companion
> Though, in effort, I struggled

The motifs of unrequited love in this painting move among homosocial subjects, whether female or male. The artist has drawn all the accoutrements of longing and lovesickness, from the cup and jug of wine to the disheveled state of the lover. However, the face of the beloved, drawn on the jug, tells the audience about the subject of desire, inscribing the sex of the beloved friend who may be receiving the painting as a gift. A necklace around the beloved's neck represents sisterhood. The exchange of ritual vows between two sisters was officiated through the gift of a necklace, not unlike that of a wedding ring. The poetry underscores the ritual and the meaning of the necklaces. Physical and carnal, the neck is impressed on the memory of the beloved as a sensuous memento. Yet this homoerotic desire must be hidden. The poetry framing Muhammad Qasim's portrayal of melancholia

FIGURE 5.5 Muhammad Qasim, *Woman Smoking a Pipe*, dated 1650. Topkapi Museum, TSMK, H 2137, fol. 21r. Presidency of the Republic of Turkey, Directorate of National Palaces.

makes the secret explicit. And for those sisters who share dispositions (*tabʿ*) that desire other women, it is in another world, perhaps in the imaginary world of word and image, that female homoerotic love can be materialized and woven into experience.

Female friendships, like their male equivalents, were sanctioned by religious custom. Vows of sisterhood (*sigha-yi khwahar khwandagi*) are recorded in seventeenth-century anthologies belonging to religious judges practicing in Isfahan. In the context of Shi'a law a *sigha* is a legal contract more commonly deployed for contractual relationships such as temporary marriages (*mutʿa*).[18] On the anniversary of Ghadir Khumm, the day when Muhammad purportedly chose Ali as his brother and successor, two sisters take each other's hands and declare, "I seek protection for you in God, I shake hands with you before God, I pledge myself to you for God, and I pledge myself to God, His angels, [His] books, messengers, and sent prophets. And praise be to God, Lord of the Two Worlds." To which the partner replies, "I accept and forfeit all the rights of sisterhood in favor of proximity to God. I take you as a sister before God."[19] Sisters legally entered into sworn friendships as means of attaining intimacy with God, which also allowed for intimacy with one another.

Within the confines of the practice of sisterhood, female intimacy, whether platonic, romantic, or sexual, was a point of contention for some practitioners of Islamic law. For example, female friendships were the subject of a parody by the cleric Aqa Jamal Khwansari (d. 1710), whose family anthology we explored in Chapter 2.[20] His *ʿAqaʾid al-Nisaʾ* (Beliefs of Women), belongs to the genre of essays written by religious scholars that address social issues emerging in their communities, often to clarify practice for those believers who questioned how sharia affected daily life. Aqa Jamal Khwansari derides such female practices as "superstition." The women he ridicules in his social commentary are caricatures, but their beliefs and rituals undoubtedly represent a larger collective culture that impinged on the religious establishment's project of transforming Isfahan residents' social and sexual practices. Comparable to the disciplinary effects that edicts and religious treatises on ethics and morals intended to provoke, the *ʿAqaʾid al-Nisaʾ* endeavors to produce a similar effect through the injurious bite of sarcasm. Aqa Jamal articulates male anxiety around female intimacy through humor, as he speaks of, for instance, husbands who worry about what women might share about their sexual performance in the intimacy of gossiping in the hammam. Moreover, elite circles in Isfahan were small and thrived on gossip and rumors, and it is quite likely that Aqa Jamal Khwansari had caught wind of the scandal that led to the separation between Mirza Khalil's wife and her female companion.

In his *'Aqa'id al-Nisa'* Aqa Jamal describes such friendship rituals: A reputable (*mu'tabar*) and trustworthy woman, a kind of intermediary (*pasabz*), would prepare a wax doll called the *'aruschak* (little bride) and place it on a decorated platform, which she would then send to a prospective sister (*khwahar khwanda*).[21] Accepting an offer of sisterly marriage entailed returning the *'aruschak* crowned with a necklace and rewarding the *pasabz* with a ceremonial honorary robe (*khil'at*). If the offer was refused, a black veil was instead wrapped around the head of the doll before it was sent back. According to Aqa Jamal, the practice could take place between two women unknown to one another. He makes no mention, however, of their marital status. The Urdubadi widow's example shows that female unions occurred between married women, and some, as represented by Muhammad Qasim, struggled with their disposition (*tab'*) when forced to take another path and relinquish their love for a sister, should their relationship fall under societal suspicion. Muhammad Qasim's painting may have been a gift, like a book of poetry inspired by love for another sister, commissioned for a female beloved and never read or shared with another.

In another painting by Muhammad Qasim, three women are drawn in a scene that captures a moment of exchange (Figure 5.6). Two friends sit in front of a bearded man. The woman directly facing the bearded man is engaged in conversation with him as he offers a talisman to the young girl. An inkstand and several loose sheets of paper by his side denote his profession. His extended right hand is cupped, signifying a transaction, as he presents the talisman of magical squares he has drawn on wood. Her right hand is open to its reception. His body language gestures humility, but hers commands respect as a female client who has wrapped her left hand with her robe. She may be bargaining over the price of the commissioned work, while the friend sitting behind her suggests another exchange transpiring on the painting's right margin. This friend has placed one hand on the first woman's shoulder while pointing to her transaction with the bearded man. She looks away from the exchange between patron and client to speak with an elderly woman, perhaps one of the girls' maidservants. The elderly woman holds a flower in her hand, which in poetry symbolizes love, signaling to the viewer that the transaction has to do with the subject of love. With her left hand she points to a location behind the scene, alerting the girls that someone is coming and that

FIGURE 5.6 Muhammad Qasim, *Girls, Woman, and Dervish*, signed "the work of the humble Muhammad Qasim, the painter" and dated 1655. Opaque watercolor and gold on paper (16 cm × 24 cm). Victoria and Albert Museum, Clive Album, I.S. 133-1964, fol. 43r.

they must hurry. The girl seems to be stalling, explaining to the older woman that her friend has not completed her business. It is difficult to speculate who or what the old woman is pointing at, but the fact that she holds a flower in her hand indicates the commissioned talisman's sentimental topic. Although both women wear identical necklaces, the object of the female patron's love is ambiguous. Is the talisman meant for the love of sisterhood? Could the object of love be the absent person beyond the drawing? Is there a love triangle involved? What is clear, at least, is that the woman depicted by Muhammad Qasim is acquiring a talisman to determine an important decision she intends to make. And, as a buyer of this work, she has requested the moment be celebrated with a drawing. Muhammad Qasim encapsulates the fleeting instance of commissioning; with his quick strokes he draws the parties and conditions involved in the inscription of love and fortune. The incitement to communicate and record this talismanic event, which has the power to read and alter the patron's fate, is captured by the painter as proof: another charmlike object to avert melancholy and an ill-fated amorous future.

The sex of the object of love and friendship is unstable in this painting as well as in Muhammad Qasim's representation of melancholia and the Isfahani widow's narrative. All three encapsulate a moment of time in Isfahan when mystic love had been transformed into human love and friendship and where practices of sisterhood, though authorized by religious custom, were subject to scrutiny and discipline. It is in this context that we should read the inclusion, by the Urdubadi scribe, of the widow's *masnavi* in her family anthology. He prefaces her account as one that describes places and names throughout her journey from Isfahan to Mecca and Urdubad, but he draws on the features of a genre of travel writing in which the widow also engages (see Map 0.1). He does not remark on the way that she transforms this genre to express her own emotional experiences. Nor does the scribe consider the emotions the widow divulges in her encounter with her female companion as suspect or taboo, because she writes within the conventions of friendship. She situates herself in the affective language of sisterhood and piety, where friendship is a form of amity that guides partners toward the true friend, the divine. Perhaps the scribe reads her ambivalence as evidence of false rumors circulating about their friendship; that she did not act on her love for her companion is proof of her piety and love for God. We will never know exactly how the scribe interpreted the widow's writing; what is certain is that he did not consider her narrative as blemishing her honor or that of the family. His honorific inscription of the widow has little to do with her transgressive friendship. Every powerful Muslim woman had to be purified to appear in premodern writings; for the Urdubadi woman to be inscribed in her family archive, she had to be cleansed of any possible stain of impurity. The widow's story therefore draws on ambiguity to allow for her inscription. Just like the talismanic event depicted by Muhammad Qasim in his painting of the melancholic female lover, these ambiguous records are preserved in anthologies as archival traces of the past containing possibilities for future friendships.

Leaving Isfahan: On Friends and Kin

What the historical archive silences, the family archive can make visible. The secret in the context of archiving has been the subject of conversations inspired by Michel Foucault's reading of the archive as shadows that bring into focus what the collector foregrounds.[22] In thinking about the anthology as an archive or as an act of writing, collecting, and selecting, it is not just what is in the shadows, what is hidden or lost to history, that is inscribed in Isfahan's household anthologies; the secret itself appears as a sign of the sacred that selectively reveals to the reader what is being concealed.[23] The secret marked in the anthology does not operate as an erasure or as a mechanism for forgetting traces from the past; rather, it protects the sacred from the ordinary space of the anthology. In the politics of curating Isfahan's household archives, what is concealed and revealed together provide a way of seeing and knowing where and how the everyday and the spiritual merged in the lives of residents. Analogous to the widow's spiritual journey, as captured in her narrative, it is in the absence of the human beloved that love for the divine is materialized on paper. We recall that for the urbane city disturber Aqa Mansur, the conflict between one's devotion to God and one's devotion to earthly friendships was resolved; love for one did not preclude love for the other. As we listen to the voice of the Isfahani widow, however, we find these tensions at the core of her emotional turmoil.

Born into a genealogy of masters of the word, it is not surprising that the nameless widow of Mirza Khalil is an erudite poet; what stands out is not the exceptionalism of her literacy but her gendered introduction. The scribe presents the female poet as "the pure, chaste, and honorable one, the Queen of Sheba and the Khadija of our age, the beautiful lawful one [*hilya-yi jalila*], the graceful [widow of] Mirza Khalil." We do not know her name. It is only by association with her deceased husband, the personal secretary of the Safavi Shah Sulayman, along with wise and powerful Muslim female icons—the prophet's first wife, herself a widow, and the Queen of Sheba—that the scribe identifies her. In his foreword to her *masnavi* (1,200 verses), the scribe informs us that she composed her poetry as she exited Isfahan on her journey to Mecca. She "uttered and wrote names and depicted landscapes, close and afar, between Isfahan and the Ka'ba during her travels to her place of origin [*makan-i asli*], Urdubad."[24] The three cities of Isfahan, Urdubad, and Mecca, all familiar homes of sorts, emerge as intimate spaces of attachment that she recalls, it turns out, by way of three beloveds, three objects of her love (*yar*): God, her husband, and her female companion.

The Urdubadi widow is called to reassess her own ethical and sentimental commitments at a historical moment when affective languages of friendship, kinship, and romance are being reconfigured; as a result of the hardening of lines between friendship and eros, the contours of love for her three *yar*s surface in tension and in writing. Inspired by poetry and didactic manuals describing devotional practices at the holiest of Muslim shrines, this woman's narrative draws on a variety of modes of representing love and the pilgrimage's sacred geography to write her act of repentance at the Ka'ba. An avid reader, she evokes the twelfth-century poet Nizami as her favorite, quoting from his romance *Layli and Majnun*. However, she also deploys mystic discourses on love to associate herself with the madman Majnun, a man, and translates her composition into the contemporary mode of realist expression.[25] Although *Layli and Majnun* is evoked in the preface of her family archive, it does not appear in the folios of the Urdubadi anthology. The romance was like a kindred friend that had become embedded in the family ethos. The widow was experimenting with realist poetics to speak about her attachments, love, loss, delights, and mood swings; her voice is direct and charged with psychological insight. Familiar built and natural environments trigger associations with relatives and friends, and her circular movement in and out of space divulge these connections. Between spaces of affect, her detours are the rhetorical moves she solicits to leave and then return to her melancholy. Each departure provides the audience with different layers of the ties that bind her to place and kin.

Hoping to fill the void created by her husband's death, the widow sets off on her pilgrimage around the end of the seventeenth century. She chooses to narrate her pious journey in verse, informing the audience of her decision to make the Hajj at the beginning of her story. "Since the wiles of fortune [*charkh-i hila pardaz*] left my heart burning with sorrow due to the absence [*firaq*] of my intimate companion [*yar*] . . . I vowed to circumambulate the holy Ka'ba." She continues, "I tied myself around the holy Ka'ba," perhaps turning her bodily self into a vow.[26] She tells of her sleepless nights and tormented days: "I saw no solution other than travel [*siyahat*],"[27] communicating her state in the poetic form of the *masnavi*, used to narrate romances such as that of *Layli and Majnun*. She refers to both her husband and God with the terms *rafiq* and *yar*, which are defined as "companion" and "friend" in a Sufi culture of love that places loyalty and devotion at its heart. Once she leaves Isfahan, her affective ties come into view; physical distance brings the urban landscape, her social relations of family and friends, into memory and writing.[28]

In the process of telling her story, the widow reveals another, earlier experience of loss that, as a respectable married woman in Isfahan, she had borne secretly for many years: a forced separation from another *rafiq* and *yar*, her Isfahani female companion now living in Urdubad. This friendship had generated suspicion, with rumors circulating in Isfahan about their relationship to such an extent that her friend was forced to leave the city. The widow's experience of the absence of and longing for her friend, her illness and recovery, are all narrated as part of a curative process of purification and transcendence. Messages from the divine in the guise of a birdsong, musical instrument, or a natural phenomenon such as the wind are literary motifs that suffuse the widow's poignant expression. Her spiritual quest will be solitary, for none of her relatives will accompany her on her journey: "Not one became my friend [*yar*]." But she reminds and comforts herself: "Who needs a human companion? God is the *rafiq* of the forlorn."[29] Hurt by the betrayal of relatives (*khwishan u 'azizan*), she leaves Isfahan like a "violent wind [*sarsar*]." Using the figure of Majnun, who, destitute and deprived of his beloved Layli, wanders the desert, the widow writes, "Alone I rode off to circumambulate the House of the Dispenser of Justice."[30] Audiences familiar with this romance would certainly sympathize with Majnun, who was refused for a son-in-law by Layli's father before going on the Hajj, at the behest of his own father, to remedy his lovesickness. Pressing him to embrace God, the supreme patriarch with the ultimate authority to decide the fate of human lives, Majnun's father attempts to dissuade his son from earthly love and urges him to recite a prayer at the Ka'ba, asking God to cure him of his love for Layli.

Like Majnun, the widow chooses to fill her absence with the fullness of God at the Ka'ba and to walk through the very spaces that the prophet Muhammad and his family had inhabited. There, she trusts she will unite with the Truth. A persistent call, which she hears and at times describes as a song, draws her toward Mecca, filling her with excitement and propelling her forward along an arduous terrain: from Isfahan, northward to the Caucasus, through eastern Anatolia, Syria, and ultimately southward to Arabia. The pilgrim, aware of the journey's difficulties, is afraid. But her fear must be conquered, and so the brave widow, using the language of chivalry at the start of her journey, "tied her belt and wore her armband." We admire her decision taking: "I washed my heart from the fear of danger. I wrote my trip's divination as auspicious."[31]

The journey to Mecca and Medina was arduous and challenging for pilgrims, requiring travel through rough terrain, including mountains, highlands, rivers, and finally deserts, and across territories held by the hosts of the Hajj, the Ottomans.[32] In this narrative of separation and longing with mystical themes, symbols, and metaphors, the widow divulges herself in both familiar and foreign landscapes. How, then, might the consistent use of Sufi terminology related to absence and longing configure her subjectivity, let alone shape the representation of her journey, which is punctuated by religious experiences, nostalgia for Isfahan, the discovery of such kindred cities as Aleppo, and a return to her birthplace, Urdubad? One answer is that, although she relies on conventional Sufi rhetoric of absence and longing to explain her condition, the Isfahani widow also inscribes her narrative within the male-dominated poetics of the realist school. In her ability to become a historical subject, she deliberately intervenes in changing and shaping the masculinist language, moving among discursive possibilities in writing her affective and ethical commitments. She constantly enters and exits the modes of realist poetry to particularize her experiences and variegated moods. Hence the widow's decision to embark on the pilgrimage and her self-association with Majnun manifest the contours of her imaginal structure, giving shape to a habitus wounded by loss. Tensions arise as she assimilates a relationship of similitude among her three *yar*s. She draws from devotional practices of pilgrimage to the Ka'ba and the familiar image of Majnun as a melancholic prototype to create categories of affinity across genders, which, though identical in name (*yar* or *rafiq*), are nonetheless distinct in their essence.

What are we to make of our penitent's evocation of the example of Majnun, who failed in his endeavor to repent from loving Layli? The pious act of repentance, she hopes, will provide the cure for her love toward another woman, which was condemned by Islamic law and seventeenth-century Isfahani society.[33] However, unlike the Layli and Majnun story, the widow evokes not a singular beloved but rather three. She wishes to relinquish the love she had for her old companion, but her pilgrimage is also prompted by the death of her husband and further inflamed by complex feelings of grief and anxiety; these are the emotions she foregrounds as critical to her decision to go on the Hajj. Is the husband's early appearance in the narrative something of a social requirement and pretext that preface the account of her female friend? I suggest that for the Isfahani widow, love was an albeit problematic emotion that she felt for both of her life companions. But, as we will see, the modalities of her love are different.

On her way out of Isfahan, the widow first stops at her husband's grave, her friend's (*yar*'s) "rose garden." Tears pour from her eyes, "turning into a stream of blood." When she walks away from his tomb, "a wail sounded off my bones like a reed flute" and cried, "Since you are deprived of union with your dear friend, become a nightingale in his rose garden."[34] So she stays the night, like the symbolic nightingale that sings in the secret language of divine love. There, beside her husband, she dozes peacefully until dawn, when she suddenly weeps aloud like the nightingale. Heavyhearted, she picks herself up and begins her journey of pilgrimage. This is the last time the widow mentions her deceased husband.

We are not told why she decides to travel north to the Caucasus and visit her Isfahani friend. Perhaps in this passionate moment, she felt freed of her husband; certainly her loss of him made the sting of her previous loss fresh again. As the story unfolds, it becomes clear that their separation was forced because of rumors of their intimacy when they both still resided in Isfahan. Now the widow travels to reunite with her other lost love, whom she describes with the very terms of endearment she used for both her husband and God (*yar u rafiq*). In Tabriz, located in northwestern Iran, where she makes a detour drawn by the proximity of the homeland, she begins to long to visit her birthplace: "Once I encountered Tabriz, I was overwhelmed by desire for my Urdubad" (see Map 0.1).[35] The desire to visit a friend and the desire to visit her homeland are intimately related. We find a consistent sense of the power of space associated with the holy house of God, Isfahan, and her birthplace; sacred and profane sites alike stimulate a physical pull in her, merging in a sanctifying process and providing momentary relief from her melancholy state. Over the Aras River, she travels by boat to "my Urdubad." Having heard of her arrival, relatives and acquaintances—old and young, men and women—assemble along the banks of the river (*pishvaz*): "With kindness and affection my relatives greeted me and took me to the house of my generous companion [*rafiq*]," she says.[36]

> Together in Isfahan we had been companions [*yar*],
> in spirit we ate each other's sorrow
> She was a relative better than any sister,
> kinder than any of my other relatives
> But suddenly, Heaven's playful tricks
> appeared on the stage of deceit
> So much so that it [Heaven] hid that kind one from my gaze,
> as a body is separated from its soul

> Forty houses they placed between us,
> and inflicted separation between our two bodies
> For our hearts no cure save constraint,
> in separation [*hijran*], both of us have waited a century
> 'Til, at last, the end of the night of torturous separation
> turned into the morning of spiritual union
> After a century, I saw the face of that friend [*yar*]
> and I threw my baggage into her house
> The remedy [*dava'*] for the incurable [*bidarman*] pain of separation
> was patience and endurance, O dear one.[37]

The structure of affect communicated by the widow moves between the social and the physical: whether in invoking the city of Isfahan, where their friendship evolved, or in the forced bodily separation rendered material by the distance of forty houses, she associates her friend with the intimacy of kinship; her friend is better than even a sister, kinder than a relative. The widow inhabits the world through significant attachments to Isfahan, her kin, and her friends and through the relationality she conjures among them. She weaves poetic conventions that draw on hegemonic metaphors of longing and separation, sensibilities engraved in the hearts of those acquainted with mystical epics and romances, to perform and represent her own lived experience. Although she was inspired by a repertoire of mystic poets, such as Rumi and Nizami, we hear the unfolding of the widow's story through her own compositional agency and her selective assembly of words and images.

In the encounter with her long-lost female companion, the widow collapses. She "throws [down] her baggage in her friend's house" and shows her vulnerability, at least physically. She often shifts from the first person to the second and third person when addressing her audience and friend, as though blurring the boundaries between her self, her beloved, and society.

> Happily, I spent some time at my hostess's,
> that Isfahani companion of mine
> O kind friend, O old companion
> you did not deny me your sweet soul
> I was so nurtured by you
> as though fallen from the heavens

But my fortune did not comply,
I was exhausted, the whole time I was suffering,
afflicted with fever [*tab*] and torment [*azar*]
Not for a moment was I able
to be her partner in conversation [*ham suhbat*].[38]
I did not become intimate [*ulfati*]
with that good-natured one.[39]

The widow is sick and aloof, unlike her friend who is openly emotional, expressive, and giving. "I was ashamed in front of my friend," the widow tells us. "You bore pain constantly on my behalf. You grieved over my suffering. You became even more brokenhearted because of my distance [*duri*]."[40] Her bodily condition or disposition undergirds a particular modality of relation to her friend; in her friend's presence she breaks down and perhaps recovers from her malady of love. In contrast to the scene at her husband's grave, where she experiences peace and calm, the torment she felt before her journey, back in Isfahan, returns to haunt her at her friend's house. Only in God's abode will she experience feeling in a nonbodily manner and temporarily unite with the divine beloved. However, as we will see in Mecca, her experience of the divine will be of another essence.

In reunion with her female beloved, the widow undergoes a role reversal: She relinquishes her narrative persona as lover (*'ashiq*), transforming herself into the object (*mahbub*) of her companion's desire. But on the day of her departure, when she hears the nightingale's song once more, her loyal companion reverts to the status of the beloved who sinks into sorrow. "That day, until dinner, that dear one had no bread, water, or any other food," the widow declares. "You hid the world-illuminating love by drowning your face in the abyss of the deep sea. She cried bloody tears—purple tears poured from her eyelashes like rain onto her skirt. She cried so much, this loyal relative, that a new grief befell me [*matam-i naw shud padidar*]." Addressing us, the widow confesses that the sorrow she had felt during the first separation was again renewed, in all its pain and agony. But the widow remains withdrawn. Instead, her female relatives commiserate and comfort (*yari numudand*) the aggrieved beloved; together "they cried over my departure."[41] Why this cold impassiveness toward her old companion, especially when the widow admits her renewed grief? Was she afraid of divulging the extent of the love she felt for her friend, particularly in the presence of her relatives? Perhaps she wanted to publicly deny the old rumors and declare her renunciation of this illicit love. Although her relatives seem to have known about their secret love, nonetheless they step in to support her, ironically arresting the widow's complete reconciliation with her friend. Was she ambivalent about leaving her friend, about continuing on the pilgrimage despite her vow? Did grief rekindle the widow's love for her old companion to such a degree that it cast doubt on the real object of true love? Or, again, was her grief part of the trope of longing and separation, constituent of the experience of pilgrimage and of mystical writing about love?

The widow reveals how much she loves her friend the minute she leaves her, her family, and her native land of Urdubad. Although she had missed Urdubad and voiced joy at seeing her family members again, her focus was trained on her friend. Once she leaves Urdubad, she resumes the role of amorous lover (*'ashiq*). She does not sleep well that night and the next day cannot enjoy a stroll in a beautiful garden: "What good is it for me to seek pleasure in a rose garden empty of the ultimate soul? I saw no rose, nor plucked one from that garden. I only cried there from loneliness and separation."[42] Still the song, which from the beginning had drawn her out of Isfahan, pulls her again toward the Ka'ba. "Since you have become saddened after the separation from your companion, go toward the House of Truth," the song seems to convey. "Do not be gloomy due to parting from your sweetheart. Hurry up, ride your camel, place your load atop the melancholy [*sawda'*] of separation from your friend [*yar*]."[43]

Stepping into the Ottoman domains in the city of Karamanlar, the widow feels out of place. The familiarity and kinship she had experienced on her long journey provided a comforting security in the "domains of the Shah of Iran."[44] This refuge is lost when she exits Safavi Iran, where "we are like valiant lions [*shir-i zhiyan*]," and enters the Ottoman lands, "where in fear we turn into mice [*mush*]."[45] But in Aleppo, which she visits for the first time, she experiences an uncanny vision of her longtime home.

> I recognized Aleppo as resembling Isfahan
> A twin to Iran, I saw Aleppo
> Its stalls, its bazaars and its *maydan*
> Well-endowed like Isfahan
> Of every kind of fruit, there was plenty
> Lending force and tranquility to the body

> Eat of its figs, they are like sugar candy
> No, I misspoke; [they're] more like the water of life
> Its people kinder than sisters
> Sisters, no better even, sacrificial mothers
> I saw Aleppo as Isfahan's twin
> Bloody tears poured down my eyes
> That day, I recollected [*yad*] my home [*vatan*]
> Releasing a burning [*jahansuz*] shriek
> I remembered my children and relatives
> Like a reed flute, I cried and screamed[46]

In riveting, emotionally wrought verse, the rhythms of her encounters and her reflections come to the fore as Aleppo's built environment and the kindness of its residents recall her affective associations with Isfahan. We walk with her through the central square, surrounded by stalls and bazaars, the streets full of people shopping and tasting seasonal fruits sold in stalls; we recognize the urban habits that have inscribed her every day in Isfahan. Exposure to Aleppines' native warmth, the familiarity of social forms and urban architecture, and the abundance of provisions and goods in the streets produce a cascading effect in her, summoning a visceral memory of her adopted home. Although the widow was born in Urdubad and she continues to refer to it as "my Urdubad," it is Isfahan that is her home, her *vatan*, where her children and relatives reside and where a particular aesthetics of urbanity fashions her appreciation of cities.[47] The distribution of the sensible by means of a familiar urban sensibility leads her to cry as she remembers her home (*vatan*), her children (*farzandan*), and her relatives (*khwishan*). Once again, it is in absence that she conjures Isfahan as her *vatan* and voices her affection for her kin. The way people communicate their warmth, the measure of sacrificial care, and a familiar urban sensibility not only stir a recognizable longing in the widow but also, just as important, allow her to read Aleppo. These urban features mark her experience of Aleppo, a new city that she assimilates into her affective landscape.

Still, the anticipation of Mecca, of walking in the footsteps of the prophet Muhammad and performing the Hajj, incites her to move on. As she first espies, from a distance, the holy city of Mecca, her ecstasy is almost palpable. "The night of separation between spirits has ended," she declares. "Eyes have been illuminated in union with the Friend. Everyone has washed their hearts from Satan's whispers;

they have expelled the kindness of friends from their chests. Toward the Ka'ba's stone they all face. Sorrow and grief they cast away."[48] The medieval poet Nizami's verse comes to her mind: "How wonderful it is, after a wait, for the hopeful to attain their hope [*umid*]."[49] She even proclaims that her "fortune came to such fruition, that from the excitement [*shawq*] of union, I lost consciousness." Then, stepping through the Gate of Peace (*salam*)—the first entryway to the Ka'ba—she sets her eyes on the house of God and begins to weep, feeling beyond words to describe the holy site. She cannot utter a word to thank God, nor does she have the presence of mind to laugh and be happy. She faints, and even though she regains consciousness after an hour, she remains speechless. But once able to "untie the knot that had restricted her tongue," she begins her surrender to God, praising his omnipotence, knowledge, and endless grace. She thanks her creator for the favor (*tawfiq*) he has granted: "You gave me both wealth and life. You brought me to my goal [*maqsad*] and my desire [*matlub*]."[50] She humanizes the Ka'ba, cloaked in black with a golden belt tied around its waist; its face covered with the kisses of pilgrims, the Ka'ba is her beloved.[51] Although she claims that it is incomparable, she associates the Ka'ba with a beautiful youth (*nawjavani*) and a lofty flowing cypress tree (*sarv-i ravani*), deploying Persianate mystic poetry's ungendered metaphors of divine beauty. Standing before the Ka'ba, she cannot tell if she is dreaming or awake.

> Carrying the weight of a hundred tons of crimes and sins,
> I turned my face toward the circumambulating God's Alley
> After seven circles my shoulder became lightened,
> from the weight of my sins [*gunah*]
> As I began to enumerate my transgressions,
> I emptied my leather bag all the way to the bottom
> I cleansed my crimes [*jurm*] with water from my eyes,
> My sins were numerous and the path so short
> Upon the seventh turn of my guilt I repaired my ruined heart,
> I sought the road of forgiveness and washed away my filthy crime
> I drank a sip of Zamzam's water,
> Sorrow, pain, and affliction were all forgotten
> The water's purity enlivened my body and cured my diseased [*bimar*] heart,
> At the House of God, I apologized for my crime
> Like a beggar I began to cry,

> What shall I say, in negligence my life was wasted
> In Your Abode no honor remains for me,
> Woe to me if You do not forgive my crime,
> Hell shall be my dwelling place,
> Since performing the pilgrimage of women, I have kicked Satan's face,
> my heart has been cleansed of his whispers
> I shall not allow my heart to engage in bad deeds[52]

The widow vividly illustrates her remorse and shame. Although she deploys mimetic rituals of preforming the Hajj, she communicates her psychological and spiritual experience through external, visual means; thus the architecture of Mecca, from its gate to the House of God to its alleys and the path that surrounds it, all become part of her realist aesthetic. To recount her ways of inhabiting the Hajj, she divulges her negligence and apologizes for what she characterizes as her filthy crimes; it is in body and virtue that she renounces her diseased heart, kicking Satan's face in accordance with the rites of the pilgrimage of women. To atone for her satanic sins, she cuts her hair and has a camel sacrificed. She expels the human kindness of her companion from her chest and turns her face toward the divine beloved to cure her "diseased" heart. The widow seeks forgiveness from God; it is in relationship to God that friendship reaches its apotheosis.

This pilgrim's devotional act comes to naught. Only when circumambulating the Ka'ba and encountering God does she feel cleansed of this forbidden love. The moment she leaves the Ka'ba, her grief and longing come flooding back to haunt her. Once the pilgrimage has been completed, she turns back toward Isfahan, passing again through Aleppo. Woefully she cries, "How pleasant was the Ka'ba! How worthy was the going, and how empty is the return."[53] The tensions between profane and sacred love and friendship that torment the widow motivate her journey away from Isfahan toward her three *yar*s; however, these tensions are never resolved. The figure of the friend gives form to the widow's relationships with her husband, her female companion, and God. Friendship, for the widow, is an emotional experience of that cardinal virtue of love, and it is through the language of kinship that she weaves strangers and acquaintances together to establish her communal ties and the affinities that construct home and city. Even though friendship is the practice that produces her social attachments and her deep spiritual relationship with the divine, her ethical commitment requires a choice between friendship with her female companion and friendship with God. And so, the widow's story also brings to the fore a tension in the Urdubadi family anthology, which proclaims itself to be a reflection of divine assembly, its very pages bound as though according to the logic of creation. Yet here, in the journey from Isfahan to Mecca, the valences of both human and divine friendship rest in an uneasy balance; human friendship is never entirely erased in mystical union, just as divine friendship never recedes from the profane sights and sounds of the cityscape. The anthology not only collects and curates these tensions but also teaches us to read them; perhaps, we might speculate, it also helped early modern anthologizers to live with them.

We do not know if the widow makes it back to Isfahan. Her narrative ends in the middle of a folio with another blank page following the scribe's recording. Was there more to her story that the scribe anticipated he would include? Did she go back to Urdubad or did she die on the road? We probably will never know. What we do know is that the widow's tormented, ambivalent affections provide spaces of reflection; like the letter or the face of the beloved, these affects are mirrors of the soul. Separation and melancholy are themselves sites of knowing God as well as the unfolding of the religious and desiring self. Revealed in her writing and preserved in her household anthology, the widow's story has become a space for the genesis of other female friendships, an example of the agency of the anthology itself.

CONCLUSION

The Erotics of Urbanity

In *The City as Anthology* I read household anthologies as verbal and visual archives of an entwined urban and erotic form of knowledge that is typically overlooked in the historiography of seventeenth-century Isfahan. Eight residents acted as protagonists in this early modern history of Isfahan (see Map 0.1). By anthologizing their experience of the city, they wrote their relationship to the habitus they helped shaped. Seven men and one woman enacted the gestures, manners, and sensibilities of a shared culture of *adab* that configured their social and erotic relations. Schooled in the politics and aesthetics of Isfahan, residents deployed different media to embody what I have termed urbanity, displaying their mastery of the *adab* of sociability and flaunting their knowledge of the city and its ways. From king to widow, painter to religious scholar, poet to bureaucrat, their authorial voices and habits of writing, reading, seeing, and desiring have grounded my analysis of the urban. A shared phenomenology emerges from these anthologies as residents learned to see the beauty of Isfahan, realized how to read eros in its beauty, cultivated desire for the coy gestures of the beloved, and studied the protocols of writing love in letters to friends. These intimately entangled acts—seeing, reading, desiring, and writing—converge to fashion the urban self through the sensual and the sexual. As authors, the eight protagonists of this book made the city their own, writing their quotidian engagement with friends, kin, and clients and dynamically divulging the many dimensions of the social, cultural, and religious spheres of life in Isfahan.

Furthermore, these anthologies posit a highly refined sensuality as the prism through which the recognition of a subjective self, family, and beloved friend become tangible in the context of the beauty of Isfahan. The prominence of 'ishq—the mystic love that is desiring—in household anthologies underscores the emotional apparatus that enables us to trace these protagonists' encounter with Isfahan. Inhabitants deployed the idiom of mystic love to produce their urbanity and exhibit their refinement. Whether as collectors or authors of letters, poetry, drawings, manuals, or essays, men mobilized the idealized rhetoric of beauty and love, fetishized in the figure of the male youth, to engage in politics and to fashion their masculine bonds. Among the cast of characters in this history, one king, Shah Abbas I, composed his anthology in the form of a central square (the Naqsh-i Jahan, analogized to the image of the world) adorned with wall paintings and epigraphy illustrating paradise with all its material delights, including homoerotic pleasures, for residents and visitors to view and to be seduced by. Shah Abbas I's authorizing act, aimed at converting his subjects to Shi'ism, drew men and women into the urban public sphere, which, as this book has shown, was also a sphere of intimate affects. Although it was articulated in a range of idioms and scales, the representation of male homoerotism was ideologically and materially central to Isfahan's social and moral fabric, engraved as it was from the walls of the city center to the images and words collected on sheets of paper in households. Even though household anthologies and their male authors speak in the privileged language of patriarchy, the anthologies themselves were domestic objects, pedagogical tools with which family members across gendered lines could educate themselves and cultivate their relations with kin and friends. In particular, the pedagogical material gathered in anthologies served to educate household members in the *adab* of sociability and decorum. In this respect, gender difference does not seem to matter much in the practice of intimate friendship, where *'ishq* is the ubiquitous emotion that signifies spiritual, familial, and amical ties. The words of one female resident, the Urdubadi widow, illustrate that she too marshaled the rituals and language of mystic love to inscribe her relationship to God, her deceased husband, and a beloved female friend. Although the Urdubadi widow provides suggestive evidence for the practice of intimate female friendships, the question of the practice and acceptance of female homoeroticism more broadly remains speculative. Nonetheless, as manifest in the central square, homoerotic affects were nothing less than world-making, and embodied desire was imagined and lived as a site of both power and resistance.

Muhammad Qasim's drawing of the bastinade on the cover of my book encapsulates the social shape and significance of erotic desire for the experience of masculine *adab* in Isfahan. Educating the male child entailed the solicitation but also the taming of homoerotic desire with a disciplinary stick, a technique with which youth were trained into the patriarchal order. The initiation of an apprentice into the circle of his master painter, Muhammad Qasim, reproduces communal hierarchies and symmetries according to age and rank. Men with beards and mustaches bear the regalia of power, from the stick to the book, the pen, and the rosary. A shared performance of *adab* marks the bodily comportment of Muhammad Qasim; in gesture and gaze he embodies the knowledge of the arts and eros, authorizing its transmission to initiate subservient beardless youth into the proper politics of sexuality. Asymmetries of standing between master and student intersect with symmetric associations between friends under the scrutiny of two masters, one of the craft and the other of the spiritual brotherhood. Model affective ties, arranged according to the concepts of *'ishq* and the protocols of friendship, bound together men of all ages in configuring fraternal communities of learning. The didactic message of the bastinade signals to the audience that *'ishq* must also be governed by the *adab* of urbanity to safeguard the prescribed moral and social order. Inscribed in students' notebooks as a first lesson, *'ishq* is to be practiced according to established codes of behavior to ensure the apprentices' submission to their master painter and loyalty to their friends and co-workers. In this context of patronage and apprenticeship, erotic desire operates both through resistance and disavowal, highlighting the social condition that produces sensual affirmation. A traffic of affect, involving pain, pleasure, fear, and agony, forge the emotional bonds that establish social relations. Muhammad Qasim's *Bastinade* signals how sexual desire is experienced through intimate contact with male bodies, as it gives visual form to the epistemology of sexuality that renders intelligible the mutual obligations and the reciprocal relationship binding men in networks at work, at court, in the seminary, and in the city.

In *The City as Anthology* I draw on the analytical purchase of eroticism to provide a distinct vantage point onto the connections between urbanity, friendship, and spirituality. Although this project began by treating the anthology as a genre to understand the city that incited its production, the homoerotic vista provided by the anthologies I consider here tendered a cognitive panorama of Isfahan with a view into how the city was materially and affectively performed. Adopting a different way of doing history in the field of early modern Persianate studies, I focus on a discrete moment in the story of Isfahan—when the lines of force between eroticism and passionate friendship were being reinforced—to think more broadly with historians of sexuality about the valences of erotic desires that bound together networks of friends living in previous centuries. Inspired by historian Alan Bray's scholarship on sworn friendships, I adopt his mode of social history by locating religiously sanctioned male bonds within systems of affect and kinship.[1] One of the important contributions of his analysis of Western Europe is that intimate male friendship provided both the terms of social cohesion and the means of its disruption. Moreover, I take up literary critic Valerie Traub's invitation to "think sex with the early moderns," which involves confronting those moments when the meanings of sexuality and eroticism are far from transparent.[2] In an effort to bring the practices of history into dialogue with queer and feminist methodologies, Traub exploits the opacity of sex as a productive way to lay bare the difficulties and impasses historians elide when, and if, we write about our conceptual frames and processes of making sexual knowledge. To this methodological common purpose, I bring the multiple representations and significations of the Persianate concept of *'ishq* to bear through my eight character studies. Considerable historical context informs my reading of the contours and tensions with which residents of Isfahan mobilized the power and pleasures of eros to write and display their *adab* in anthologies.

In this book I explore the capacity for social cohesion that homosocial and homoerotic intimacy awarded and the threat of disruption such intimacy carried over the course of the seventeenth century in a city experiencing exponential growth in wealth, immigration, and public surveillance. To properly historicize the emotions that animated friendships, I focus on the figure of the friend represented in letters, paintings, and love poetry. Collected in household anthologies, the presence of so many epistolary manuals and model letters to a friend (*rasa'il-i ikhvaniyyat*), as well as the personal letters exchanged by friends, first struck me as remarkable. But as I collated fragments of evidence of vows of friendship (*sigha-yi ukhuvvat*), gifts of drawings to friends, and model and personal letters, I began to understand them as speaking to a convention that was far from unusual for the residents who collected them, gifted them, learned from them, and wrote their own loving letters to friends in and outside Isfahan. The visual and verbal language of eroticism that friends deployed to convey their moods and dispositions, drawn from already resonant mystic love poetry (*ghazal*), have guided my critical inquiry into the urban history of Isfahan. This language has directed me toward the built environment and the material experience of urban objects, to see, smell, taste, and hear so as to consume eros, for it is these sensual experiences that engendered the lived experience of Isfahan for the one female and seven male characters in this book.

Although my focus is on my protagonists' shared epistemic affinities of sexuality—grounded in affect, kinship, and intimacy—I also compare the affinities to those of other temporalities and geographies. My aim is to provide sufficient historical specificity to the practice of friendship and the forging of social relations so as to facilitate a dialogic engagement between early modern Persianate studies with early modern sexuality studies. By means of my analysis, we can see both similarities and differences with the Western world while adding some thickness to our broader knowledge of sexuality. Thinking sex with the early moderns has compelled me to see erasures that today silence passionate friendships and that obscure the entangled history that love shares with eros and beauty. The early modernity of homoeroticism archived in seventeenth-century household anthologies extends the possibility of the analysis of gender and sexuality to loving friendships that established amical communities in other geographies and temporalities.[3] Whether moving the dialogue eastward to Delhi or westward to Istanbul, Damascus, Cairo, Paris, and London, my project details how erotic sensibilities forged social collectives that shaped the habitus of early modern Isfahan. By the middle of the seventeenth century, residents of Isfahan lived under a new regime of public surveillance, in which a range of techniques and procedures were deployed by the Safavi court, together with the Twelver Shi'a mosque and seminary, to discipline the body's sexuality and the homoerotic culture of urbanity. The stigmatization of homoeroticism and its association with sodomy and boy gazing would reemerge with nationalist projects that rewrote gender roles and sexual desires for Iranian citizens. Here, I posit an early modern genealogy for the *longue durée* history of tensions operative in the erotics of beauty and embodied desire. In her *Women with Mustaches and Men Without Beards*, Afsaneh Najmabadi has masterfully demonstrated how, by the turn of the twentieth-century, Iran's nationalism closeted the male beloved (*amrad*) and unveiled women to cleanse homosocial spaces from the taint of erotic desire.[4] My history of Isfahan presents an *early* emergence of heteroerotic anxieties, provoked by the *adab* of urban love and Sufi homoerotic desire, that in the twentieth century were recuperated to make Iran modern. The contradiction of the sex-gender system underpinning the early modern gendered order at the Safavi court and the city of Isfahan illustrates how male sexual patronage and apprenticeship was practiced through asymmetries of age and rank, authorizing the possibility and visibility of behaviors subversive to that order, to simultaneously cultivate heteroerotic or disguised male homoerotic desire, thus laying the conditions for modernity in Iran to produce its heterosexuality.

* * *

Even though I assume that households discussed, enacted, shared, and compared their curations, I am unable to hear these exchanges. Given this, it is important to acknowledge my choice of the noun *curation* and the verb *curating* to describe the work of both my subjects and myself. As I probe the subjective processes of making urban knowledge, my curation of these anthologies highlights my subject's own curatorial process of collecting material, recording segments of essays and poems, and choosing personal and private letters or talismans. It is these processes, I argue, that composed not only the anthologizing of the city but also the procedures and methods of sex and gender knowledge production.

To investigate the power and the resistance that embodied ideals of love and eros elicited—from the scripted city square to the conventions of model friendship letters—I provide a contrapuntal example of Aqa Mansur's city disturber, because this figure makes public the tensions between spiritual and carnal love. Aqa Mansur's city disturbance is a revelation; he divulges the identity of his beloved Aqa Husayn Ali and makes his secret love a public certainty. Disrupting the *adab* of love's decorum, he evokes the eyelashes of his beloved wrestler, which have "the force of the arm of love," with "the power to pierce open the gazer's heart," so much that he loses consciousness in the *maydan* (central square) and faints in the face of his beloved's beauty in the very space of sovereign authorization. Aqa Mansur explicitly voices the emotional and material processes that his disturbance entailed: "I restrain myself from the tip of my pen upon the page of tulip quality because according to the law [sharia] of *adab*, it is forbidden to write about these hidden secrets [*raz-i nihan*] and unveil them [*parda gusha*] in public."[5] Aqa Mansur deploys the city and sensory travel through it as a remedy, a means to experience love and transform the mystic state of abstention and separation from God into a state of ecstatic carnal encounter. In the street of the rag sellers, he guides the reader to imagine the collective body of male beloveds, which he disrobes, starting with the belt and moving all the way to the belly button. Crossing the lines between secrecy and disclosure, Aqa Mansur points his pen at the rag seller's belly button, inviting his readers to imagine the rest. Of significance here is the symbolic language that Aqa Mansur uses to produce erotic knowledge, a shared repository of signs familiar to the entire cast of characters, which gives meaning to the range of erotic sensibilities that fashion urban selves.

Aqa Mansur ends his education of the senses on the rag seller's street with a rebuke to his readers, critiquing those who falsely accused these men of sodomy (*livat*). Rag sellers are sincere lovers whose papermaking craft is the medium for representing intercourse (*sukhan*).[6] Playing on the meaning of the word *intercourse*, Aqa Mansur equates the *adab* of speech (*sukhan*) with the *adab* of erotic desire (*sukhan*), unambiguously merging these two semantic fields of *sukhan* implicit in the discourse of *adab*. His speech classifies eloquence as a modality of the art of flirtation. It was the flamboyant mannerism of sellers of rags, according to Aqa Mansur, that ironically gave them a bad reputation in Isfahan: "Being accused of sodomy, they have been thrown into the abyss of infamy and disgrace."[7] This is the subversive act of transgression with which Aqa Mansur's city disturber troubles the sexual order, transforming shame into piety, in his "religion of love."

As I curate the productions of these seven writers and one painter, certain patterns reveal themselves. The erotic trope of moon-faced beauties who bedazzle the heart of the lover with their coy and colorful styles is a recognizable metaphor for all of them; yet how each fashioned their playful flirtation in deploying these tropes depends on the mannerism of *adab* they embody. Consider, for example, the religious scholar Aqa Husayn Khwansari (d. 1686), who participated in the moral panics and religious refutations against Sufi ecstatic practices of boy gazing. Although Aqa Husayn does not reveal a taste for male homoerotic poetry, he curates essays and poetry on heteroerotic love whose subjects speak to carnal desire and renunciation, mobilizing the very idioms that signify homo-eros in a language of beauty that is genderless. Are these silences in Aqa Husayn's collection indicative of his sexual preference, writing himself as a male youth composing the beauty of spring, figured as a female bride? We will never know with certainty, but male homoerotic desire configured Aqa Husayn's *adab*, whether in his negation of boy gazing or in his representation of loving friendships among men. The lines between homo- and heteroerotic desire were mobile and mutable. For Aqa Husayn's son, Aqa Jamal Khwansari (d. 1710), who must have studied the family anthology, his anxiety was transferred onto female friendships and the practice of sworn friendships. In his essay "Beliefs of Women," he imagines the erotic secrets that female friends share as a threat to the reputation of men. By the middle of the seventeenth century, both male and female friendships came under social scrutiny. It is possible that in the environment of male sexual surveillance, the friendship of the Urdubadi widow sparked rumors in her own family circle. In the widow's words, her female companion (*yar*) was "a relative better than any sister, kinder than any of my other relatives";[8] her intimate ties with her surrogate sister exposed the vulnerability of her relations with both male and female kin.

* * *

I have separated anthologies that assembled specialized subjects, such as diplomatic letters, philosophical, medical, or theological treatises, from those interspersed with professional and personal or familial objects. Categorizing anthologies along the lines of genre and modes of curation provides me with the model or rubric of what I have termed household anthologies, which are family archives distinct from single-subject anthologies that were compiled for institutional purposes, such as the transmission of power and knowledge in courtly or religious circles. My retrospective creation of this genre is supported by the table of contents present in both the Khwansari and Urdubadi anthologies; the material is ordered in such a way as to clearly indicate deliberate choices that gave meaning to the multitude of urban texts circulating in Isfahan. Both Aqa Husayn Khwansari's and Muhammad Mu'in Urdubadi's anthologies preserve networks of texts that connected households together with the intersecting lives of teachers, students, friends, and relatives who mattered to each respective family. Helpfully, the two household scribes, Riza Quli and the anonymous Urdubadi scribe, state the exact date they began to assemble their anthologies: 1672 and 1664, respectively. Riza Quli dates the completion of the Khwansari anthology three years later, in 1675. Marking time and labor from the first moment of recording to the finished product illustrates the collective process of how long it took to locate, to curate, and to transform loose sheets of texts, preserved in family libraries and personal city archives, into a distinct codex. Such archival details distinguish the Khwansari and Urdubadi anthologies, but they also provide a useful conceptual map of probabilities that I have brought to the hundreds of other anonymous household anthologies I have consulted.

We can glean from these anthologies a surprising amount of information about what mattered to authors and scribes as they collected, selected, inscribed, and rearranged. Originals mattered for the two scribes employed in the Urdubadi and Khwansari households, for these scribes painstakingly note when they record texts from the original, times when they have consulted a fair copy (*raq'a*), a duplicate (*savad*), or a facsimile (*bayaz*). Aqa Husayn's scribe, Riza Quli, makes sure to note when the hand of his patron or that of the religious dignitary Navvab Isfahani validates the copy (*raq'a*) of a letter he records. The authenticity of contents assembled not only is a confirmation of accuracy but also becomes a convention of the practice. Time and again, Riza Quli makes his appearance as he collects and archives material for his patron with his own eyes, noting the place and date of copying in Isfahan. Moreover, the Urdubadi practice of collecting, which involved dismantling the codex to incorporate the continued life of the family and reconfiguring the anthology (recorded in red ink), illustrates the temporal process of archiving. The significance of the authorial status of Muhammad Mu'in Urdubadi, who first assembled his family anthology, speaks to the simultaneous importance of the originary and the replicative practice of self-fashioning, where new subjects read past curations to compare, relate, and rewrite their refined selves.

Habits of collecting visual and verbal texts in the domestic sphere generated family archives that simultaneously document the intimate lives of kin and the household's professional and social life *outside* the confines of the home. Not every household had the financial ability to hire a scribe to anthologize the family, of course. Friends must have exchanged poetry, essays, and letters among themselves, engaging their networks in the process of circulating and recording urban knowledge. For example, Mirza Ali Akbar's euphoric love letter to Zahid Khan must have been copied from Mirza Ali's private collection by a trustworthy friend. Even though not widely preserved in Isfahan's household anthologies, Mirza Ali's letter became a model for collectors to delight in, to imitate, and to write their own passion for their beloveds or their fury toward friends who had betrayed the most valued trust of custodianship (*amanat*). The process of inscription, however, is only part of the process of anthologizing the city. Male friendships developed around shared habits of viewing and collecting images, which were to be read, discussed, and performed in the bazaars, coffeehouses, and streets of Isfahan. Even when apart, friends communicated their desire to exchange gifts of portraits (*surat*) of beautiful male youth. As we recall, during his travels in Hindustan, Nasira Hamadani (d. 1620) sent a letter to his famous friend in Isfahan, Riza Abbasi. Nasira asks his artist friend to send him a "life-giving human image" as a memento of Isfahan's beauty to gratify his longing and erotic desire (*havas*). The request for a portrait (*surat*) of a male Isfahani beauty was part of the *adab* of masculinity that connected Riza Abbasi to Nasira and his acquaintances in Mughal India. This gift of friendship had the power to forge bonds, as men viewed and communicated the *adab* of aesthetics and erotics beyond imperial dominions.[9] Even as Nasira was boasting about his friendship with the celebrated painter, it was the exchange and the subject of the gift that mattered: "Let me [Nasira] show them [his acquaintances] how your [Riza Abbasi's] paintings encapsulate the beauty of Isfahan."[10]

The homoerotic vista that household anthologies expose brings into sharp focus the materiality of Isfahan with a view onto how the city was affectively seen, read, written, and desired. Nasira's letter to Riza Abbasi circulated widely; written in eloquent poetry and prose, it was prized for its value as an exemplary object of *adab*. The letter quickly became a classic model to emulate and to read in households and friendship circles. Yet Nasira's letter also encapsulates the phenomenology of experience shared by the seven other protagonists of this book. As he lays out the work that portraits perform, he draws on the mystical vocabulary of transcendence to write his yearning for Isfahan's beauty in a language that merges sexual desire with spirituality. Nasira evokes Shah Abbas I's ideal city, analogized to the image of the world, which today remains a metonym for Isfahan (see Map 1.1). But the intimate connections between urbanity, friendship, and spirituality operative in the seventeenth century have been lost to the significance of the central square, Naqsh-i Jahan. Thousands of friendship letters assembled in anthologies sit in Tehran's manuscript libraries, and thousands of portraits of male youth are housed in museums worldwide; their bond and affinity have been severed by our modern taxonomies and habits of collecting. *The City as Anthology* reunites the visual with the verbal to make the city familiar and provides a new and enticing panorama of what it meant to experience early modern Isfahan.

APPENDIX

Aqa Husayn Khwansari Majmuʻa

Tehran University Library, MS 7116, folio 1v (see Figure 2.2).

That which is in this majmuʻa

1. Imam Ali's *Book of Divination* [*Falnama*]
2. Book on the oneness of God in poetry [*Tawhidnama*]
3. *Divination of Zamir* by his holiness, Imam Jafar al-Sadiq (peace be upon him) and the particularities of some verses of the Quran in Persian (dated 1083)
4. *Ikhtilajat*
5. Translation of an Almanac that the prophet Muhammad composed
6. Sahih Hadith about the benefits of rosewater
7. 10th *rasha* from the divine words of Hazrat-i Khwaja, who is the founder of the human *tariqat*
8. From Muhaqqiq Sabzivari, seven pages from the author of *Jamiʻ al-Lazzat* about virility [*quva-yi bah*]
9. Calculating the time of prayer [*raziya*]
10. Essay [*risala*] on the *Ikhtiyar al-ayyam* [almanac] by Muhammad Baqir Majlisi, the author of *Bihar*, in Persian
11. Preface [*dibacha*] to the *Gulzar*, written by Ibrahim Mawlana Zuhuri (recorded by Riza Quli in 1083)
12. Preface [*dibacha*] of *Nawras*, Mawlana Zuhuri
13. Preface of a copy [*dibacha-yi bayaz*] from the writings of Aqa Husayn [Khwansari]
14. Copy [*savad*] of the *raqʻa* [letter] that Aqa Husayn wrote to Mir Zulfaqar
15. Preface [*dibacha*] that the children of Aqa Husayn wrote to Muhammad Baqir Yazdi
16. [in the margins] *Raqʻa* [letter] that his holiness Aqa Husayn wrote to Mir Abu-l-Qasim Findiriski

17. [in the margins] *Raq'a* that *khan-i khanan* wrote in response to the illness of Mawlana 'Urfi
18. Essay on love [*'ishq*] by Husayn ibn Nimatullah
19. Concerning sleep and awakeness
20. Excerpts from an essay by Mawlana Jalal al-din [Rumi]
21. Story [*hikayat*] of Shaykh Ali Daqqaq and his *zamir guftan*
22. Copies of letters [*raq'at*] about requesting prayer beads, eyeglasses, etc.
23. Essay titled "Nuriyya" from among the *tasnifat* of the drunken lover of God, Pir Kia 'Ala al-din, may God bless his soul
24. Sufi sects
25. *Risala Nuriyya* by the holy Nurbakhsh, may God bless his soul
26. A story about Sayyid Jalal 'Azud Yazdi
27. *Farhad and Shirin* by Mawlana Vahshi
28. Endowment deed that the children of Aqa Husayn bequeathed to Mirza Raziyya
29. Letter from the librarian [*kitabdar*] in Najaf
30. Excerpts from the *Nafas al-funun* about physiognomy, *dar qal'-i* from the *Nuzhat al-Qulub*, *istidlal* of the *kammiyyat* of horses, *dar zarf va mutayyibat*, and about the knowledge of houses
31. On almanacs assumed to be by Sipahani
32. Copies [*savad*] of written miscellanea
33. Knowledge of the calendar [*taqvim*] written in 1082 with an introduction and two chapters and a conclusion, written in 1082 on the 9th of Safar, including the sayings of Khwaja Abdullah Ansari, written on the 3rd of Safar 1082, on the *ahkam-i tali'* of the Turks according to the learned Turkish philosophers

The date of writing this book [*kitab*], beginning in 1083 [1672–1673] and ending in 1086 [1675]

NOTES

Introduction: The Adab of Urbanity

1. Babaie, *Isfahan*; Babaie, "Safavid Palaces"; Blake, *Half the World*; Dale, *Indian Merchants*; Haneda, "Urbanisation of Isfahan"; Jafariyan, *Safaviyya*.
2. Matthee, *Politics of Trade*.
3. Aslanian, *From the Indian Ocean*.
4. Babaie et al., *Slaves of the Shah*.
5. Roland Barthes attributes the concept of reading to Levi-Strauss's *Tristes Tropiques*, a study of the village of Bororo deploying the semantic approach. See Barthes, "Sémiologie et urbanisme"; and Lynch, *Image of the City*.
6. Lefebvre, *Production of Space*; Wheatley, "Levels of Space Awareness."
7. Literacy, that is, the use of particular literary forms as part of a larger complex of social practices in early modern Islamicate societies, has recently received some scholarly attention, but the significant role that manuscripts played in the production, preservation, transmission, and transformation of discourses and practices beyond the court and the religious seminary remains unexplored. My research begins to address these important lacunae.
8. Henkin, *City Reading*, 5. I would like to thank Will Glover for introducing me to David Henkin's work.
9. Abu Lughod, "The Islamic City."
10. My reading of Isfahan has also been inspired by the work of medievalist Armando Petrucci on the Roman Empire; Petrucci reads cities like Rome through the ubiquitous presence of monumental writing. See Petrucci, *Public Lettering*. Henkin draws on Petrucci's work, in his case to distinguish between writing and the figurative arts. In my reading, I blur the visual and verbal values of public texts.
11. Fletcher, "Integrative History"; Bentley, "Cross-Cultural Interaction." I would like to thank Sebouh Aslanian for these sources, which discuss the correlation between the global rise of literacy, urbanization, and the centralization of large states.
12. The first stage of development of the central square probably took place over a five-year period (1590–1595) after Shah Abbas I issued a decree to construct the new city center in 1590. I have adopted the date of 1593, recorded by the contemporaneous historian Afushta Natanzi, when Shah Abbas I's celebrated the inaugural

ceremony of Isfahan as the capital. For a detailed discussion, see Chapter 1. Also see McChesney, "Four Sources."

13. Subtelny, "Visionary Rose."

14. Hunarfar, *Ganjina*, 430.

15. For Shaykh Baha'i's works on ethics and conduct, see his *Jami'-i 'Abbasi*, *Kashkul*, and *Nan u Halva*.

16. Natanzi, *Naqavat al-Asar*, 107.

17. Herzig, "Rise of the Julfa Merchants"; Matthee, *Politics of Trade*; Baghdiantz-McCabe, *The Shah's Silk*. Sebouh Aslanian draws on this scholarship for his own research in the Venetian archives. Aslanian dates the first appearance of Julfans in the Venetian archives to 1571. Ghevont Alishan confirms these Julfan merchants as agents in Venice depositing, as early as 1571, money in Venice's Banco Dolfin. Old Julfans were the suppliers of Iranian silk to European merchants in Aleppo; see Aslanian, *From the Indian Ocean*, 28.

18. McChesney, "Four Sources," 122.

19. On the history of the Persian *ghazal*, see de Bruijn, "Ghazal"; Lewis, "Reading, Writing and Recitation"; and Meisami, *Medieval Persian Court Poetry*, 237–98.

20. I discuss the city disturber, or *shahrashub*, in Chapter 3.

21. See Aslanian, *From the Indian Ocean*.

22. Chardin, *Voyages*, 4: 69.

23. The Jesuit missionary Monsigneur Levesque de Berite estimated in August 1662 that there were 25,000–30,000 Armenian residents (6,000 families) in New Julfa (Berite, "Extrait d'un Journal," Gal 97 1-3, fol. 114). Thanks to Sebouh Aslanian for providing me with this information.

24. Pierre Bourdieu coined the term *symbolic capital* to refer to the symbolic meaning of objects with a perceived or concrete value that established social rank based on the ability to deploy these objects to claim certain class and status. See Bourdieu, *Distinction*.

25. Konrad Hirschler makes a similar argument for medieval Damascus in his *Written Word*.

26. I explore this seemingly paradoxical practice of anonymizing anthologies in Chapter 2, where I discuss authorship and the many different hands, mostly anonymous and some identified, in the context of ownership and household productions.

27. Most of these anthologies bear different seals of ownership, notes in multiple hands, and various types of marginalia. They are rich sources for a diachronic history of reading practices. Many questions remain unanswered about the process of collecting material, recording segments of essays and poems, or the choice of personal and private letters or talismans that went into anthologizing the city;

these are important subjects of inquiry concerning the material fabric of anthologies for future scholars to investigate.

28. Malik Library, MS 2551.

29. Malik Library, MS 2551, fol. 50v.

30. Some anthologies, such as the anthology belonging to the religious judge Kazim, were sold in the bazaar or at book stands in the central square and were repossessed by new owners who wrote into the folios of anthologies to make them their own. Even as we discovered the name of the owner through his daughter Jahan Banu, many more hands and dates were inserted into the margins of this anthology. Dates of ownership range from the seventeenth century all the way to the turn of the twentieth century (Malik Library, MS 2551, fol. 22r). The owner notes the date, Monday 1289/1910, in the margin). From loans and debts accrued by new owners to the record of the marriage of a son in 1761, wishing him and his bride good fortune, anthologies continued to generate and animate the lives of multiple owners well into the twentieth century, when lithography and print took over the economy of the book in Isfahan.

31. Farhad, "Safavid Single-Page Paintings"; Farhad, "The Art of Muʿin Musavvir."

32. The realistic turn in poetry has been studied by Ahmad Golchin Maʿani; see Golchin Maʿani, *Maktab-i Vuquʿ dar Shiʿr-i Farsi*. Also see Losensky, *Welcoming Fighani*; and Andrews and Kalpakli, *Age of Beloveds*. Massumeh Farhad has touched on this subject in her work on single-page paintings; see Farhad, "Safavid Single-Page Paintings." This turn to historicity remains to be explored in the writing of history, portraiture, murals, and the production of court chronicles.

33. Hirschler, *Written Word*; Toorawa, *Ibn Abi Tahir Tayfuur*; Touati, *L'armoire à sagesse*; Pedersen, *The Arabic Book*.

34. See Chapter 1 for a detailed discussion of the mural.

35. Barthes, "Sémiologie et urbanisme," 445.

36. Theoretically, both partners in a penetrative act were to be executed. See Rowson, "Homosexuality."

37. See Dror Ze'evi's discussion on the Kadizadeli movement in mid-seventeenth-century Istanbul in his *Producing Desire*, 78–98. On the Kadizadeli, also see Zilfi, "The Kadizadelis"; and Terzioğlu, "Sunna-Minded Sufi Preachers."

38. For an account of these transformations, see Babayan, *Mystics, Monarchs, and Messiahs*, 403–39.

39. Danishpazhu, "Yik Parda az Zindigani-yi Shah Tahmasb-i Safavi."

40. Muhammad Tahir Vahid Qazvini was writing his *ʿAbbasnama* under the rule of Abbas II (r. 1642–1655) and dates the edict to 1064/1653. See Vahid Qazvini, *ʿAbbasnama*, 70–72.

41. For detailed studies of these refutations (*radd*) against Sufis, see Jafarian,

Din va Siyasat; Jafarian, "Ruyaru'-i Faqihan"; Newman, "Clerical Perceptions"; and Babayan, *Mystics, Monarchs, and Messiahs*.

42. In practice, it was acceptable for adult men to have anal intercourse with young boys. Similar to the practice of politics and sex in ancient Greece, the passage into adult masculinity assumed the passivity of the male youth being penetrated by the adult male, a sexual act that marked social hierarchies. However, once the adolescent attained the age of maturity, he was expected to become sexually active with boys and/or with women. Mature men who sought the passive role in sex were considered diseased, suffering a pathological condition.

43. I am referring here to Jacques Rancière's "distribution of the sensible," a system of palpable facts held in common based on a "distribution of spaces, times and forms of activity that determines the very manner in which something in common lends itself to participation" (Rancière, *Politics of Aesthetics*, 12). I would like to thank Will Glover for his insights and for introducing me to Rancière's work.

Chapter 1: Imperial Visions of Sovereignty

1. On the concept of the public secret, see Taussig, *Defacement*; and on the secret as sacred knowledge, see Johnson, *Secrets, Gossip, and Gods*.

2. The conjunction of Saturn and Jupiter occurs every twenty years in a cycle of trigons, a set of three signs of the zodiac, each 120 degrees from one another, referred to as the triplicity. Every 240 years the greater conjunction moves into a new triplicity, and every 960 years the greatest conjunction makes a full cycle of all four trigons. This theory of great conjunctions was elaborated by Abu Ma'shar (d. 868), who in his *Zij al-hazarat* interpreted these conjunctions as symbolizing the advent of a prophet and a change in religion.

3. There is much discussion as to when exactly Isfahan was designated the new capital of the Safavi Empire. Robert McChesney offers the most convincing dates based on contemporaneous chronicles from Shah Abbas I's reign: McChesney, "Four Sources." McChesney relies on the source closest to the period of the making of the capital city, Natanzi's *Naqavat al-Asar*. Natanzi narrates the inauguration of Isfahan as a consequence of the dramatic rebellion and suppression of the Nuqtavis. Although Natanzi relates several encampments of Shah Abbas I in Isfahan between 1593 and 1595, he records 1591–1592 (AH 1000) as the year when the shah ordered the building of a bazaar to rival the one in Tabriz and named Isfahan as the capital city (*misr-i jami'*). The dramatic performance of entry into the capital is recorded in the middle of Muharram 1002/October 1593, two months after the mock coronation of Ustad Yusufi; this is the date I have adopted for the inauguration of Isfahan as capital city.

4. Natanzi intersperses a series of Quranic verses on earthquakes, famine, and flood in his narrative, which includes Sura 99, *The Earthquake* (*al-Zalzala*).

5. Natanzi, *Naqavat al-Asar*, 107.

6. Although seven colors traditionally form the color spectrum, here the addition of eight colors signals the ingenuity of the textile weavers and dyers. On contemporaneous art historical treatises delineating how colors are made from natural products in Safavi painting studios, see Munshi Qummi, *Gulistan-i Hunar*; and Dust Muhammad's *Dibacha*, translated as "Preface to the Bahram Mirza Album" in Thackston, *A Century of Princes*, 335–49.

7. According to Natanzi, there was an old seminary, built by Khwaja Malik Mustawfi, in the space where the *maydan* would be constructed. Natanzi, *Naqavat al-Asar*, 539.

8. Natanzi, *Naqavat al-Asar*, 539.

9. Natanzi, *Naqavat al-Asar*, 577.

10. Natanzi, *Naqavat al-Asar*, 577.

11. "The Marvels of Creatures and Strange Things Existing" had become a popular genre by the early modern period, inspired by medieval cosmographer al-Qazvini, who wrote his marvels, the *'Aja'ib al-makhluqat*, in 1203.

12. Quran 56:32–33.

13. Natanzi, *Naqavat al-Asar*, 578.

14. The inauguration ceremonies were an expensive endeavor that the historian Natanzi makes sure to enumerate: Natanzi, *Naqavat al-Asar*, 579. Natanzi had heard from court supervisors and officials that, for the preparation of these festivities, 400 tomans had been spent on the four fortresses alone. Along with the 15,000 foot soldiers, their clothes and military accoutrements, and a toman each for their personal expenses, the total cost of this inauguration was set at 20,000 tomans, equivalent to the yearly revenue of the Royal Treasury from the tax on prostitution or from tobacco duties. Chardin states that in the 1660s, during the reign of Abbas II, the royal treasuries' total yearly revenue amounted to 700,000 tomans—the equivalent of 32 million livres. [Sami'a], *Tazkirat al-Muluk*, 182. On tobacco duties, see [Sami'a], *Tazkirat al-Muluk*, 176.

15. Descriptions of Isfahan as the city of paradise appear throughout anthologies under the title of *ta'rif-i Isfahan* (In Praise of Isfahan), both in prose and in verse.

16. This is according to Shah Abbas I's court historian, Iskandar Beg Munshi. See Munshi, *Tarikh-i 'Alam Ara-yi Abbasi*, 2: 545.

17. Although Shah Ismail (r. 1501–1524) had visited Isfahan several times and had camped in the gardens where the Ali Qapu palace would stand, he renovated two religious 'Alid structures in the old city, where his name is inscribed along with the Qizilbash general and governor of Fars. On the Harun-i Vilayat and Masjid-i Ali, see Hunarfar, *Ganjina*, 360–79.

18. See Necipoğlu, "Framing the Gaze."

19. Construction began in 1012/1603 and was completed in 1028/1618. For the biography of Shaykh Lutfullah Maysi, see Abisaab, *Converting Persia*, 82–87.

20. "Qala Allah wa inna al-masajid li-Allah fa-la tadʿu maʿ Allah ahadan." Hunarfar, *Ganjina*, 406.

21. Medieval Muslim theologians have labeled the ninety-nine names of Allah as the most beautiful of names, *al asmaʾ al-husna*. Derived from the Quran and the Hadith, these names of God designate his essence and his qualities, and believers memorize and recite the names during prayer and Sufi rituals of *zikr* as a means of transcendence and entry into paradise.

22. On the debates over the permissibility of Friday prayer during the absence of the Mahdi, see Babayan, *Mystics, Monarchs, and Messiahs*; and Jafarian, *Davazda Risala-yi Fiqhi*.

23. Shaykh Bahaʾi, *Jamiʿ-i ʿAbbasi*, 59.

24. Hunarfar, *Ganjina*, 428. Recorded in the contemporaneous chronicle by Iskandar Beg Munshi: Munshi, *Tarikh-i ʿAlam Ara-yi ʿAbbasi*, 2: 841.

25. Hunarfar, *Ganjina*, 430–31.

26. Hunarfar, *Ganjina*, 433.

27. In her revised master's thesis, Nuha Khoury reads the epigraphic program of the Friday Prayer Mosque as a book written by Shaykh Bahaʾi to educate the believer in Shiʿa doctrine and belief. She refers to his *Kitab al-Arbaʿin* as the main source for the epigraphy. See Khoury, "Ideologies and Inscriptions," 38. Khoury's reading has inspired mine, though I argue that Shaykh Bahaʾi gathers fragments, bits, and pieces from a variety of his works, creating a new collection: an anthology of inscriptions to educate worshippers in Shiʿa Islam.

28. Hunarfar, *Ganjina*, 439–40; Khoury, "Ideologies and Inscriptions," 61.

29. Hunarfar *Ganjina*, 430; Khoury, "Ideologies and Inscriptions," 69.

30. Quran 76, translated by Mohammad M. Pickthall, with my additions. Pickthall, *Glorious Qurʾan*, 672–73.

31. Khoury, "Ideologies and Inscriptions," 95.

32. The chronogram in the foundation text dates the palace to 1057/1647, in Hunarfar, *Ganjina*, 566.

33. The Qizilbash were the Turkman military and spiritual backbone of the early Safavis. They typically wore a red headdress with twelve folds representing the twelve Imams as well as initiation into the Safavi order. We no longer see these headdresses on the walls of the Forty Pillars Palace. On the introduction of slavery at the Safavi court, see Babaie et al., *Slaves of the Shah*.

34. "Midahad dar paykar-i afsurda-yi divar jan." Tabrizi, *Kulliyat*, 835, verse 18.

35. The original three hosting scenes of the renegade princes: Humayun, to Vali

Muhammad Khan and Nadir Muhammad Khan. On the wall paintings commissioned in 1647, see Hunarfar *Ganjina*, 560; and Babaie, "Shah 'Abbas II."

36. Currently six grand mural paintings survive in the Chihil Sutun; however, two of these paintings where added in the nineteenth century. For a discussion on the four paintings commissioned by Abbas II (r. 1639–1666), see Hunarfar, *Ganjina*, 557–574; and Babaie, "Shah Abbas II."

37. On the emergence of portraiture and the drawing of portraits on paper and then on walls, see Farhad, "Safavid Single-Page Paintings"; and Rizvi, "Suggestive Portrait."

38. On the *saqi* (cupbearer) and the poetic form of the *saqinama* (book of the cupbearer), see Losensky "Saqi-Nama."

39. The Safavi dynasty had its genesis in a Sufi order (1301–1501), a successful brotherhood that prospered under the dynastic founder Shaykh Safi al-din (d. 1334), Shah Ismail's charismatic ancestor. Located in northwestern Iran close to the Caspian Sea region, Ardabil lay on important east-west and north-south trade routes traveled by merchants on their way to Anatolia or north to the Caucasus. Shaykh Safi al-Din actively engaged his followers' conversion, and his mystical teachings and rituals introduced them to Islam's basic tenets. Merchants, craftsmen, bureaucrats, and rulers came to patronize this saintly man after whom the Safavi dynasty was named.

40. *Zikr* is a Sufi ritual of remembrance of Allah, in which God's ninety-nine names are recited.

41. The tambourine, or *tambur* in Persian, is a musical instrument often played by female entertainers in seventeenth-century paintings and drawings. The Persian term is *tabaq zan*, from the root *t.b.q.*, which describes a flat and round plate or tray. Because of the flat surface and round shape of the tambourine and the movement of the fingers on its skin, I assume that it is a visual signifier for female homoeroticism.

42. The term used to designate these friendships—*khwahar khwanda*, or "adopted sister"—came to imply a *tabaq zan*, or "lesbian," in modern Persian literary usage.

43. The obligation has become famously referred to as "commanding right and forbidding wrong" (*al-amr bi-l-ma'ruf wa-l-nahy 'an al-munkar*) (Quran 3:104). Seven more Quranic verses (Quran 3:110, 3:114, 7:157, 9:71, 9:112, 22:41, 31:17) refer to this duty. See Cook, *Commanding Right*, 26.

44. Mirza Sami'a comments on the position of the *muhtasib* al-Mamalik and delineates his duties to control prices of goods in the bazaar to prevent the inflation of prices. See [Sami'a], *Tazkirat al-Muluk*, 83. The French jeweler Chardin, who resided in Isfahan between 1665 and 1677, confirms this; see Chardin, *Voyages*, 5: 259.

45. Shah Safi (r. 1629–1642) reissued the *firman* in Zu al-Hijja 1038/July 1629. The original *firman* that was issued by Shah Abbas I is dated Zu al-Hijja 1021/January 1613.

46. The term for barbers, *salmani*, comes from Salman Farsi, the Persian convert to Islam and the companion of the prophet who had shaved Muhammad's head after the conquest of Mecca. Traditionally, Ali is the patron of the barber's guild, and Salman Farsi is named as a private patron. The poet Quli Khaki Khurasani (1627–1646) wrote about patron saints of guilds in Isfahan. See Khaki Khurasani, *Abbreviated Version*, 48, verses 770–78.

47. Other bathhouse employees mentioned are the mirror holders (*ayinadaran*), garment keepers (*jamidaran*), scrubbers (*kisamalan*), water carriers (*abgiran*) in both the male and female hammams, and the makers of razor blades and grinding wheels. The decree reiterates Shah Abbas I's *firman*s, transcribed in Hunarfar, *Ganjina*, 434.

48. Shah Abbas I's personal barber (*khassatarash*), Ustad Ali Riza, is also referred to as his personal masseur, *dallak-i khassa-yi sharifa*. Hammam employees were ordered to pay their master the requisite customary dues (*rusum*).

49. On the obsession of religious scholars who wrote about nudity (*'awra*) and shame (*haya'*) and the need to have proper covering around male and female genitalia in the hammam, see Katz, "Shame."

50. Majlisi, *Hilyat al-Muttaqin*, 160; Bauer, "Male-Male Love."

51. Majlisi, *Hilyat al-Muttaqin*, 128.

52. For a comparable process in early modern Germany, see Puff, *Sodomy in Reformation Germany*. Puff argues that Protestant discourses defaming sodomy deployed matrimony to construct sodomy. Reform-minded theologians recognized the purchase of drawing on established values on marriage and same-sex desire to help create communal identity in Reformation Germany and Switzerland.

Chapter 2: Collecting, Self-Fashioning, and Community

1. Tehran Library, MS 4660, fol. 67v (dated 1059/1649).

2. Julie Scott Meisami links the conventional Persianate garden poetics to medieval habits of analogical thought that perceive parallels between the garden as allegory to paradise; see Meisami, "Allegorical Gardens."

3. My use of *self-fashioning* invokes the work of Stephen Greenblatt, in that he highlights the reciprocal relationship between writing and structures of power to think about the ways that individuals are shaped by social conventions and taboos. See Greenblatt, *Renaissance Self-Fashioning*. I use Greenblatt's coinage to focus on the anthology as a medium for writing the self, a space where individuals creatively curate themselves in relation to the codes of urbanity. Moreover, my read-

ing of self-fashioning that anthologies archive refines this reciprocal relationship to allow for agency and for subjective acts of resistance against normative versions of power.

4. The one exception is the study by Massumeh Farhad on single-page paintings: "Safavid Single-Page Paintings." The subject of her study, however, is not the transmission and the processes of knowledge production but rather the content and proliferation of single-page paintings beyond court ateliers.

5. There are, of course, exceptions, particularly in the study of poetry, calligraphy, and architecture, because these were connected and complementary professional skills in Safavi Iran. See Babaie, *Isfahan*; Losensky, *Welcoming Fighani*; and Roxburgh, *Persian Album*. However, the linkages across the disciplines of theology, letter writing, painting, poetry, the sciences, and literature are yet to be explored.

6. On the historiographical turn to experience in Islamic history, see Ahmed, *What Is Islam?*

7. Azhand, *Sadiqi Beg Afshar*, 28. For an illuminating discussion and translation of this treatise on painting, see Dickson and Welch, *Houghton Shahnameh*, 1: 259–69 (Appendix I: The Canons of Painting by Sadiqi Bek).

8. Taymuri, "Sarguzasht-i Kitabkhana-ha-yi Isfahan," 2: 125. Ali ibn Ahmad Asadi Tusi (d. 1072) was a poet, linguist, and copyist who completed his *Garshaspnama* in 1066 CE. This epic tells the story of Garshasp, the grandfather of the *Shahnama* hero Rustam. According to Khaleghi Mutlaq, Asadi's attempt to portray Garshasp as a greater hero than Rustam was a failed endeavor. However, the fact that in seventeenth-century Isfahan a merchant commissioned the copying of the *Garshaspnama* rather than the *Shahnama* points to its popularity into the early modern period. This is one example that illustrates the purchase of studying *majmu'a*s to write a history of reading, copying, and collecting Persianate medieval epics and romances. See Khaleghi-Motlagh, "Asadi Tusi."

9. One of 'Itiqad Khan's commissioned manuscripts of the *Bustan* of Sa'di (d. 1291) was copied by Mir 'Imad and is now housed in the Majlis Library in Tehran. Taymuri, "Sarguzash-i kitabkhana-ha-yi Isfahan," 2: 122.

10. We have good examples of the practice of hiring binders and scribes to repair or produce new manuscripts in documents collected at the holy shrine of Imam Riza in Mashhad. The largest archive of documents comes from the seventeenth century and lists the names of scribes and bookbinders, their salaries, the cost for repairs, and the materials needed for these repairs, such as thread, paper, glue, and silk. For example, the salary of Ustad Muhammad Zaman (d. 1680), who worked at the shrine between 1667 and 1669, was paid 1 toman and 8,000 Iraqi dinars plus 17 *kharvar* of wheat in 1669. This salary of 1 toman (in silver equivalent to 8–9 Russian rubles in the late seventeenth century) seems to be the average pay for bookbind-

ers who worked on repairing manuscripts at the shrine library in the seventeenth century; most did receive salaries in kind and cash. See Mahbub-Farimani, "Sahhafi," 71.

11. Hamori et al., "Mukhtarat."

12. After Timur's death in 1405, the Timuri realm was divided among his male descendants, each occupying seats of princely power in Samarqand, Herat, Shiraz, and Isfahan, which became centers of cultural patronage in the fifteenth century.

13. Roxburgh, *Persian Album*, 112.

14. The "new habit of assembling," as David Roxburgh puts it in his work on the Persian album, came to be shaped by and to shape the simultaneous pleasures of seeing, reading, and learning. Roxburgh's study of three sixteenth-century Safavi royal albums demonstrates how each album is distinctly shaped by its collector and his social networks. See Roxburgh, *Persian Album*, 12–25.

15. Roxburgh, *Persian Album*, 140–47.

16. Losensky, *Welcoming Fighani*, chaps. 5 and 6.

17. On anthologies and bookmaking in the European context, see Benedict, *Making the Modern Reader*; Chartier, *Order of Books*; Gillespie, "Caxton's Chaucer and Lydgate Quartos"; Lerer, "Medieval English Literature"; and Nichols and Wenzel, *The Whole Book*.

18. Losensky, "Sa'eb Tabrizi."

19. Milli Library, MS 4672. Theoretically, according to Shi'a law, inheritance from fathers was to be equally divided among female and male children. In practice, however, different proportions were allocated to children, depending on whether the mother was alive and how many children constituted the family. This will states that 14 shares out of 73 shares are inherited by the son of Hajj Muhammad.

20. Chardin, *Voyages*, 4: 275.

21. Chardin, *Voyages*, 4: 281. Chardin notes that this scribal fee is quite expensive, surmising that rarely could regular people afford to pay for 1,000 lines at the cost of 27 sols. Twenty sols made 1 livre. Around 1640, the average daily salary of a hired worker in France was about 10 sols. A kilo of bread cost 2 sols, a bottle of wine 3 sols, and a chicken 1 livre. I would like to thank Helwi Blom for this information.

22. Jafarian speculates that the number of manuscripts produced in the religious sciences in seventeenth-century Isfahan was equivalent to what one prominent press would produce today in Tehran. Jafarian, "Isharati dar Bab-i Kitab va Kitabkhana."

23. Mans, *Estat de la Perse*, 33.

24. The manuscript is housed in the Majlis Library, MS 5557, and was found by Rasul Jafarian. See Jafarian's blog post "Fihrist-i Kitab-ha-yi yik kitabfurushi."

25. Sadra, "Sharh Hidayat al-Hikma."

26. Fazil, *Fihrist*.

27. Safavi shahs also gifted religious books, such as the Quran, to the holy shrines in Ardabil, Mashhad, and Ray.

28. Marʿashi Najafi Library, MS 9607.

29. In addition, the jeweler-traveler Jean Baptiste Chardin, who lived in Isfahan between 1655 and 1677, had access to workshops at court as a jeweler; see Chardin, *Voyages*.

30. On two seventeenth-century Safavi administrative manuals, see [Samiʿa], *Tazkirat al-Muluk*; Ansari, *Dastur al-moluk*; and Danishpazhu, "Yik Parda az Zindigani-yi Shah Tahmasb-i Safavi," which contain detailed descriptions of royal workshops.

31. Safavi princes in the sixteenth century were art collectors and patrons who drew talent from the bazaar; they were connoisseurs who patronized the crème de la crème of artists in their respective provincial seats of power. Bahram Mirza and Ibrahim Mirza, two younger brothers of Shah Tahmasb, were patrons of the arts of the book in Mashhad (1550s). They invested in thriving ateliers that produced spectacular illustrated manuscripts and histories of art. See Shreve-Simpson and Farhad, *Sultan Ibrahim Mirza's Haft Awrang*. For Dust Muhammad's preface to Bahram Mirza's album, see Roxburgh, *Prefacing the Image*. Beyond royal ateliers, the city of Shiraz (southwestern Iran), for example, was an important center of manuscript production that in the sixteenth century traded in the commercial market, where manuscripts were sold in the Ottoman Empire. See Uluç, "Ottoman Book Collectors." For a recent study on the Ottoman royal album of Sultan Ahmad I (r. 1603–1617), see Fetvaci, *Album of the World Emperor*.

32. Paper was available in sheets and used by scribes, who provided their services to booksellers and individual buyers in the bazaar.

33. ʿItiqad Khan commissioned Mir ʿImad to create his copy of the *Bustan* of Saʿdi (d. 1291), currently housed in the Majlis Library in Tehran.

34. Several Iranian scholars, namely, Rasul Jafarian, Mortiza Taymuri, and Rukn al-Din Humayun Farrukh, have explored the libraries of men of religion, providing a threshold for my inquiry into literacy in seventeenth-century Isfahan. My book, however, assembles the arts and sciences together to explore the visual and literary texts produced, collected, and housed in private households in the seventeenth century.

35. ʿItiqad Khan and Hajj Hasan Beg were two merchants who hired the calligrapher, Ali Riza Abbasi, and the painter, Riza Abbasi for their libraries. Two generals of Shah Abbas I, Zaynal ibn Zakariyya and Farhad Khan, also employed Riza Abbasi.

36. Jafarian, "Isharati dar Bab-i Kitab va Kitabkhana"; Farrukh, *Tarikhcha*. Known private collections during the reign of Shah Abbas I were held by merchants and notables (Ibn Khatun, Mirza Abu Turab Isfahani, Hajj Hasan Beg, ʿItiqad Khan,

Muhammad Muqim, Shaykh Najib), generals (Zaynal Ibn Zakariyya, Rustam Khan Shamlu, Farhad Khan), and *ulama* (Mirza Abdullah Afandi, Hazin Lahiji, Khatunabadi, Aqa Husayn Khwansari, Shaykh Abu Talib Zahidi, Shaykh Baha'i, Mirza 'Inayat Isfahani, Mulla Muhsin Fayz Kashani, Muhammad Baqir Majlisi, Shaykh Ali Minshar 'Amili, Mir Findiriski).

37. For a biography of Husayn b. 'Abd al-Samad 'Amili, see Stewart, "Husayn b. 'Abd al-Samad al-'Amili's Treatise"; and Stewart, "An Episode."

38. Taymuri, "Sarguzash-i kitabkhana-ha-yi Isfahan," 2: 122.

39. On the production of paper in Isfahan, see Afshar, *Kaghaz*, 96.

40. Tehran University, MS 7116, fol. 53. Riza Quli writes his name and the date 1083/1672–1673 as well as the name of the city, Isfahan, where he is assembling this *majmu'a*. The other four Khwansari *majmu'a*s are housed in Malik Library, MSs 2454, 4727, and 8235/193, and in the Tehran University Library, MS 4758.

41. These anthologies should be studied for a project on the history of reading.

42. Ahmadi, *Dar Bab-i Awqaf-i Safavi*. Huri Khanum was probably a Georgian slave concubine, the mother of Shah Safi (r. 1629–1642). The endowment deed is dated 1058/1648 and enumerates the shops (butcher, tobacco, condiments, perfume, green grocer, confectionary, bakery, and hookah maker) in its vicinity owned by the shah's mother. The rent, in kind, is guaranteed for the upkeep of the seminary. A list of manuscripts endowed to the seminary are also mentioned; it is interesting to note that beyond books on law, medicine, philosophy, and theology, there are anthologies of poetry and commentaries on two famous poets, Rumi (d. 1273) and Jami (d. 1492).

43. Nasrabadi Isfahani, *Tazkira-yi Nasrabadi*; and Sefatgol, *Sakhtar*.

44. See the Appendix for the entire list of contents.

45. Tehran University Library, MS 7116, fols. 2r–24v.

46. For more on divination in the Persianate world, see Farhad and Bagci, *Falnama*; and Gruber, "Divination."

47. The Safavi Empire began as a mystical brotherhood centered on the shrine of their eponymous founder, Shaykh Safi al-Din (d. 1334), in the city of Ardabil, northwestern Iran.

48. An essay on the qualities and powers of precious stones, which were objects that Aqa Husayn Khwansari collected, ends the section on divination and the occult. Turquoise, for example, is to be kept close to the body during sleep so that when one wakes and gazes upon it, one's day will be filled with pleasure and play.

49. See Chapter 1 for a discussion on the public debates by members of the Shi'a clergy who engaged in the defamation of Sufis, writing treatises in condemnation of Sufi practices, especially treatises that prohibited the practices of boy gazing and sodomy as well as beard shaving, practices that targeted men who delayed taking on their productive social roles in marriage as fathers and husbands.

50. Muharram is the first month of the Muslim lunar calendar; it also marks for the Shi'a the first ten days of mourning that commemorates the martyrdom of Imam Husayn (d. 680) in Karbala.

51. The *Falnama* is ascribed to Ali and the *Ikhtiyarat al-Ayyam* to Jafar al-Sadiq. This last essay is written by Aqa Husayn's teacher, Muhammad Taqi Majlisi (d. 1640).

52. Aqa Husayn Khwansari's collection of sixty-five letters has been copied in multiple manuscripts under the title of *Munsha'at-i Aqa Husayn Khwansari*. See Zamani Nizhad, *Munsha'at va Makatibat*.

53. Navvab Isfahani's letter is a response to a letter he had received from Mir Findiriski informing him of his safe entry into the city of Lahore. Navvab Isfahani writes that he is thrilled to have received firsthand news from Mir Findiriski. The content of the letter acknowledges the importance of Mir Findiriski's travels to Mughal India, where he was involved in a translation project of Sanskrit texts, such as the *Mahabharata* and the *Razmnama*, into Persian. "Even though you have been prohibited from attaining the place of your desire, you will nevertheless attain the lofty stations of the mystic. Whether or not a heart as talented and intelligent as yours is confronted with obstacles, you will acquire ample fortunes and shining earnings." Navvab Isfahani encourages Mir Findiriski to pursue his desired goal; failure, he writes, is put forth by the "intention of the lofty God" to activate the seeker toward himself. Even though "shortsighted people" come in the way of one's aspirations, these are impotent men who "have recourse to prohibitions which is the way of Satan, and they will fall themselves from the ranks of humanity. . . . The almighty God will preserve you from the deceits of these people." The letter by the scholar Navvab Isfahani, in his own hand, endorses Mir Findiriski's desire to learn Indian thought and practice Hinduism despite the critique it generated by Shi'a religious scholars. Aqa Husayn choice of including this letter in his anthology is to validate his teacher. Navvab Isfahan's letter to Mir Findiriski, "Khwansari majmu'a," Tehran University, MS 7116, fol. 8ov.

54. "Khwansari majmu'a," Tehran University Library, MS 7116, fol. 53v.

55. Form letters on the subject of requesting a rosary or a pair of glasses appear to be objects that Aqa Husayn Khwansari possessed. Several responsa against Sufis are followed by selections from the romance of *Farhad and Shirin* composed by a near contemporaneous poet, Vahshi Bafiqi. Aqa Husayn himself composed poetry, both in Persian and Arabic. An endowment deed that belonged to the family of Aqa Husayn sits with an essay on physiognomy, ending with a series of almanacs and notes on calculating the days of the year according to the Turkish animal year and its equivalency with the Muslim lunar year.

56. Twelve *majmu'a*s from seventeenth-century Isfahan containing Aqa Husayn's letter in praise of spring have been identified by Zamani Nizhad, *Munsha'at va Makatibat*.

57. "Khwansari majmuʿa," Tehran University Library, MS 7116, fol. 75v.

58. "Khwansari majmuʿa," Tehran University Library, MS 7116, fol. 75v.

59. Zuhuri had traveled throughout the Iranian plateau, from Khurasan in the northeast to Yazd, Shiraz, and Isfahan, where he composed a poem (*tarjiband*) for Shah Abbas I. For a biography of Zuhuri, see Munshi, *Tarikh-i ʿAlam Ara-yi ʿAbbasi*. For his poetry, see Zuhuri Tarshizi, *Divan*. Mawlana Zuhuri is known for his three masterpieces on composition: the *Gulshan-i Ibrahimi*, a preface referred to as *Nawras* for the sovereign of the Bijapur Sultanate; Ibrahim ʿAdilshah II's composition in the local Deccani language on prose writing; and the preface for *Khan-i Khalil*.

60. Zuhuri Tarshizi, *Divan*, 46, no. 2.

61. Mawlana Zuhuri, *Gulzar-i Ibrahimi*, Tehran University Library, MS 7116, fol. 58v.

62. Tehran University Library, MS 7116, fol. 81v.

63. Tehran University Library, MS 7116, fol. 81v.

64. Tehran University Library, MS 7116, fol. 82r.

65. Tehran University Library, MS 7116, fol. 81v.

66. Tehran University Library, MS 7116, fol. 81v.

67. Eighteen copies of Aqa Husayn's fatwa against the shaving of beards and the consumption of wine appear in seventeenth-century *majmuʿa*s. See Zamani Nizhad, *Munshaʾat va Makatibat*.

68. Losensky, "Vahshi Bafqi"; Losensky, "Wahshi Bafki."

69. Tehran University Library, MS 7116, fols. 75v–162v.

70. Herzog, *Sex in Crisis*.

71. Nasrabadi Isfahani, *Tazkira-yi Nasrabadi*, 139–40. I would like to thank Cameron Cross for his help in translating these verses.

72. We will return to Muhammad Qasim's paintings for a female clientele in Chapter 5. Here I focus on his self-representations.

73. Farhad dates Muhammad Qasim's *Bastinade* to 1650–1655 on the basis of style; she notes that the inscribed date 114 (i.e., 1014/1605) appears to be a later addition. Farhad, "Safavid Single-Page Paintings," 309.

74. My reading of this drawing has been informed by Massumeh Farhad's reading in "Safavid Single-Page Paintings."

75. Nasrabadi Isfahani, *Tazkira-yi Nasrabadi*, 152.

76. Mauss, "Techniques of the Body."

77. Muhammad Qasim composed these lines of poetry, which he repeats in another of his drawings depicting a beautiful young male holding a sheet of poetry.

78. Manuchihr Khan (d. 1636) and grandson Qarachaqay Khan II (d. 1668).

79. See my *Mystics, Monarchs, and Messiahs*, where I narrate the cabals and provincial revolts that broke out after the death of Shah Abbas I in 1629.

80. See Babaie et al., *Slaves of the Shah*.

81. See Babaie et al., *Slaves of the Shah*; in particular, on this Armenian slave-convert family and their patronage of the arts, see the chapter "Military Slaves in the Provinces: Collecting and Shaping the Arts," 114–38.

82. Farhad, "Safavid Single-Page Paintings," 121–23.

83. Muhammad Qasim also drew for another patron in Baghdad, Vali Tuni. The subject of that drawing was of a cupbearer (*saqi*) serving coffee: Farhad, "Safavid Single-Page Paintings," 123.

84. For a reference to the painter as Khwaja Muhammad Qasim Isfahani, with the pen name "painter," see Shamlu, *Qisas al-Khaqani*, 2: 153–54.

85. On the history of the Baba Rukn al-Din Shrine in Isfahan, see Hunarfar, *Ganjina*, 493–98.

86. We have one exception, however, where the painter Mu'in Musavvir (d. 1697) captured a shocking incident in which a tiger devoured a 15-year-old apprentice grocer at the palace precinct gate (*darvazadawlat*) in Isfahan. On the drawing's top margin, Mu'in includes a detailed description of this tragedy. He dates the composition to a Monday in 1672 that marked the holy feast of Ramadan. The tiger, Mu'in informs us, had been brought to Isfahan by the Uzbek khan as a gift to the Safavi Shah Sulayman (r. 1666–1692). Although he did not witness this horrifying episode, Mu'in writes, "We heard about the grocer but did not see him; in his memory I drew this." Mu'in relates these urban details through words accompanied by an image of the grocer lying dead at the boundary of palace and nature. A man from within the palace gate holds onto the chained lion who is tearing at the face of the young boy on the ground. Mu'in's placement of the attack between the urban and the idyllic signals a shift in pictorial conventions that this event elicited. For an astute analysis of this drawing, see Farhad, "An Artist's Impression."

Chapter 3: Disturbing the City

1. "Dar safahan zi qaza naqsh-i jahan khub nishast / 'alami dar safarash az vatan avara bi-bin," Mawlana I'jaz Herati, "Dar Ta'rif-i Isfahan," Tehran University, MS 3034, fol. 44r.

2. Nasrabadi, *Tazkira-yi Nasrabadi*, 408.

3. Nasrabadi, *Tazkira-yi Nasrabadi*, 408.

4. For a sampling of anthologies that record I'jaz Herati's "Dar Ta'rif-i Isfahan," see Tehran University Library, MS 2591, fols. 76r–87v; and Tehran University Library, MS 3034, fols. 39r–52v.

5. On the defamation of Sufis as sodomites in a series of decrees, manuals on ethics, and anti-Sufi polemics, see Chapter 1.

6. A century earlier, the poet Harfi Isfahani traveled from his hometown of Isfahan to the Caspian Sea region of Gilan. There he wrote a *shahrashub* about the

male youth of Gilan that so upset the inhabitants that they accused Harfi of a crime (pederasty, or *jurm*) and cut off his tongue. The Safavi poet-prince Sam Mirza recounts this story about Harfi Isfahani in the middle of the sixteenth century, in his biography of poets, the *Tuhfat-i Sami*: Sam Mirza Safavi, *Tuhfat-i Sami*, 153.

7. On the variety of *shahrashub*s about Isfahan in seventeenth-century anthologies, see Golchin Ma'ani, *Shahrashub dar Shi'r-i Farsi*.

8. For similar transformations in European writing culture regarding the move away from parchment to paper, see Petrucci, *Writers and Readers*.

9. There is much scholarly debate about the distinct features of the poetic form of the *shahrashub*. Mas'ud Sa'd's poetry is considered an early example, depicting young males in bazaars, ranging from Christians to cross-eyed and curly-haired youths. Although he does not focus on craftsmen as later *shahrashub*s do, Mas'ud Sa'd also writes about the confessional and physical mingling of youths in the public space of the bazaar. See Sharma, *Persian Poetry*. On early modern Ottoman *shahrengiz*, see Çalis-Kural, *Sehrengiz*; and on the *shahrashub*s in Mughal India that catalog artisanal male youth, see Sharma, *Mughal Arcadia*. More recently, Farshid Emami has published a reading of the *shahrashub*: Emami, "Discursive Images." The question in and of itself as to why the *shahrashub* becomes the preferred mode of writing cities in the early modern Persianate world is fascinating.

10. Although Mahsati Ganjavi has a museum to her name in Ganja (Azerbaijan), where she is presented as the first woman to have played chess, composed music, and written poetry, few scholarly works to date have been conducted on her *Divan*. See Mihrabi, *Mahsati Ganja-'i*.

11. Sharma, *Persian Poetry*.

12. Nasiri, "Ikhvaniyyat-i Abbas Iqbal."

13. Mir Rukn al-Din's letter to Aqa Mansur Semnani and his response in the form of a manual are recorded in many anthologies from the seventeenth century, but they are not always collected together. For a sampling, see Malik Library, MSs 4671, 5403, and 1100; Tehran University Library, MSs 4864, 5634, 2591, and 3034; and Majlis Library, MS 2655. Mir Rukn al-Din's letter was collected in an anthology as a singular letter, as is the case with Tehran University Library, MS 8235. These compositions were first discovered and transcribed in Danishpazhu, "Isfahan va Tavus-khana-yi an." Danishpazhu has consulted the following manuscripts: Tehran University Library, MSs 4864, 5634, 2591, 3034, and 8235; Majlis Library, MS 2655; and Malik Library, MSs 4671 and 1100. I have noticed discrepancies in Danishpazhu's facsimile, slightly different versions of Mir Rukn al-Din's letter to Aqa Mansur Semnani as well as his response circulated in these *majmu'a*s. I have used two manuscript copies: Malik Library, MS 4671, fols. 162v–167v, and Malik Library, MS 5403, fols. 53r–57v, which are more complete versions.

14. Malik Library, MS 5403, fol. 53v.

15. For a sample text of the vows recorded in anthologies collected in Isfahan, see Chapter 5. Malik Library, MS 5085, dated seventeenth-eighteenth centuries CE and compiled by the poet 'Abd al-'Azim b. Mirza Ali Khu'i, known as Shurida.

16. Malik Library, MS 5403, fol. 53v.

17. Malik Library, MS 5403, fol. 53r.

18. Malik Library, MS 5403, fol. 53r.

19. Malik Library, MS 5403, fol. 53r.

20. Malik Library, MS 5403, fol. 53r.

21. Malik Library, MS 5403, fol. 53v.

22. Malik Library, MS 5403, fol. 54r.

23. Losensky, "Heaven's Vault."

24. Walter Benjamin provides a different vision of modernity associated with the figure of the flâneur. The flâneur's role as "gentleman stroller of city streets" is a position that allows him a key role in understanding, participating in, and portraying city life as a detached observer. See the chapter "Paris, the Capital of the Nineteenth Century," in Benjamin, *Writer of Modern Life*, 30–45; also see Clark, *Painting of Modern Life*, 63.

25. Malik Library, MS 5403, fol. 54v.

26. Malik Library, MS 5403, fol. 54v.

27. Malik Library, MS 4671, fol. 162v, titled, "Dardmandi insha'i dar ta'rif va tawsif-i Isfahan-i bihisht nishan numuda" (an afflicted one's composition describing Isfahan, the Image of Paradise).

28. See, for example, Tehran University Library, MS 8235.

29. As I argue in Chapter 1, the affective response to Shah Abbas I's imperial project to focus the public gaze on the Naqsh-i Jahan square cultivated a visual sensibility among the urban population. Spectacular displays of political, religious, and economic authority deployed architecture, graphics, and performance in the square to generate the visual power of palace and mosque, to hold the gaze of the viewer for which the new city center appeared to be intelligible and central.

30. Malik Library, MS 4671, fol. 162v; "spectate," *Oxford English Dictionary*, 2nd ed. online (University of Michigan Humanities Text Initiative, 1996), https://quod.lib.umich.edu/cgi/o/oed/oed-idx?q1=spectate&type=Lookup.

31. Malik Library, MS 4671, fol. 162v.

32. Malik Library, MS 4671, fol. 162v.

33. Malik Library, MS 4671, fol. 162v.

34. Malik Library, MS 4671, fol. 162v.

35. Malik Library, MS 4671, fol. 162v.

36. On fatwas banning tobacco, see Matthee, *Pursuit of Pleasure*, 135–42.

37. Malik Library, MS 4671, fol. 163r.

38. Malik Library, MS 4671, fol. 163r.

39. According to Hadith reports that recorded the actions and speech of the prophet, Muhammad had predicted the division of the Muslim community (*umma*) into seventy-two sects in what is called the *hadith al-tafriqa*, or the "tradition concerning division." This Hadith is preserved in Ibn Maja (d. 887), Abu Daʿud al-Sijistani (d. 889), al-Tirmidhi (d. 892), and al-Nisaʾi (d. 915), four of the six canonical Sunni collections of Hadith. See Mottahedeh, "Toward Pluralism," 32.

40. Malik Library, MS 4671, fol. 163r.

41. Malik Library, MS 4671, fol. 163r. The beauty of the prophet Yusuf/Joseph, which is the sign of his being chosen by God as prophet, is narrated in Chapter 12 of the Quran; Joseph also becomes the symbol of divine beauty in mystical poetry. See the Jami's (d. 1492) *Yusuf and Zulaykha*, where Yusuf is turned into a male homoerotic object of love.

42. Malik Library, MS 4671, fol. 163r.

43. Malik Library, MS 4671, fol. 163r.

44. Malik Library, MS 4671, fol. 163r.

45. Malik Library, MS 4671, fol. 163v.

46. Malik Library, MS 4671, fol. 163v.

47. Afshar, *Kaghaz*, 57–58.

48. On the commerce and consumption of coffee, see Matthee, *Pursuit of Pleasure*, 144–74. For the culture of coffeehouses in Isfahan, see Babayan, *Mystics, Monarchs, and Messiahs*, 439–43.

49. See, for example, Majlis Library, MS 14215, fol. 105, dated to seventeenth-century Isfahan.

50. Chardin first traveled to Iran in 1667. In 1669 he stayed in Isfahan for six months and returned to live there for a period of two and a half years (June 24, 1673–1676). Chardin, *Voyages*, 4: 68.

51. Malik Library, MS 4671, fol. 163r.

52. Malik Library, MS 4671, fol. 163r.

53. Malik Library, MS 4671, fol. 163r.

54. Mani was to have learned to paint from the Chinese, who were considered masters of the art. In fact, Chinese ideals of beauty, from the shape of the eyes to the white complexion of moon-faced youth, are archetypes in medieval and early modern Persianate literary and visual arts. The *Ardahang* is referred to as an extra-canonical book of paintings and illustrations meant to illustrate aspects of Mani's dualistic doctrine. See Asmussen, "Arzang."

55. Rancière, *Politics of Aesthetics*, 7–14.

56. Malik Library, MS 4671, fol. 164v.

57. Malik Library, MS 4671, fol. 164v.

58. Farhad, "Safavid Single-Page Paintings."

59. Malik Library, MS 4671, fol. 164v. The Talar-i Tavila is not extant today. It is unlikely that inhabitants of Isfahan had access to this pavilion. From poetry we have describing the Talar-i Tavila and descriptions of foreign ambassadors and travelers, the Talar-i Tavila was an audience hall that would have been reserved for court ceremonies and the reception of dignitaries. See Babaie, "Safavid Palaces."

60. Malik Library, MS 4671, fols. 164v–r.

61. "In the hands of the agile engraver who, with his diamond-fine pen, draws his name into the design so that no longer can the finger of description be lifted from the epigraphy!" Malik Library, MS 4671, fol. 164r.

62. Malik Library, MS 4671, fol. 164r.

63. On *takhyil*, or image evocation, see Harb, "Wonder in Medieval Arabic Aristotelian Poetics." Harb discusses the emotional dimension of poetry through the Aristotelian concept of image evocation that was evoked through speech, more particularly through the use of metaphor (*istiʿara*) to incite delight and pleasure in the audience. I would like to thank Lara Harb for generously sharing her paper with me.

64. Hundreds of copies of *tawbanama*, acts of repentance, have been collected in seventeenth-century anthologies. This practice points to the widespread act and performance of repentance, much like vows of brotherhood and sisterhood.

65. Malik Library, MS 4671, fol. 165v.

66. Malik Library, MS 4671, fol. 165v. For Ibn Sina on love, melancholy, and madness, see "Avicenna."

67. Malik Library, MS 4671, fol. 165v.

68. Malik Library, MS 4671, fol. 165v.

69. Malik Library, MS 4671, fol. 165v.

70. Malik Library MS 4671, fol. 165r. This mosque, now referred to as Ali's Mosque, was built in the early sixteenth century, dated 929/1523 in an inscription. It is noteworthy for its pairing with the shrine of Harun-i Vilayat (1513) and their location on the southern threshold of the Maydan-i Kuhna, the old *maydan*. See Hillenbrand, "Safavid Architecture," 764–65; Hunarfar, *Ganjina*, 369–79; and Babaie, *Isfahan*, 32–33.

71. Malik Library, MS 4671, fol. 165r.

72. Malik Library, MS 4671, fol. 165r.

73. Malik Library, MS 4671, fol. 166v.

74. Malik Library, MS 4671, fol. 166v.

75. Malik Library, MS 4671, fol. 166v.

76. The Sufi Muhammad Najm al-Din Razi (d. 654/1256) provides a detailed

discussion on the relationship between love and the intellect in his *'Ishq u 'aql*, explaining the cosmological basis for love's superiority. He concludes that intellect concerns itself with discernment and separation, among other things, and thus with plurality and the establishment of this world, but love bridges gaps and annihilates multiplicity. The opposition (*ziddiyat*) between intellect and love is based on the fact that "intellect is the great champion [*qahraman*] of constructing the two worlds, corporeal and spiritual, while love is a fire that consumes the haystack and overthrows the existence of both these worlds" (Razi, *Risala-yi 'Ishq u 'aql*, 63).

77. Malik Library, MS 4671, fol. 166v.
78. Malik Library, MS 4671, fol. 166v.
79. Malik Library, MS 4671, fol. 166r.
80. Malik Library, MS 4671, fol. 167v.
81. Malik Library, MS 4671, fol. 167v.
82. Malik Library, MS 4671, fol. 167v.
83. Malik Library, MS 4671, fol. 167v.
84. For a reading of the "age of beloveds" in seventeenth-century Istanbul, see Andrews and Kalpakli, *Age of Beloveds*.

Chapter 4: Cultivating and Disciplining Friendship Letters

I would like to thank Helmut Puff for his generous engagement with a panel on Persianate friendships, "Friendship in Persianate Societies and Cultures: Forms, Practices, and Significances," organized by Mana Kia at the Iranian Studies International Society biannual conference held in Istanbul in 2012. I presented an early version of this chapter at that conference, and his thoughtful comments have now become part of its conceptual framing.

1. *Ghazal* from Nasira Hamadani's letter to his friends in Shiraz, Majlis Library, MS 2665, fol. 442v.

2. Friendship letters preserve the main features of the *ghazals*' realist iteration; they clarify ambiguity and the use of metaphor to voice actual states and emotions (*halat*) of love and of being in love, based on their experiences with friends. In his *Maktab-i Vuqu'* (The Realist School), the literary scholar Ahmad Golchin Ma'ani canonizes this school of poetry in a volume where he collects biographies of poets and their *ghazal* compositions. See Golchin Ma'ani, *Maktab-i Vuqu' dar Shi'r-i Farsi*.

3. Nasira Hamadani's letter to his friends in Shiraz refers to the *adab* of letter writing as a joyful exchange (*tarabnama*): Majlis Library, MS 2665, fol. 442v.

4. See Chapter 3 for an exchange between two beloved friends, Mir Rukn al-Din and Aqa Mansur Semnani.

5. The designation of the letter, *nama*, had been deployed as the communicative means in medieval epics such as the *Shahnama*, literally "the shah's letter," to mark

the epic mode. The medieval *nama* is traditionally translated as "epic," incorporating in verse the medium of the epistle as a narrative form of exchange or speech act.

6. On the epistolary practice and chancellery culture of the medieval and early modern Persianate world, see Biran, "Diplomacy and Chancellery Practices"; Kinra, *Writing Self, Writing Empire*; and Mitchell, "Safavid Imperial *Tarassul*."

7. Friendship letters (*ikhvaniyyat*) for any period of Persianate history remain to be studied. In the medieval Persianate world, the term *ikhvaniyyat* referred to a form of letter writing between poet friends, who wrote in verse to display their skills and elicit eloquent responses. An aesthetic and at times boastful exchange of poetry, the *ikhvaniyyat* resemble the *munazara*, the performance of poetry in courtly and literary assemblies. Friendship letters have been categorized by the Iranian scholar Abbas Iqbal as distinct from royal (*sultaniyyat*) and chancellery (*divaniyyat*) epistles because of their personal content and poetic form. See Nasiri, "Ikhvaniyyat-i Abbas Iqbal."

8. Letters by Nasira Hamadani were the most popular epistles collected in seventeenth-century Isfahan. In the Majlis Library alone at least 100 anthologies curate his letters. For a sampling, see Majlis Library, MSs 266, 732, 908, 1122, 1168, 1346, 1665, 3455, 3547, 5996, 9087, 10180, 13443, 13777, 14145, 14209, 14215, and 16732.

9. Nasira Hamadani to his friends in Shiraz, Majlis Library, MS 1398, fol. 16v; Majlis Library, MS 10180, fol. 19v; and Majlis Library, MS 8982, fol. 162r.

10. Sa'ib Tabrizi to Zafar Khan, Malik Library, MS 4671, fol. 437r.

11. Tughra to the merchant Amina, Majlis Library, MS 3215, fol. 265r.

12. Nasrabadi, *Tazkira-yi Nasrabadi*, 339–40.

13. Derrida, "Hospitality."

14. For examples of letters of invitation to a friend for a morning coffee, see Majlis Library, MS 14215, fol. 105r; for *ash* (soup), see Majlis Library, MS 14215, fol. 208v; for *kuku* (frittata), see Majlis Library, MS 14215, fol. 207v; for *kala pacha* (sheep trotters), see Majlis Library, MS 14215, fol. 53r.

15. Such tropes are pervasive; see, for example, Majlis Library, MS 14215, fol. 105v, where an anonymous friend invites his beloved for a morning coffee at his home.

16. Mir Ilahi to Mir Munir, Majlis Library, MS 3455, fol. 375v.

17. Nasira Hamadani to his friends in Shiraz, Majlis Library, MS 2665, fol. 442v.

18. He begins his genealogy with Ibn 'Ibad, the epistles of Ibn al-Hamid, the letters of 'Abd al-Hamid, the *Maqamat* of Hamadani, Muhammad Jariri (d. 923), Hamid al-din Balkhi, the *Kashkul* of Shaykh Baha'i, the letters of Qutb ibn Muy, *Tarikh-i Wassaf*, letters of Sharaf al-Din Ali Yazdi, Shaykh Abu-l-Fazl Hindi, Anvari, Nizami, Khaqani, Sa'di, Hafiz, and Afzal Kashi.

19. Nasira Hamadani to his friends in Shiraz, Majlis Library, MS 2665, fol. 442v.

20. Copies of Nasira Hamadani's letter to his friends in Shiraz are collected in several anthologies. See, for example, Majlis Library, MS 1080, fol. 25r, and MS 3455, fol. 125r.

21. Nasrabadi, *Tazkira-yi Nasrabadi*, 164–65.

22. Quran 4:125.

23. Nasira Hamadani to Husayn Kashi, Majlis Library MS 3455, fol. 125v.

24. Although Husayn Kashi was lame, he often traveled from his hometown of Kashan to Isfahan to enjoy the pleasures of the city and maintained a cloister (*hujra*) in Isfahan. Nasrabadi, *Tazkira-yi Nasrabadi*, 164–65.

25. Nasrabadi, *Tazkira-yi Nasrabadi*, 164–65.

26. Kaykavus b. Iskandar b. Qabus (b. 1021), in his mirror-for-princes, the *Qabusnama*, speaks of the practice of friendship as a social reality—as an institution characterized by rituals and obligations akin to those of marriage and government. Although he differentiates between blood kin and friends when he quotes from the dictum that "even if one has a brother, it is better to have a friend" (*baradar ham dust bih*), he places the chapter on the rules and protocols (*ayin*) of friendship in the context of kinship, after his advice about taking a wife and raising children. Kaykavus enumerates a variety of types of friends, from boon companions (*nadim*) to feigned (*majazi*) friends. Yet the ideal of friendship is represented as a form of voluntary kinship through which the individual can publicly demonstrate his humane virtues (*mardumi*) of loyalty and generosity. A worthy partner in friendship is one who regularly renews his social bonds through the act of gifting. So long as he lives, he must withhold nothing from a friend in need. The obligations of friendship continue beyond the death of a friend, for the survivor must preserve his ties with the children and blood relatives of his dead friend, caring for them financially and emotionally. True friendship (*dusti-yi haqiqi*) is portrayed as a single-hearted (*dusti-yi yik dil*) relationship, something Kaykavus recognizes to be rare but integral to the stages of becoming a model human being as one embarks on the path of humanness (*tariq-i mardumi*). Sections from the *Qabusnama* are recorded in seventeenth-century anthologies as models of ideal friendship. Kaykavus ibn Iskandar ibn Qabus, *Nasihat-nama*, 149.

27. For a discussion on the moods and intentions of the *ghazal* in realist poetry of the sixteenth-century, see Losensky, "Poetics of Eros."

28. Mirza Ali Akbar to Zahid Khan, Tehran University Library, MS 5645, fol. 51r.

29. Ibn Muqla al-Shirazi (d. 940) was a scribe at the Abbasid Chancellery in Baghdad who rose to high positions at court, first heading the library and then taking on the post of vizier. He wrote about the art of calligraphy and is said to have codified six Arabic calligraphic scripts (*al qalam al-sitta*). His life ended in prison after first having his right hand chopped off, then his left hand, and finally his tongue.

30. Mirza Ali Akbar to Zahid Khan, Tehran University Library, MS 5645, fol. 51r.

31. Letters collected in anthologies record famous love stories between men in Isfahan. See, for example, Malik Haydar, the brother of Malik Hamza Sistani, and his beloved Zaqhu, who worked in a coffeehouse in Isfahan. Muhammad Salih Isfahani's love affair with Muhammad Riza, son of Hajji Yusuf Qahvachi, is said to have been the impulse behind him leaving his painting profession to work at the coffeehouse of his beloved, Muhammad Riza's father. These are a couple of the celebrated love affairs archived in household anthologies.

32. Copies of the *Munsha'at-i Sulaymani* and similar epistolary manuals appear in many anthologies from the seventeenth century; see, for example, Majlis Library, MSs 8895, 5162, and 5996; Malik Library, MSs 2551, 2361, and 3424; and Tehran University Library, MS 3525. I have found one manual dated to the reign of Shah Safi (r. 1629–1642), the *Munsha'at-i Shah Safi*, copied in an anthology written in Tehran and Ray; see Malik Library, MS 3850. The *Munsha'at-i Sulaymani* has been published and edited by Rasul Jafarian; see Jafarian, *Munsha'at-i Sulaymani*.

33. I have consulted about 200 anthologies housed in the Majlis, Malik, and University of Tehran manuscript libraries that include friendship letters. My analysis is drawn from this archive.

34. See, for example, Malik Library, MS 3850, fols. 48–63 and fols. 79–146.

35. *Munsha'at-i Sulaymani*, Majlis Library, MS 8835, fol. 50v.

36. In a letter written by the poet 'Urfi, he thanks Mulla Zuhuri for the gift of a scarf, writing that he wears the scarf around his neck, considering it the pride and glory of their friendship. Majlis Library, MS 3457, fol. 166r.

37. *Munsha'at-i Sulaymani*, Majlis Library, MS 8835, fol. 50v.

38. The typology of friendship letters that appear as lists in anthologies are the following: requests to meet the friend (*mulaqat*), complaints against the friend (*shikayat*), making peace (*sulhnama*), and repenting (*tawbanama*).

39. *Munsha'at-i Sulaymani*, Majlis Library, MS 8835, fol. 50r.

40. *Munsha'at-i Sulaymani*, Majlis Library, MS 8835, fol. 50r.

41. *Munsha'at-i Sulaymani*, Majlis Library, MS 8835, fol. 52v.

42. *Munsha'at-i Sulaymani*, Majlis Library, MS 8835, fol. 52v.

43. See Chapter 5 for the wording of a sample text of brotherhood vows recorded in anthologies.

44. *Munsha'at-i Sulaymani*, Majlis Library, MS 8835, fol. 53r.

45. We have several drawings by Riza Abbasi and Mu'in Musavvir as gifts for their friends. I would like to thank my friend and colleague Massumeh Farhad, who has generously informed me about this visual archive.

46. Tehran University Library, MS 8465, fol. 40r.

47. Majlis Library, MS 14209, fol. 382v.

48. There are several examples that Sheila Canby has studied in her work on Afzal Husayni. See Canby, *Rebellious Reformer*.

49. Harb, "Wonder in Medieval Arabic Aristotelian Poetics."

Chapter 5: Family Archives and Female Spaces of Intimacy

A version of Chapter 5, especially the section "Leaving Isfahan: On Friends and Kin," was previously published as "'In Spirit We Ate of Each Other's Sorrow': Female Companionship in Seventeenth-Century Safavi Iran," in *Islamicate Sexualities: Translations Across Temporal Geographies of Desire*, ed. Kathryn Babayan and Afsaneh Najmabadi, 239–74 (Cambridge, MA: Harvard Middle Eastern Monographs, 2008). I have, however, significantly reshaped my reading here to foreground a widow's family archive, her city of Isfahan, and her female beloved friend.

1. Mirza Muʿin Urdubadi, Tehran University Library, MS 2591, fol. 1r.

2. See Muhanna, *World in a Book*. Muhanna reads a fourteenth-century compendium written in Cairo by Shihab al-Din Nuwayri to think about the context and impetus for the production of such an enormous work. The seventeenth-century anthologies produced in Isfahan attempt to organize the many bodies of knowledge circulating in the city, but their authors or scribes are not interested in compiling a compendium of the humanities and the sciences, nor is the literate public their audience.

3. Recent scholarship on the dearth of official archives from the premodern Islamicate world has focused on state archives. Jurgen Paul asks a simple question: Should we not be looking elsewhere? For a summary of these debates, see Paul, "Archival Practices"; Bauden, "Du destin des archives en Islam"; Hirschler, "From Archive to Archival Practices"; Hirschler, "Text Reuse"; el-Leithy, "Living Documents"; and Sartori, "Seeing Like a Khanate."

4. On the epistolary manual, the *Munshaʾat-i Sulaymani*, see Chapter 4.

5. Consider, for example, a preserved letter by Hatim Khan Urdubadi (d. 1611), the grand vizier who served Shah Abbas I during the first two decades (1591–1611) of Isfahan's transformation into a capital city. This curatorial choice marks the 100th anniversary of the Urdubadi family in seventeenth-century Isfahan, populating the content of the anthology. Hatim Khan Urdubadi was the grandson of Bahram Khan, the amir of Urdubad who had been awarded a land grant by the founder of the Safavi dynasty, Shah Ismail (d. 1524), and was named Malik, or Lord of Urdubad.

6. This innovative feature appears, for instance, in the contemporaneous anthology of the Khwansari family of religious scholars, as both families shared the desire to organize the vast bodies of knowledge circulating in the city. For a discussion of Khwansari's anthology, see Chapter 2.

7. Mirza Muʿin Urdubadi, Tehran University, MS 2591, fols. 742–743.

8. There are a number of dates ranging from 1664 all the way to 1842.

9. On the *majlis nivis*, the secretary of the shah and rapporteur of courtly sessions, see [Samiʿa], *Tazkirat al-Muluk*, 52–54.

10. I am thinking about Gaston Bachelard's poetics of space, where he talks about "sites of our intimate lives," imagining the house as place for dreaming, an archive of dreams that resonates in "objects that may be opened," like caskets of the dead. The labor of the historian who reads the archive allows for the possibility of opening up a world, a social order collected and filed in a box, or in an anthology. See Bachelard, *Poetics of Space*.

11. Mirza Muʿin Urdubadi, Tehran University Library, MS 2591, fol. 326v.

12. Several famous *dibacha* composers appear in the Urdubadi anthology—namely, Mirza Muhammad Ibrahim, Khan Khalil Mawlana Zuhuri, Nasira Hamadani, and Aqa Husayn Khwansari—and their clearly famous prefaces were collected in many anthologies of seventeenth-century Isfahan.

13. Other practices of archiving appear in the anthology. For example, *surat* and *savad* are used to refer to different kinds of facsimile collected in the Urdubadi household archive. The *savad* is a duplicate copy, whereas the *surat* is a replica or reproduction (image), indicating two different techniques of recording from the original. And when the scribe records from an original source that was not part of the household archive, he makes sure to indicate it, stating that he has seen with his own eyes (*nazar*) the text he is copying. Clearly such practices of copying shed light on the complexities of knowledge production through the archives.

14. The terminology used for recording is indicative of the practice of archiving. *Bayaz* refers specifically to the act of copying from a bound anthology. Other terms are frequently used for copying different types of source material. *Savad*, literally "the ability to read or write," or simply "a copy," refers to reproducing from copies of letters. On the other hand, *surat*, literally "a face," "an image," or "a copy," indicates an inscription written from the original. Whether *surat-i maktub* or *savad-i maktub*, the *savad* is a duplicate copy, whereas the *surat* is a replica or reproduction (image), both indicating two different techniques of recording from the original.

15. On the *tazkira* compiled by the Safavi prince Sam Mirza Safavi in the 1550s, see Sam Mirza Safavi, *Tuhfat-i Sami*. Mirza Tahir Vahid's (1645–1666) anthology of letters (*munshaʾat*) are assembled together with those penned by two grand viziers, Muhammad Beg (1654–1661) and Sultan al-Ulama (d. 1654). And they continue beyond his death, because his son Mirza Talib Khan followed in the footsteps of his father, as *majlis nivis* (1629–1632), becoming the private secretary of the shah, the official historiographer at court, who recorded the official exchanges at the shah's assemblies and at his audiences for Shah Safi. As rapporteur to the king, Mirza

Talib Khan officially recorded and answered all forms of communications and petitions received at court. A copy of what he and his father penned was then preserved as the collective property of the Urdubadi family.

16. The Urdubadi anthology measures 11 by 7 inches (27 × 18 cm); its binding is 5 inches thick.

17. The well-preserved tablet is a phrase used in Quran 85:22 to refer to the original codex or document on which the Quran, according to traditional commentators, was originally inscribed and which has always existed in heaven. Associated with another description of the divine archetype of revelation is "mother of the book" (Quran 3:6, 13:39, 43:3; Quran 43:4, 56:78 for *kitab maknun*).

18. On the institution of temporary marriages in Shi'a Islam termed *mut'a*, literally "pleasure," which were contracted for sexual pleasure and limited to a definite period of time, see Haeri, "Mot'a."

19. Malik Library, MS 5085, dated seventeenth–eighteenth century CE and compiled by the poet 'Abd al-'Azim b. Mirza Ali Khu'i, known as Shurida.

20. Aqa Jamal Khwansari (d. 1710) was the son of Aqa Husayn Khwansari (d. 1686), the Shi'a scholar who originally collected the Khwansari household anthology in 1672–1673. See Chapter 2.

21. Khwansari, *'Aqa'id al-Nisa'*, 37.

22. Foucault's *Archeology of Knowledge* has inspired Jacques Derrida, Antoinette Burton, and Carolyn Steedman's conceptualization of the archive as housing something hidden, forgotten, or lost. Antoinette Burton refers to the practice of archiving, the process of collecting traces from the past as a "history of loss," whereas for Derrida it is a space to discover the hidden. But the archival methods of seeing and knowing the past that elicit a reading "against or along the grain" may benefit from the example of seventeenth-century household anthologies that conjure the secret to call to mind sacred knowledge as an act of signifying that which is concealed. See Foucault, *Archaeology of Knowledge*; Derrida, *Archive Fever*; Burton, *Archive Stories*; and Steedman, *Dust*.

23. See Paul Johnson's study on the Afro-Brazilian religion of Candombè, where he discusses the relationship between the secret and the sacred as a body of knowledge that is concealed and revealed in degrees to the initiate. Johnson, *Secrets, Gossip, and Gods*.

24. Mirza Mu'in Urdubadi, Tehran University Library, MS 2591, fol. 764r.

25. A century earlier, the realist school had seen the turn of another poetic mode, the *ghazal*, to realism. On the *maktab-i vuqu'*, see the Introduction and Chapters 2 and 3.

26. Mirza Mu'in Urdubadi, Tehran University Library, MS 2591, fol. 764r.

27. Mirza Mu'in Urdubadi, Tehran University Library, MS 2591, fol. 764r.

28. As earlier chapters detail, expecting a level of sharing both in spiritual and

material matters, friendship with God and with humans was an ethical practice that helped fashion a virtuous community; sincere friendships, meaningful companionship, and sociability were critical philosophical and mystical ideals prescribed for the healthy functioning of both material and moral communities.

29. Mirza Mu'in Urdubadi, Tehran University Library, MS 2591, fol. 764r.
30. Mirza Mu'in Urdubadi, Tehran University Library, MS 2591, fol. 764r.
31. Mirza Mu'in Urdubadi, Tehran University Library, MS 2591, fol. 764r.
32. On the pilgrimage to Mecca during the early modern period and the possibilities of different routes, see Faroqhi, *Pilgrims and Sultans*; Pearson, *Pilgrimage to Mecca*; Subrahmanyam, "Persians, Pilgrims, and Portuguese"; and McChesney, "Central Asian Hajj-Pilgrimage."
33. Love (*'ishq*) and melancholy (*malikhuliya*) were classified as twin maladies in Islamicate medical and ethical literature. See, for example, Biesterfeldt and Gutas, "Malady of Love"; and Seyed-Gohrab, *Layli and Majnun*.
34. Mirza Mu'in Urdubadi, Tehran University Library, MS 2591, fol. 764r.
35. Mirza Mu'in Urdubadi, Tehran University Library, MS 2591, fol. 765v.
36. Mirza Mu'in Urdubadi, Tehran University Library, MS 2591, fol. 766r.
37. Mirza Mu'in Urdubadi, Tehran University Library, MS 2591, fol. 766r.
38. For the contemporaneous use of *suhbat* to mean intercourse in heterosexual matrimonial contexts, see Khwansari, *'Aqa'id al-Nisa'*, 20.
39. Mirza Mu'in Urdubadi, Tehran University Library, MS 2591, fol. 766r.
40. Mirza Mu'in Urdubadi, Tehran University Library, MS 2591, fol. 766r.
41. Mirza Mu'in Urdubadi, Tehran University Library, MS 2591, fol. 766r.
42. Mirza Mu'in Urdubadi, Tehran University Library, MS 2591, fol. 766r.
43. Mirza Mu'in Urdubadi, Tehran University Library, MS 2591, fol. 766r.
44. She calls the Safavi dominion the *vilayat-i 'ajam* and the *sarzamin-i shah-i Iran*. Mirza Mu'in Urdubadi, Tehran University Library, MS 2591, fol. 767r.
45. Mirza Mu'in Urdubadi, Tehran University Library, MS 2591, fol. 767r.
46. Mirza Mu'in Urdubadi, Tehran University Library, MS 2591, fol. 768v.
47. Mirza Mu'in Urdubadi, Tehran University Library, MS 2591, fol. 766r.
48. Mirza Mu'in Urdubadi, Tehran University Library, MS 2591, fol. 769v.
49. Mirza Mu'in Urdubadi, Tehran University Library, MS 2591, fol. 771r.
50. Mirza Mu'in Urdubadi, Tehran University Library, MS 2591, fol. 769v.
51. Mirza Mu'in Urdubadi, Tehran University Library, MS 2591, fol. 771v.
52. Mirza Mu'in Urdubadi, Tehran University Library, MS 2591, fol. 771r.
53. Mirza Mu'in Urdubadi, Tehran University Library, MS 2591, fol. 771v.

Conclusion: The Erotics of Urbanity

1. Bray, *The Friend*. Although the religious genealogy of sworn friendships in England resonates with early modern Isfahan's practice of friendship, the mystical

and erotic terrain of Isfahan presents a quite different historical context for the affective bonds that fashion social relations.

2. Valerie Traub, in her magnum opus *Thinking Sex with the Early Moderns*, initiates a dialogue between the field of queer and feminist studies and the many insights that Alan Bray brought to the scholarship on homosexuality and the history of friendship in England to offer analytical and methodological rigor to the field of sexuality studies.

3. In addition to the seminal work of Alan Bray on the history of friendship in England from the medieval to the modern, my project is in particular dialogue with Andrews and Kalpaklı's *Age of Beloveds*; El-Rouayheb, *Before Homosexuality in the Arab-Islamic World*; Flatt, *Courts of the Deccan Sultanates*; and Walkowitz, *City of Dreadful Delight*.

4. Najmabadi, in *Women with Mustaches*, initiates her readers into the visual practices and aesthetics of the late Qajar period to elucidate how male and female concepts of beauty were undifferentiated, possessing attributes that, until the final decades of the nineteenth century, were mobile and genderless.

5. Malik Library, MS 4671, fol. 167v.

6. Malik Library, MS 4671, fol. 167v.

7. Malik Library, MS 4671, fol. 167v.

8. Mirza Muhammad Muʿin Urdubadi, Tehran University Library, MS 2591, fol. 766r.

9. Kia, *Persianate Selves*.

10. Tehran University Library, MS 8465, fol. 40r.

BIBLIOGRAPHY

Manuscript Anthologies (*majmuʿa*)
Majlis Library, Tehran. MS 266; MS 732; MS 908; MS 1080; MS 1122; MS 1168; MS 1346; MS 1398; MS 1665; MS 2655; MS 2665; MS 3215; MS 3455; MS 3457; MS 5162; MS 5557; MS 5996; MS 8835; MS 8895; MS 8982; MS 9087; MS 10180; MS 13443; MS 13777; MS 14145; MS 14209; MS 14215; MS 16732.
Majlis Library, Tehran. *Munshaʾat-i Sulaymani*, MS 8835.
Malik Library, Tehran. MS 1100; MS 2361; MS 2454; MS 2551; MS 3424; MS 3850; MS 4671; MS 4727; MS 5085; MS 5403; MS 8235/193.
Milli Library, Tehran. MS 4672.
Tehran University Library. Aqa Husayn Khwansari, MS 7116.
Tehran University Library. Mirza Muʿin Urdubadi, MS 2591.
Tehran University Library. MS 3034; MS 3525; MS 4660; MS 4758; MS 4864; MS 5634; MS 7116; MS 8235.

Sources
Abisaab, Rula Jurdi. *Converting Persia: Religion and Power in the Safavid Empire.* London: I. B. Tauris, 2004.
Abu Lughod, Janet. "The Islamic City: Historic Myth, Islamic Essence, and Contemporary Relevance." *International Journal of Middle East Studies* 19, no. 2 (May 1987): 155–76.
Afshar, Iraj. *Kaghaz dar Zindigi va Farhang-i Irani.* Tehran: Markaz-i Puzhuhishi-yi Miras-i Maktub, 2011.
Ahmadi, Nozhat. *Dar Bab-i Awqaf-i Safavi.* Tehran: Majlis-i Shura-yi Islami, 1390/2011.
Ahmed, Shahab. *What Is Islam? The Importance of Being Islamic.* Princeton, NJ: Princeton University Press, 2016.
Andrews, Walter G., and Mehmet Kalpakli. *Age of Beloveds: Love and the Beloved in Early-Modern Ottoman and European Culture and Society.* Durham, NC: Duke University Press, 2005.
Ansari, Mohammad Rafiʿ al-Din. *Dastur al-moluk: A Safavid State Manual*, trans. Willem Floor and Mohammad H. Faghfoory. Costa Mesa, CA: Mazda, 2007.

Aslanian, Sebouh. *From the Indian Ocean to the Mediterranean: The Global Trade Networks of Armenian Merchants from New Julfa*. Berkeley: University of California Press, 2011.

Asmussen, J. P. "Arzang." *Encyclopaedia Iranica*, online edition, 2011. http://www.iranicaonline.org/articles/arzang-mid.

"Avicenna." *Encyclopaedia Iranica*, online edition, 2011. http://www.iranicaonline.org/articles/avicenna-index.

Azhand, Ya'qub. *Sadiqi Beg Afshar*. Tehran: Intisharat-i Amir Kabir, 1387/2007.

Babaie, Sussan. *Isfahan and Its Palaces: Statecraft, Shi'ism, and the Architecture of Conviviality in Early Modern Iran*. Edinburgh: Edinburgh University Press, 2008.

Babaie, Sussan. "Safavid Palaces at Isfahan: Continuity and Change (1590–1666)." PhD diss., New York University, 1993.

Babaie, Sussan. "Shah 'Abbas II, the Conquest of Qandahar, the Chihil Sutun, and Its Wall Paintings." *Muqarnas* 11 (1994): 125–42.

Babaie, Sussan, Kathryn Babayan, Ina Baghdiantz McCabe, and Massumeh Farhad. *Slaves of the Shah: New Elites of Safavid Iran*. London: I. B. Tauris, 2004.

Babayan, Kathryn. "'In Spirit We Ate Each Other's Sorrow': Female Companionship in Seventeenth-Century Safavi Iran." In *Islamicate Sexualities: Translations Across Temporal Geographies of Desire*, ed. Kathryn Babayan and Afsaneh Najmabadi, 239–74. Cambridge, MA: Harvard Middle Eastern Monographs, 2008.

Babayan, Kathryn. *Mystics, Monarchs, and Messiahs: Cultural Landscapes of Early Modern Iran*. Cambridge, MA: Harvard University Press, 2002.

Bachelard, Gaston. *The Poetics of Space*, trans. Maria Jolas. Boston: Beacon Press, 1994.

Baghdiantz-McCabe, Ina. *The Shah's Silk for Europe's Silver: The Eurasian Trade of the Julfa Armenians in Safavid Iran and India (1530–1750)*. Atlanta: Scholars Press, 1999.

Barthes, Roland. "Sémiologie et urbanisme." In *Roland Barthes, Oeuvres complètes: 1966–1973*, ed. Éric Marty, 2: 439–46. Paris: Éditions du Seuil, 1994.

Bauden, Frédéric. "Du destin des archives en Islam: Analyse des données et éléments de réponse." In *La correspondance entre souverains, princes et cités-États: Approches croisées entre l'Orient musulman, l'Occident latin et Byzance (XIIIe–début XVIe siècles)*, ed. Denise Aigle and Stéphane Péquignot, 27–49. Turnhout: Brepols, 2013.

Bauer. Thomas. "Male-Male Love in Classical Arabic Poetry." In *The Cambridge History of Gay and Lesbian Literature*, ed. E. L. McCallum and Mikko Tuhkanen, 107–24. Cambridge, UK: Cambridge University Press, 2014.

Benedict, Barbara M. *Making the Modern Reader: Cultural Mediation in Early Modern Literary Anthologies*. Princeton, NJ: Princeton University Press, 1996.

Benjamin, Walter. *The Writer of Modern Life: Essays on Charles Baudelaire*, ed. Michael W. Jennings. Cambridge, MA: Belknap Press of Harvard University Press, 2006.

Bentley, Jerry H. "Cross-Cultural Interaction and Periodization in World History." *American Historical Review* 101, no. 3 (June 1996): 749–70.

Berite, Levesque de. "Extrait d'un Journal de Monsigneur Levesque de Berite escrit de sien a la fin du mois d'Aouit 1662." Gal 97 1-3, folio 114. Missio Ad Persas, Jesuit Archives, Rome.

Biesterfeldt, Hans Hinrich, and Dimitri Gutas. "The Malady of Love." *Journal of the American Oriental Society* 104, no. 1 (January–March 1984): 21–55.

Biran, Michal. "Diplomacy and Chancellery Practices in the Chagataid Khanate: Some Preliminary Remarks." *Oriente Moderno* 88, no. 2 (2008): 369–93.

Blake, Stephen P. *Half the World: The Social Architecture of Safavid Isfahan, 1590–1722*. Costa Mesa, CA: Mazda, 1999.

Bourdieu, Pierre. *Distinction: A Social Critique of the Judgment of Taste*, trans. Richard Nice. Cambridge, MA: Harvard University Press, 1987.

Bray, Alan. *The Friend*. Chicago: University of Chicago Press, 2003.

Burton, Antoinette, ed. *Archive Stories: Facts, Fictions, and the Writing of History*. Durham, NC: Duke University Press, 2006.

Çalis-Kural, Deniz. *Sehrengiz, Urban Rituals, and Deviant Sufi Mysticism in Ottoman Istanbul*. Surrey, UK: Ashgate, 2014.

Canby, Sheila. *The Rebellious Reformer: The Drawings and Paintings of Riza-yi 'Abbasi of Isfahan*. London: Azimuth, 1996.

Chardin, Jean. *Voyages du chevalier Chardin en Perse et autres lieux de l'Orient*, ed. L. Langlès, 10 vols. Paris: Le Normant, Imprimeur-Librairie, 1811.

Chartier, Roger. *The Order of Books: Readers, Authors, and Libraries in Europe Between the 14th and 18th Centuries*. Stanford, CA: Stanford University Press, 1992.

Clark, Timothy J. *The Painting of Modern Life: Paris in the Art of Manet and His Followers*. New York: Knopf, 1985.

Cook, Michael. *Commanding Right and Forbidding Wrong in Islamic Thought*. Cambridge, UK: Cambridge University Press, 2000.

Dale, Stephen. *Indian Merchants and Eurasian Trade, 1600–1750*. Cambridge, UK: Cambridge University Press, 1994.

Danishpazhu, Muhammad Taqi, ed. "Isfahan va Tavuskhana-yi an." Special issue of *Farhang-i Iranzamin* 18 (1350/1971–1972): 157–243.

Danishpazhu, Muhammad Taqi. "Yik Parda az Zindigani-yi Shah Tahmasb-i Safavi." *Danishkada-yi Adabiyyat va 'Ulum-i Insani-yi Danishgah-i Ferdowsi-yi Mashhad* 7, no. 28 (1350/1972): 915–97.

de Bruijn, J. T. P. "Ghazal, i. History." *Encyclopaedia Iranica*, online edition, 2012. http://www.iranicaonline.org/articles/gazal-1-history.

Derrida, Jacques. *Archive Fever: A Freudian Impression*, trans. Eric Prenowitz. Chicago: University of Chicago Press, 1996.

Derrida, Jacques. "Hospitality." *Angelaki: Journal of the Theoretical Humanities* 5, no. 3 (2000): 3–18.

Dickson, Martin Bernard, and Stuart Cary Welch. *The Houghton Shahnameh*, 2 vols. Cambridge, MA: Harvard University Press, 1981.

el-Leithy, Tamer. "Living Documents, Dying Archives: Towards a Historical Anthropology of Medieval Arabic Archives." *al-Qantara* 32, no. 2 (July–December 2011): 389–434.

El-Rouayheb, Khaled. *Before Homosexuality in the Arab-Islamic World, 1500–1800*. Chicago: University of Chicago Press, 2005.

Emami, Farshid. "Discursive Images and Urban Itineraries: Literary Form and City Experience in Early Modern Iran." *Journal for Early Modern Cultural Studies* 18, no. 3 (2018): 154–86.

Farhad, Massumeh. "An Artist's Impression: Muʿin Musavvir's *Tiger Attacking a Youth*." *Muqarnas* 9, no. 1 (1992): 116–23.

Farhad, Massumeh. "The Art of Muʿin Musavvir: A Mirror of His Times." In *Persian Masters: Five Centuries of Persian Painting*, ed. Sheila R. Canby, 113–28. Bombay: Marg, 1990.

Farhad, Massumeh. "Safavid Single-Page Paintings, 1629–1666." PhD diss., Harvard University, 1987.

Farhad, Massumeh, and Serpil Bagci, eds. *Falnama: The Book of Omens*. Washington DC: Arthur M. Sackler Gallery, Smithsonian Institution, 2009.

Faroqhi, Suraiya. *Pilgrims and Sultans: The Hajj Under the Ottomans, 1517–1683*. London: I. B. Tauris, 1994.

Farrukh, Rukn al-din Humayun. *Tarikhcha-yi Kitabkhana-ha-yi Iran va Kitabkhana-ha-yi ʿUmumi*. Tehran: Intisharat-i Ittihad, 1344/1965.

Fazil, Mahmud. *Fihrist-i Nuskha-ha-yi Khatti-yi Kitabkhana-yi Jamiʿ-i Gawharshad*, 4 vols. Mashhad: Kitabkhana-yi Masjid-i Jamiʿ-i Gawharshad, 1363/1984.

Fetvaci, Emine. *The Album of the World Emperor: Cross-Cultural Collecting and the Art of Album-Making in Seventeenth-Century Istanbul*. Princeton, NJ: Princeton University Press, 2019.

Flatt, Emma J. *The Courts of the Deccan Sultanates: Living Well in the Persian Cosmopolis*. Cambridge, UK: Cambridge University Press, 2019.

Fletcher, Joseph. "Integrative History: Parallels and Interconnections in the Early Modern Period, 1500–1800." In *Studies on Chinese and Islamic Inner Asia*, ed. Joseph F. Fletcher Jr. and Beatrice Forbes Manz, 37–58. Aldershot, UK: Variorum, 1995.

Foucault, Michel. *The Archaeology of Knowledge and the Discourse on Language*, trans. A. M. Sheridan Smith. New York: Pantheon, 1972.

Gillespie, Alexandra. "Caxton's Chaucer and Lydgate Quartos: Miscellanies from Manuscript to Print." *Transactions of the Cambridge Bibliographical Society* 12, no. 1 (2000): 1–25.

Golchin Ma'ani, Ahmad. *Maktab-i Vuqu' dar Shi'r-i Farsi*. Mashhad: Intisharat-i Danishgah-i Ferdowsi, 1374/1995.

Golchin Ma'ani, Ahmad. *Shahrashub dar Shi'r-i Farsi*. Tehran: Intisharat-i Amir Kabir, 1346/1967.

Greenblatt, Stephen. *Renaissance Self-Fashioning: From More to Shakespeare*. Chicago: University of Chicago Press, 1980.

Gruber, Christiane. "Divination." In *Medieval Islamic Civilization*, ed. Josef W. Meri, 1: 209–11. New York: Routledge, 2006.

Haeri, Shahla. "Mot'a." *Encyclopaedia Iranica*, online edition, 2005. http://www.iranicaonline.org/articles/mota.

Hamori, A., J. T. P. de Bruijn, Günay Alpay Kut, and J. A. Haywood. "Mukhtarat." *Encyclopaedia of Islam*, 2nd ed., online edition, 2012. *http://dx.doi.org.proxy.lib.umich.edu/10.1163/1573-3912_islam_COM_0791*.

Haneda, Masashi. "The Character of the Urbanisation of Isfahan in the Later Safavid Period." In *Safavid Persia: The History and Politics of an Islamic Society*, ed. Charles Melville, 369–88. London: I. B. Tauris, 1996.

Harb, Lara. "Wonder in Medieval Arabic Aristotelian Poetics." Paper presented at the 222nd Meeting of the American Oriental Society, Boston, MA, March 18, 2012.

Henkin, David. *City Reading: Written Words and Public Spaces in Antebellum New York*. New York: Columbia University Press, 1998.

Herzig, Edmund M. "The Rise of the Julfa Merchants in the Late Sixteenth Century." In *Safavid Persia: The History and Politics of an Islamic Society*, ed. Charles Melville, 305–22. London: I. B. Tauris, 1996.

Herzog, Dagmar. *Sex in Crisis: The New Sexual Revolution and the Future of American Politics*. New York: Basic Books, 2008.

Hillenbrand, Robert. "Safavid Architecture." In *The Cambridge History of Iran 6: The Timurid and Safavid Periods*, ed. Peter Jackson and Lawrence Lockhart, 759–842. Cambridge, UK: Cambridge University Press, 1986.

Hirschler, Konrad. "From Archive to Archival Practices: Rethinking the Preservation of Mamluk Administrative Documents." *Journal of the American Oriental Society* 136, no. 1 (January–March 2016): 1–28.

Hirschler, Konrad. "Text Reuse in Medieval Syrian Manuscripts." Paper presented at the Comparative Oriental Manuscript Studies workshop "Looking Back—Looking Ahead," Hamburg, Germany, September 26, 2016.

Hirschler, Konrad. *The Written Word in the Medieval Arabic Lands: A Social and Cultural History of Reading Practices*. Edinburgh: Edinburgh University Press, 2012.

Hunarfar, Lutfullah. *Ganjina-yi Asar-i Tarikhi-yi Isfahan*. Isfahan: Kitabfurushi-yi Saqafi, 1344/1965.

Jafarian, Rasul. *Davazda Risala-yi Fiqhi dar bara-yi Namaz-i Jumaʿ az Ruzigar-i Safavi*. Qom: Intisharat-i Ansariyan, 1381/2003.

Jafarian, Rasul. *Din va Siyasat dar Dawra-yi Safavi*. Qom: Intisharat-i Ansariyan, 1370/1991.

Jafarian, Rasul. "Fihrist-i Kitab-ha-yi yik kitabfurushi dar akharin sal-ha-yi dawra-yi Safaviyya." *Kitabkhana-yi Takhassusi-yi Tarikh-i Islam va Iran* (blog). Bahman 22, 1394/February 11, 2016.

Jafarian, Rasul. "Isharati dar Bab-i Kitab va Kitabkhana dar Dawra-yi Safaviyya." In *Maqalat-i Tarikhi*, by Rasul Jafarian, 4: 739–76. Qom: Intisharat al-Hadi, 1372/1994.

Jafarian, Rasul. *Munshaʾat-i Sulaymani*. Tehran: Majlis-i Shura-yi Islami, 1388/2009.

Jafarian, Rasul. "Ruyaruʾ-i Faqihan va Sufiyan dar ʿAsr-i Safaviyya." *Kayhan-i Andisha* 33 (1369/1990): 101–27.

Jafariyan, Rasul. *Safaviyya dar ʿArsa-yi Din, Farhang, va Siyasat*, 3 vols. Qom: Puzhuhishkada-yi Hawza va Danishgah, 1379/2000.

Johnson, Paul. *Secrets, Gossip, and Gods: The Transformation of Brazilian Candomblé*. Oxford: Oxford University Press, 2004.

Katz, Marion. "Shame (Hayaʾ) as an Affective Disposition in Islamic Legal Thought." *Journal of Law, Religion, and State* 3 (2014): 139–69.

Kaykavus ibn Iskandar ibn Qabus. *Nasihat-Nama, Known as Qabus-Nama*, trans. and ed. Reuben Levy. E. J. W. Gibb Memorial Series, n.s., 18. London: Luzac, 1951.

Khaki Khorasani, Imam Quli. *An Abbreviated Version of the Divan of Khakhi Khorasani*, ed. Vladimir Ivanow. Bombay: Islamic Research Associate Series, 1933.

Khaleghi-Motlagh, Dj. "Asadi Tusi." *Encyclopaedia Iranica*, online edition, 2012. http://www.iranicaonline.org/articles/asadi-tusi.

Khoury, N. N. Nuha. "Ideologies and Inscriptions: The Epigraphy of Masjid-i Shah and the Ahmediye in the Context of Safavid-Ottoman Relations." Unpublished, 1997.

Khoury, N. N. Nuha. "Safavid Epigraphy in Isfahan: The Masjid-i Shah." MA thesis, University of Victoria, British Columbia (Canada), 1983.

Khwansari, Aqa Jamal. *ʿAqaʾid al-Nisaʾ va Mirat al-Balhaʾ*, ed. Mahmud Katiraʾi. Tehran: Intisharat-i Tahuri, 1349/1970.

Kia, Mana. *Persianate Selves: Memories of Place and Origin Before Nationalism*. Stanford, CA: Stanford University Press, 2020.

Kinra, Rajeev. *Writing Self, Writing Empire: Chandar Bhan Brahman and the Cultural World of the Indo-Persian State Secretary*. Oakland: University of California Press, 2015.

Lefebvre, Henri. *The Production of Space*, trans. Donald Nicholson-Smith. Malden, MA: Blackwell, 1991.

Lerer, Seth. "Medieval English Literature and the Idea of the Anthology." *Publications of the Modern Language Association* 118, no. 5 (October 2003): 1251–67.

Levi-Strauss, Claude. *Tristes Tropiques*, trans. John and Doreen Weightman. New York: Penguin, 1992.

Lewis, Franklin D. "Reading, Writing, and Recitation: Sana'i and the Origins of the Persian Ghazal." Ph.D. diss., University of Chicago, 1995.

Losensky, Paul. "'The Equal of Heaven's Vault': The Design, Ceremony, and Poetry of the Hasanabad Bridge." In *Writers and Rulers: Perspectives on Their Relationship from Abbasid to Safavid Times*, ed. Beatrice Guendler and Louise Marlow, 195–216. Wiesbaden: Reichert, 2004.

Losensky, Paul. "The Poetics of Eros in Early Modern Persia: The Lovers' Confection and the Glorious Epistle by Muhtasham Kashani." *Iranian Studies* 42, no. 5 (2009): 745–64.

Losensky, Paul E. "Sa'eb Tabrizi." *Encyclopaedia Iranica*, online edition, 2003. http://www.iranicaonline.org/articles/saeb-tabrizi.

Losensky, Paul. "Saqi-Nama." *Encyclopaedia Iranica*, online edition, 2016. http://www.iranicaonline.org/articles/saqi-nama-book.

Losensky, Paul. "Vahshi Bafqi." *Encyclopaedia Iranica*, online edition, 2004. http://www.iranicaonline.org/articles/vahshi-bafqi.

Losensky, P. E. "Wahshi Bafki." *Encyclopaedia of Islam*, 2nd ed., online edition, 2012. https://referenceworks.brillonline.com/entries/encyclopaedia-of-islam-2/wahshi-bafki-or-yazdi-SIM_7828.

Losensky, Paul. *Welcoming Fighani: Imitation and Poetic Individuality in the Safavid-Mughal Ghazal*. Costa Mesa, CA: Mazda, 1998.

Lynch, Kevin. *The Image of the City*. Cambridge, MA: MIT Press, 1960.

Mahbub-Farimani, Elaheh. "Sahhafi, az Safaviyya ta Qajar." *Nama-yi Baharistan* 11, no. 16 (1389/2006): 61–144.

Majlisi, Muhammad Baqir b. Muhammad Taqi. *Hilyat al-Muttaqin*. Qom: Intisharat-i Masjid-i Muqaddis-i Jamkaran, 1388/2009.

Mans, Raphaël du. *Estat de la Perse en 1660*, ed. Charles Scheffer. Paris: Ernest Leroux, 1890.

Matthee, Rudolph P. *The Politics of Trade in Safavid Iran: Silk for Silver, 1600–1730*. Cambridge, UK: Cambridge University Press, 1999.

Matthee, Rudi. *The Pursuit of Pleasure: Drugs and Stimulants in Iranian History, 1500–1900*. Princeton, NJ: Princeton University Press, 2005.

Mauss, Marcel. "Techniques of the Body." *Economy and Society* 2, no. 1 (1973): 70–88.

McChesney, R. D. "The Central Asian Hajj-Pilgrimage in the Time of the Early

Modern Empires." In *Safavid Iran and Her Neighbors*, ed. Michel Mazzaoui, 129–56. Salt Lake City: University of Utah Press, 2003.

McChesney, R. D. "Four Sources on Shah 'Abbas's Building of Isfahan." *Muqarnas* 5 (1988): 103–34.

Meisami, Julie Scott. "Allegorical Gardens in the Persian Poetic Tradition: Nezami, Rumi, Hafez." *International Journal of Middle East Studies* 17, no. 2 (May 1985): 229–60.

Meisami, Julie Scott. *Medieval Persian Court Poetry*. Princeton, NJ: Princeton University Press, 1987.

Mihrabi, Mu'in al-Din. *Mahsati Ganja-'i: Buzurgtarin Zan Sha'ir-i Ruba'isara*. Tehran: Intisharat-i Tus, 1382/2003.

Mitchell, Colin. "Safavid Imperial *Tarassul* and the Persian *Insha'* Tradition." *Studia Iranica* 26 (1997): 173–209.

Mottahedeh, Roy. "Toward Pluralism: The Use and Reuse of the Seventy-Odd Divisions." In *Diversity and Pluralism in Islam: Historical and Contemporary Discourses Amongst Muslims*, ed. Zulfikar Hijri, 31–42. London: I. B. Tauris, 2010.

Muhanna, Elias. *The World in a Book: al-Nuwayri and the Islamic Encyclopedic Tradition*. Princeton, NJ: Princeton University Press, 2018.

Munshi, Iskandar Beg. *Tarikh-i 'Alam Ara-yi 'Abbasi*, 2 vols. Tehran: Intisharat-i Amir Kabir, 1350/1971.

Munshi Qummi, Ahmad b. Husayn. *Gulistan-i Hunar*, ed. Ahmad Suhayli Khwansari. Tehran, Intisharat-i Manuchihri, 1366/1987.

Najmabadi, Afsaneh. *Women with Mustaches and Men Without Beards: Gender and Sexual Anxieties of Iranian Modernity*. Berkeley: University of California Press, 2005.

Nasiri, Muhammad Riza. "Ikhvaniyyat-i Abbas Iqbal." *Faslnama-yi Nama-yi Anjuman* 5, no. 21 (1385/2006): 165–86.

Nasrabadi Isfahani, Muhammad Tahir. *Tazkira-yi Nasrabadi*, ed. Vahid Dastgirdi. Tehran: Intisharat-i Armaghan, 1351/1973.

Natanzi, Mahmud bin Hidayatullah Afushta. *Naqavat al-Asar fi Zikr al-Akhyar dar Tarikh-i Safaviyya*, ed. Ihsan Ishraqi. Tehran, Instisharat-i 'Ilmi va Farhangi, 1350/1971.

Necipoğlu, Gülru. "Framing the Gaze in Ottoman, Safavid, and Mughal Palaces." *Ars Orientalis* 23 (1993): 303–42.

Newman, Andrew. "Clerical Perceptions of Sufi Practices in Late Seventeenth-Century Persia, II: Al-Hurr al-'Amili (d. 1693) and the Debate on the Permissibility of Ghina." In *Living Islamic History: Studies in Honour of Professor Carole Hillenbrand*, ed. Yasir Suleiman, 192–207. Edinburgh: Edinburgh University Press, 2010.

Nichols, Stephen G., and Siegfried Wenzel, eds. *The Whole Book: Cultural Perspectives on the Medieval Miscellany*. Ann Arbor: University of Michigan Press, 1996.

Paul, Jurgen. "Archival Practices in the Muslim World Prior to 1500." In *Manuscripts and Archives: Comparative Views on Record-Keeping*, ed. Alessandro Bausi, Christian Brockmann, Michael Friedrich, and Sabine Kienitz, 339–60. Berlin: De Gruyter, 2018.

Pearson, M. N. *Pilgrimage to Mecca: The Indian Experience, 1500–1800*. Princeton, NJ: Markus Wiener, 1996.

Pedersen, Johannes. *The Arabic Book*, trans. Geoffrey French. Princeton, NJ: Princeton University Press, 1984.

Petrucci, Armando. *Public Lettering: Script, Power, and Culture*, trans. Linda Lappin. Chicago: University of Chicago Press 1993.

Petrucci, Armando. *Writers and Readers in Medieval Italy: Studies in the History of Written Culture*, trans. and ed. Charles M. Radding. New Haven, CT: Yale University Press, 1995.

Pickthall, Mohammad M. *The Glorious Qur'an: Arabic Text and English Rendering*, 10th ed. Des Plaines, IL: Library of Islam, 1994.

Puff, Helmut. *Sodomy in Reformation Germany and Switzerland, 1400–1600*. Chicago: University of Chicago Press, 2003.

Rancière, Jacques. *The Politics of Aesthetics*, trans. Gabriel Rockhill. London: Bloomsbury, 2006.

Razi, Muhammad Najm al-Din. *Risala-yi 'Ishq u 'aql*, ed. Taqi Tafazzoli. Tehran: Bungah-i Tarjuma va Nashr-i Kitab, 1345/1966.

Rizvi, Kishwar. "The Suggestive Portrait of Shah 'Abbas: Prayer and Likeness in a Safavid *Shahnama*." *The Art Bulletin* 94, no. 2 (June 2012): 226–50.

Rowson, E. K. "Homosexuality, ii. In Islamic Law." *Encyclopaedia Iranica*, online edition, 2012. http://www.iranicaonline.org/articles/homosexuality-ii.

Roxburgh, David. *The Persian Album, 1400–1600: From Dispersal to Collection*. New Haven, CT: Yale University Press, 2005.

Roxburgh, David. *Prefacing the Image: The Writing of Art History in Sixteenth-Century Iran*. Leiden: Brill, 2001.

Sadra. Mulla. "Sharh Hidayat al-Hikma." MS 9607. Mar'ashi Najafi Library, Qom.

Sam, Mirza Safavi. *Tuhfat-i Sami*, ed. Vahid Dastgirdi. Tehran: Intisharat-i Armaghan, 1314/1935.

[Sami'a, Mirza]. *Tazkirat al-Muluk*, trans. Vladimir Minorsky. E. J. W. Gibb Memorial Series, n.s., 16. London: Luzac, 1943.

Sartori, Paolo. "Seeing Like a Khanate: On Archives, Cultures of Documentation, and Nineteenth-Century Khvarazm." *Journal of Persianate Studies* 9, no. 2 (2016): 228–57.

Sefatgol, Mansur. *Sakhtar-i Nihad va Andisha-ha-yi Dini dar Iran-i ʿAsr-i Safavi*. Tehran: Intisharat-i Risa, 1389/2010.

Seyed-Gohrab, Ali Asghar. *Layli and Majnun: Love, Madness, and Mystic Longing in Nizami's Epic Romance*. Leiden: Brill, 2003.

Shamlu, Vali Quli b. Davud Quli. *Qisas al-Khaqani*, ed. Sayyid Hasan Sadat Nasiri, 2 vols. Tehran: Vizarat-i Farhang va Irshad-i Islami, 1371/1992.

Sharma, Sunil. *Mughal Arcadia: Persian Literature in an Indian Court*. Cambridge, MA: Harvard University Press, 2017.

Sharma, Sunil. *Persian Poetry at the Indian Frontier: Masʿud Saʿd Salman of Lahore*. Delhi: Permanent Black, 2000.

Shaykh Bahaʾi, Muhammad b. Husayn. *Jamiʿ-i ʿAbbasi*. Bombay: Intisharat-i Gulzar Husayni, 1319/1940.

Shreve-Simpson, Marianna, and Massumeh Farhad. *Sultan Ibrahim Mirza's Haft Awrang: A Princely Manuscript from Sixteenth-Century Iran*. New Haven, CT: Yale University Press, 1997.

Steedman, Carolyn. *Dust: The Archive and Cultural History*. New Brunswick, NJ: Rutgers University Press, 2002.

Stewart, Devin J. "An Episode in the ʿAmili Migration to Safavid Iran: Husayn b. ʿAbd al-Samad al-ʿAmili's Travel Account." *Iranian Studies* 39, no. 4 (December 2006): 481–508.

Stewart, Devin. "Husayn b. ʿAbd al-Samad al-ʿAmili's Treatise for Sultan Suleiman and the Shiʿi Shafiʿi Legal Tradition." *Islamic Law and Society* 4, no. 2 (1997): 156–99.

Subrahmanyam, Sanjay. "Persians, Pilgrims, and Portuguese: The Travails of Masulipatnam Shipping in the Western Indian Ocean, 1590–1655." *Modern Asian Studies* 22, no. 3 (1988): 503–30.

Subtelny, Maria. "Visionary Rose: Metaphorical Application of Horticultural Practice in Persian Culture." In *Botanical Progress, Horticultural Innovations, and Cultural Change*, ed. Michel Conan and W. John Kress, 22–31. Washington, DC: Dumbarton Oaks, 2007.

Tabrizi, Saʾib. *Kulliyat-i Saʾib Tabrizi*, ed. Jahangir Mansur. Tehran: Intisharat-i Khayyam, 1373/1995.

Taussig, Michael. *Defacement: Public Secrecy and the Labor of the Negative*. Stanford, CA: Stanford University Press, 1999.

Taymuri, Mortiza. "Sarguzasht-i Kitabkhana-ha-yi Isfahan dar Dawran-i Safaviyya." In *Majmuʿa-yi Maqalat-i Hamayish Isfaha va Safaviyya*, ed. Mortiza Dihqan Nizhad, 2 vols. Isfahan: Danishgah-i Isfahan, 1380/2001.

Terzioğlu, Derin. "Sunna-Minded Sufi Preachers in Service of the Ottoman State:

The Nasihatname of Hasan Addressed to Murad IV." *Archivum Ottomanicum* 27 (2010): 241–312.

Thackston, W. M. *A Century of Princes: Sources on Timurid History and Art*. Cambridge, MA: Aga Khan Program for Islamic Architecture, 1989.

Toorawa, Shawkat M. *Ibn Abi Tahir Tayfuur and Arabic Writerly Culture: A Ninth Century Bookman in Baghdad*. London: Routledge Curzon, 2005.

Touati, Houari. *L'armoire à sagesse: Bibliothèques et collections en Islam*. Paris: Aubier, 2003.

Traub, Valerie. *Thinking Sex with the Early Moderns*. Philadelphia: University of Pennsylvania Press, 2016.

Uluç, Lale. "Ottoman Book Collectors and Illustrated Sixteenth Century Shiraz Manuscripts." *Revue des mondes musulmans et de la Méditerranée* 87–88 (1999): 85–107.

Vahid Qazvini, Muhammad Tahir b. Husayn. *'Abbasnama*, ed. Ibrahim Dihqan. Arak: Kitabfurushi-yi Davudi Arak, 1329/1950.

Walkowitz, Judith. *City of Dreadful Delight: Narratives of Sexual Danger in Late-Victorian London*. Chicago: University of Chicago Press, 1992.

Wheatley, Paul. "Levels of Space Awareness in the Traditional Islamic City." *Ekistics* 42, no. 253 (December 1976): 354–66.

Zamani Nizhad, Ali Akbar. *Munsha'at va Makatibat*. Markaz-i Tahqiqat-i Rayana-'i Hawza-yi 'Ilmiya-yi Isfahan, 1393/2015.

Ze'evi, Dror. *Producing Desire: Changing Sexual Discourse in the Ottoman Middle East, 1500–1900*. Berkeley: University of California Press, 2006.

Zilfi, Madeline C. "The Kadizadelis: Discordant Revivalism in Seventeenth-Century Istanbul." *Journal of Near Eastern Studies* 45, no. 4 (October 1986): 251–69.

Zuhuri Tarshizi, Nur al-din Muhammad. *Divan-i Ẕuhuri Tarshizi: Ghazaliyyat*, ed. Aṣghar Babasalar. Tehran: Majlis-i Shura-yi Islami, 1390/2011.

INDEX

Page references in italics indicate illustrative material.

Abbas I, Safavi Shah of Iran: as beloved cupbearer, 17–18, 46–50, *48*, 54, 58, 100–102, *101*; divine genealogy, 37, 40, 42, 46; imperial building project, overview, 5, 7, 8–9; inaugural program, 32–36, 213n14; masculine courtly love toward, 50–55, *51*, *53*, *55*, 95–96; and Nuqtavi movement, 18, 30–31; as patron of the arts, 34, 40, 46; public presence in Isfahan, 36, 58, 109; religious endowments, 37, 41–42
Abbas II, Safavi Shah of Iran, 46, 62, 213n14
Abdullah ibn Abbas, 45
absence and presence: mediated through friendship letters, 112, 114–17, 151–54; mediated through portraits, 155–57, *157*, 160–62, *161*, 178, *179*; and melancholy, 121, 178, 185–92
abstention, 61, 90, 123, 131, 136, 202
Abu-Lughod, Janet, 4
adab (rules of etiquette and conduct): as concept, 11–12; of sociability (*see* male friendship; homoerotic/homoeroticism; masculinity; mystic love; social order; urbanity); of literature (*see* male friendship letters)
'Adilshah II, Ibrahim, 86
Afandi, Mirza Abdullah, 77, 78, 220n36

Afshar, Sadiqi Beg, 66
Afushta Natanzi, Mahmud b. Hidayatullah, 31–36, 209n12, 212–13nn3–4, 213n7, 213n14
Afzal Husayni (painter), 160, *161*, 178
Afzal Kashi, 229n18
Ali, Imam: in *dibacha*s, 172, 175; in New Friday Prayer Mosque epigraphic program, 5, 9, 40, 42–46, 130–31; as patron of barber's guild, 216n46; *Sahifat al-Kamila*, 82
Ali Qapu (Imperial Gate), 7, 37, *38*, 45, 46
Ali Riza (barber), 36, 58–59, 216n48
Ali Riza Abbasi Tabrizi (calligrapher), 40, 42, 66
Allah. *See* God
almanac (*taqvim*), 83, 84, 221n55
al-'Amili, Shaykh Ali Minshar, 77, 220n36
al-'Amili, Shaykh Baha'i: *Jami'-i'Abbasi*, 9, 41; *Kashkul*, 229n18; library, 77, 220n36; Nasira Hamadani as guest of, 144; New Friday Prayer Mosque epigraphic program, 41–42, 214n27; role as Shaykh al-Islam, 8–9, 57
Andrews, Walter G., 236n3
anthologies, *13*; and city concept, 10–17; curated subjects, 73–75; and habits of collecting, 67–70, 218n14;

household genre, overview, 65–66, 68, 69–70, 165–66; and literacy, 16–17, 70–71, 209n7; materiality, 10–11, 76, 219n32; ownership, 14, 70, 211n30; process of compiling, overview, 12–16, 210–11n27; and reading urbanity concept, 2–4; and family archives concept, 28, 68, 164–67, 183–84, 203–4, 234n22; workshops, 66, 67, 71, 75–76, 219n29. See also *majmuʿa*; *muraqqaʿ*

apocalypse, 18, 31–32, 36

Aqa Husayn Ali (wrestler), 134

Aqa Husayn Khwansari (religious scholar): burial, 83–84, 103; compared to Muhammad Qasim (painter), 106–7; condemnation of beard shaving, 88–89, 222n67; as *dibacha* composer, 233n12; and Khwansari household library, 77, 220n36, 220n40; as Shiʾa scholar, 78–79; as translator, 78, 82; literary skills, 80, 84–86

Aqa Husayn Khwansari, anthology, 79; habits of collecting, 75–77, collaborative production of, 78, 84, 204; compared to Urdubadi anthology, 166, 232n6; composition manuals, 86–87; dating, 80, 203; divination manuals, 81–83, 220n48; essays on love, 87–90, 202–3; letter models, 84–86, 221n52; table of contents and map of Istanbul, 80, 207–8

Aqa Jamal Khwansari, 234n20; *Aqaʾid al-Nisaʾ*, 180–81, 203

Aqa Mansur Semnani (religious scholar and poet), erotic city manual: in anthologies, 117–18, 224n13; authoritative voice, 121–22; as masculine tour of Isfahan, 119, 132, 135–36; and Rukn al-Din's friendship letter, 112, 113–17; male homoerotic/homoeroticism, 117–8; as subversion of form, 113, 118; tour of bazaars, 122–26; tour of *maydan*, 133–34; tour of palace complex, 126–29; tour of rag sellers' street, 134–35, 202; tour of sacred city spaces, 130–33; writing metaphor in, 120–21. See also *shahrashub*

Aqa Qanbar Ali Khwaja, 72

Armenians, 1, 9–10, 11, 60, 102, 123

Asadi Tusi, Ali ibn Ahmad, *Garshaspnama*, 217n8

Aslanian, Sebouh, 209n11, 210n17

Bachelard, Gaston, 233n10

Balkhi, Hamid al-din 229n18

barbers, 58–59, 216n46

Barthes, Roland, 2, 18, 209n5

bastinade trope, 85, 92–96, *93*, 103, 105, 198

bathhouse (*hammam*), 10, 17, 23, 24, 36, 44, 58–59, 60, 73, 180, 216n47,48,49

bayaz (copy), as term, 70, 143, 171, 204, 233n14

bazaar, the: Aqa Mansur and, 119, 122–26, 129, 131; construction of new, 37, 212n3; in Isfahan visual program, 5, 7, *7*, 9, 33, 61; goods sold in, xii, 16, 36, 71, 76, 211n30, 219n31,32; male youth on display in, 23, 109, 119, 122–26, 129, 224n9; performance of desire in, 4, 17, 18; regulation of, 58, 215n44; as site of alternative social order, 110–11; seminary in, 78–79; as site of urbanity, 64–66, 75, 191–92; in Tabriz, 9

beards and moustaches, 22, 23, 24, 49, 50, 60, 88–89

Index 251

beauty, as erotic, 74, 90, 160, 200. *See* male youth; Isfahan
Benjamin, Walter, 225n24
bibliomancy, 81
biographies (*tazkira*), 67
bookbinders, 76, 217–18n10
Bourdieu, Pierre, 210n24
boy gazing. *See* gazing; male youth; homoerotic/homoeroticism; mystic love
Bray, Alan, 199, 236n2
Burton, Antoinette, 234n22

Canby, Sheila, 232n48
celibacy, 21, 59, 60–61, 88, 133. *See* Sufism
central square. *See* Naqsh-i Jahan square
Chardin, Jean Baptiste, 11, 71, 125, 215n44, 218n21, 219n29, 226n50
Chihil Sutun (Forty Pillars Palace) murals, 47–57, *48, 51, 53, 55, 56,* 215n36
chub-i tariqat (stick of Sufi order) ritual, *51,* 51–52, *53*
city disturbance. See *shahrashub*
coffeehouse, 10, 17, 23, 36, 58, 60, 80, 109–10, 116, 119, 122, 124–26, 129, 135, 140, 144–46, 205, 226n48, 231n31
communal worship, 8–9, 41, 44, 131
complaint letter form (*shikayat*), 152–54
conduct manuals (*dastur al-'amal*), form and function, 113, 118. *See also* adab; Aqa Mansur Semnani, erotic city manual
cosmos and divine creation, 172–75
cross-dressers, 55, *56*
curating, as concept, 24, 63, 65, 75, 77, 129, 160, 184, 201

Danishpazhu, Muhammad Taqi, 224n13
Derrida, Jacques, 234n22
desire, erotic (male-male, female-female), 28, 56, 58, 62, 89, 94–95, 107, 109, 111, 118, 120, 125, 129, 154–55, 178, 198–201; spiritual, 22, 27, 59, 95, 106, 113, 117, 133, 143, 148–49, 189, 194, 197, 221, 205. *See* absence and presence; gazing; homoerotic/homoeroticism; love; mystic love
dibacha (preface), 80, 171–77, 174, 213n6, 233n12
discipline, sexual, 22, 50–55, *51, 53, 55,* 57, 59, 62, 82, 92–96, *93,* 107, 123, 133, 149, 163, 200
divination manuals (Falnama), 81–83, 220n48
divine creation and cosmos, 172–75
divine union. *See* mystic love

education, 76, 83, 86, 92, 94, 95, 154; of the senses, 117, 120, 124, 135, 177, 202
El-Rouayheb, Khaled, 236n3
epistles. *See* male friendship letters
eros. *See* desire, love, mystic love
eroticism. *See* homoerotic/homoeroticism; sexuality

facial hair, 22, 23, 24, 49, 50, 60, 88–89
family archives, as concept, 164–65. *See also* Aqa Husayn Khwansari, anthology; Urdubadi anthology; household anthologies
Farhad, Massumeh, xiii, 211n32, 217n4, 222n74, 231n45
Farrukh, Rukn al-din Humayun, 219n34
female friendship: male ambivalence toward, 180–83, 203; sisterhood vows (*khwahar khwandagi*), 114,

180, 181; and tension between affective ties, 188–95; Urdubadi widow's friend (*yar*) 165, 177–83, 186–87
Flatt, Emma J., 236n3
Forty Pillars Palace (Chihil Sutun) murals, 47–57, *48*, *51*, *53*, *55*, *56*, 215n36
Foucault, Michel, 183, 234n22
Friday prayer mosques: Old Friday Prayer Mosque, 131–32, 227n70; and religious leadership, 41, 131. *See also* New Friday Prayer Mosque

Gabriel (angel), 45–46
Galenic philosophy, 88, 95, 106
gardens: as city metaphor, 8, 63, 103, 106, 136; male youth as flowers in, 116, 125, 135; in mystical love poetry, 121, 158, *159*; as representation of paradise, 5–8, 35, 63, 121
gazing: at beloved cupbearer, 17–18, 46–50, *48*, 54, 58, 100–102, *101*; companionate spectatorship, 116, 125–26, 129, 146–47; condemnation of boy gazing, 22, 59, 202; and ecstatic gratification, 133–34; and embodiment, 126–29; at female entertainers, 55–56, *56*, 105; and the flâneur, 116, 225n24; and ritualized discipline, 19–21, 54–55, 92; Sufi practice of, 19–21, 54, 119–20, 15. *See also* absence and presence; homoerotic/homoeroticism
ghazals (love poetry), 121, 137–44, 147–48, 151, 152, 228n2, 234n25
Ghaznavi, Mahmud, Sultan of Ghazni, 81
God: cosmos and divine creation, 172–75; forgiveness from, 193–94; names of, 39, 214n21, 215n40; in New Friday Prayer Mosque epigraphic program, 5, *6*, 42–43, 44–46; in Shaykh Lutfullah Mosque epigraphic program, 39
Golchin Maʿani, Ahmad, 211n32; *Maktab-i Vuquʿ*, 228n2
great conjunction, 30, 212n2
Greenblatt, Stephen, 216n3

Hafiz, 229n18
hair, facial, 22, 23, 24, 49, 50, 60, 88–89
Hajj Hasan Beg, 66, 219nn35–36
Hajj Muhammad, 70, 218n19
Hajj pilgrimage, 70, 185–87, 192–94
Hajji Fazlullah Beg, 72
Hajji Tahir ʿAttar, 130
Harb, Lara, 227n63
Harfi Isfahani, 223–24n6
Henkin, David, 3
Herat, 108, 109, 111, 218n12
heterosexual, 22, 56, 59–61, 201, 235n38
Hindi, Shaykh Abu-l-Fazl, 229n18
Hirschler, Konrad, 210n25
homoerotic/homoeroticism: absence and presence, dynamics of, 112, 114–17, 151–54, 160–62; anxieties about, concept, 22–24; and cultivation of the senses, 119–20, 123–26, 133–34; disclosure of love affairs, 147–49, 163, 231n31; and ecstatic gratification, 133–34; and embodied passion, 126–29; in Isfahan, 130–33; in the *maydan*, 55–56; melancholy and emotional turmoil over, 121, 143–47, 178, 188–95; and portrait exchanges, 155–56, *157*, *161*, 162; regulation of public, 23–24, 58–61, 88–89, 118; secrecy *vs.* disclosure, 114, 117, 123, 135, 148–49, 178–80, 201–2; and sensitivity of *shahrashub* genre,

108–9, 223–24n6; social hierarchies of, 49–55, 56, 57, 89, 92–96, 212n42; as spectacle, 119–20. *See also* desire; female friendship; male friendship; gazing; male youth; mystic love
homosexuality, 22, 211n36, 236n2, 236n3
homosociality, male and female, 18, 57, 62, 87, 105, 107, 111, 117, 118, 178, 199, 200
hospitality, 142–43
household anthologies, as genre, 65–66, 68, 69–70, 165–66. *See also* Aqa Husayn Khwansari, anthology; family archives; Urdubadi anthology
Huri Khanum, 79, 220n42

Ibn Arabi, 87
Ibn 'Ibad, 229n18
Ibn Khatun, 219n36
Ibn Samsamani, *Jami' al-lazzat*, 88
Ibn Sina, *Canon of Healing*, 88, 130
I'jaz Herati, 108–9, 111
Imams, religious authority of, 41. *See also* Ali, Imam
imperial building project. *See* Isfahan
Imperial Gate (Ali Qapu), 7, 37, *38*, 45, 46
inaugural program, Isfahan, 32–36, 213n14
inheritance, 14, 70, 218n19
Iqbal, Abbas, 229n7
Isfahan, *26*, *38*; Afghan invasion of (1722), 167; Chihil Sutun (Forty Pillars Palace) murals, 47–57, *48*, *51*, *53*, *55*, *56*, 215n36; as experience (*see* Aqa Mansur Semnani, erotic city manual); Imperial Gate (Ali Qapu), 37; and longing in Aleppo, 191–92; Old Friday Prayer Mosque, 131–32, 227n70 (*see also* New Friday Prayer Mosque); population, 11, 210n23; Shah Abbas I's inaugural program in, 32–36, 213n14; Shaykh Lutfullah Mosque, 37–40, *39*, 214n19; transformation into imperial city, overview, 5–10, 11, 212n3. *See also* beauty; Naqsh-i Jahan square
Isfahani, Mirza Abu Turab, 219n36
'ishq (love that is desiring). *See* mystic love
Iskandar Beg Munshi, 66, 213n16
Ismail, Safavi Shah of Iran, 18, 46, 47, 213n17
Istanbul, 22, 80, 106, 165, 200, 211n37, 228n84
'Itiqad Khan, 66, 76, 217n9, 219n33, 219nn35–36

Jafar al-Sadiq, Imam: *Falnama*, 81, 221n51; *Ikhtiyarat al-Ayyam*, 221n51
Jafarian, Rasul, 218n22, 218n24, 219n34
Jahan Banu, 14, 211n30
Jerusalem, 132, 135
Johnson, Paul, 234n23
Joseph (Yusuf), 123, 226n41

Ka'ba, 42, 46, 113, 130–31, 132, 184–87, 191, 193–94
Kalpakli, Mehmet, 236n3
Kashani, Mulla Muhsin Fayz, 131, 220n36
Kashi, Husayn 144–47, *145*, 230n24
Kaykavus b. Iskandar b. Qabus, *Qabusnama*, 230n26
Kazim (judge), 14, 211n30
Khaki Khurasani, Quli, 216n46
khalifat al-khulafa (spiritual representative of the shah), 50–52, *51*, *53*, 58
Khoury, Nuha, 214n27

Khwaja Ali's coffeehouse, 125
Khwaja Malik Mustawfi, 132, 213n7
knowledge production, spaces for, 64–65, 72–73, 75–76, 96–97

Lahiji, Nur al-din Muhammad, 21
Lahiji, Shaykh Hazin, 77, 220n36
letters. *See* friendship letters
Levi-Strauss, Claude, 209n5
libraries: family archives concept, 164–65; Khwansari family library, 77, 220n36, 220n40; private, 76–77, 219–20n36; seminary, 71–72, 75–76, 220n42. *See also* Urdubadi anthology; household anthologies
literacy, 16–17, 43, 70–71, 150–51, 209n7
longing. *See* absence and presence; gazing; homoerotic/homoeroticism; love; mystic love
Losensky, Paul, 70
love: benefits and detriments of worldly, 89–90, 106; essays on, 87–90, 202–3; and intellect, 133, 228n76; and melancholy, 19, 121, 133, 178, 185–92, 235n33. *See also* male friendship; homoerotic/homoeroticism; mystic love
Lynch, Kevin, 2–3

Madrasa-yi Jadda, 79, 220n42
Mahdi (messiah), 18, 41
Mahsati Ganjavi, 110–11, 224n10
Majlisi, Muhammad Baqir, 60–61, 220n36
Majlisi, Muhammad Taqi, 221n51
majmu'a (collected verbal texts): xii–xiii, 2, connection to *muraqqa'*, 14–17, 67–68, 70, 177; inheritance of, 14, 70; popularity of, 67, 71–75. *See also* anthologies; Aqa Husayn Khwansari, anthology; Urdubadi anthology

male friendship: *adab* of, overview, 17–19, 22–24; with Ali, 44, 45–46; and companionate spectatorship, 116, 125–26, 129, 146–47; courtly brotherhood of love for the shah, 52–53; and mystic love, 18–19, 87–88, 184–85, 194–95; single-hearted, 146–47, 153, 230n26; sworn male friendship (*sigha-yi ukhuvvat*) of, 88, 114, 153. *See also* female friendship; homoerotic/homoeroticism

male friendship letters (*rasa'il-i ikhvaniyyat*): absence and presence mediated through, 112, 114–17, 151–54, 160–62; anonymity, 140, 143; collected in anthologies, 139, 140; commercial exchanges facilitated through, 141–42; as distinct genre, 112, 138–39, 229n7; emotional turmoil expressed through, 143–47; *ghazal* tropes in, 137, 138, 139, 140, 142, 143–44, 147–48, 151, 152, 228n2; hospitality mediated through, 142–43; love affairs disclosed through, 147–49, 163, 231n31; models and manuals for, 84–86, 112, 124–25, 143–44, 149–55; *nama*, 124, 138; portraits exchanged through, 155–56, *157*, *161*, 162; as reciprocal exchange, 151, 152; transitory nature of, 124; typology, 231n38

male youth: beardless, 24, 89; commissioned portraits of, 126, *127*, *128*, 155–57, *157*, 160–62, *161*; companionate male spectatorship of, 116, 125–26, 129, 146–47; and condemnation of boy gazing, 22, 59, 202; on display in the bazaar, 122–26; and ecstatic gratification, 133–34; featured in *shahrashub*, 108–11, 223–24n6; garden imagery, 116, 125, 135; as reward in paradise, 39, 45, 113; and ritualized discipline of male courtly love, 50–55, *51, 53, 55*; self-fashioning as, 85–86, 97, *98*; and social hierarchies, 49–55, 56, 57, 89, 92–96, 212n42; and Sufi ritual gazing practice, 19–21, *20*

Mani, *Ardahang*, 125, 126, 226n54

manuscripts: borrowing, 71–73; materiality, 10–11, 76, 219n32; popularity in Isfahan, 71, 218n22; production costs, 217–18n10, 218n21; Shiraz as important producer of, 219n31; workshops, 66, 67, 75–76, 219n29

marriage: Shi'a promotion of, 59–61; temporary, 180, 234n18

Marvels of Creatures, 34, 213n11

masculinity: *adab* of 19–21, 129, 134, 205; and boyhood memories, 105; courtly, 57; entrance into manhood, 24, 89, 212n42; and facial hair, 24, 49, 88; urban 57–62, 110, 118, 122, 125. *See also* male friendship; homoerotic/homoeroticism; male youth

master-disciple relationship, 83–84, 92–96. *See also* Sufism

Mas'ud Sa'd, 110, 111, 224n9

maydan. *See* Naqsh-i Jahan square

McChesney, Robert, 212n3

Mecca, 132, 186, 192. *See also* Ka'ba

Medina, 31, 40, 186

Meisami, Julie Scott, 216n2

melancholy (*sawda'*), 19, 121, 123, 125, 133, 178, 182, 185–92, 195, 215, 227n66, 235n33. *See also* love; *'ishq*

Membré, Michele, 51–52

Mir Ali, 158, *159*

Mir Damad, 144

Mir Findiriski, 83, 84, 94–95, 96, 220n36, 221n53

Mir Ilahi, 139, 142–43

Mir 'Imad, 66, 76, 217n9, 219n33

Mir Mirza Ali Akbar, 139, 147–49, 163, 204

Mir Rukn al-Din, 112, 113–17, 224n13. *See also* Aqa Mansur Semnani, erotic city manual

Mirza Ahsanullah, Zahir Khan, 141

Mirza 'Inayat Isfahani, 220n36

Mirza Mulla's coffeehouse, 126

Moses, 131

moustaches and beards, 22, 23, 24, 49, 50, 60, 88–89. *See also* facial hair

Muhammad, prophet: almanac attributed to, 83; in *dibachas*, 172, 175; in New Friday Prayer Mosque epigraphic program, 5, 8, 40, 42–45; and sexual morality, 60–61

Muhammad Qasim: 25–28, 64–65, *Bastinade*, 92–96, *93*, 222n73; *Boys Bird Nesting*, 103–5, *104*; burial, 103; compared to Aqa Husayn Khwansari, 106–7; female clientele, 105, 178; female subjects, 105, 177–80, *179*, 181–83, *182*; *Girls, Woman, and Dervish*, *182*; nature settings, 103; patronage, 97–102, 223n83; poetry, 100, 222n77; portfolio, 90–91; *Portrait of Shah Abbas and a Page*, 100–102, *101*; self-portraits, 97–100, *98, 99*; *Woman Smoking a Pipe*, *179*; as unappreciated, 90–91

Muhanna, Elias, 232n2

Muharram, 83, 212n3, 221n50

Muhibb Ali Beg, 9, 42

muhtasib (censor of morals and commercial practices), 58, 215n44

Mu'in Musavvir, 156, *157*, 223n86, 231n45
Mulla Rawnaqi, 156
Mulla Sadra, *Sharh Hidayat al-Hikma*, 72–73
Munir, 142–43
Munsha'at-i Shah Safi, 231n32
Munsha'at-i Sulaymani, 150, 151, 167, 231n32
muraqqa' (collected visual texts), 2, 19; connection to *majmu'a*, 14, 16, 75; large format, *69*; overview, 14; as patchwork heuristic, 21–22, 25, 64, 68, 89, 90, 91, 177; reading imagery, *15*; rise in popularity, 67–68. See also Muhammad Qasim
mystic love: experienced at the Ka'ba, 193–94; and friendship, 18–19, 87–88, 184–85, 194–95; and *ghazal* poetry, 121, 137, 138, 139, 140, 158; and melancholy, 19, 121, 133; and ritualized male courtly discipline, 50–55, *51*, *53*, *55*, 95–96; and shah as beloved cupbearer, 17–18, 46–50, *48*, 54, 58, 100–102, *101*; and Sufi practice of gazing, 19–21, 54, 119–20, 151; in Sufism, 19, 61, 121, 132–33, 185

Najmabadi, Afsaneh, 236n4
Najm al-Din Razi, Muhammad, 227–28n76
nama. See male friendship letters
Naqsh-i Jahan square, *7*; dating, 209–10n12; ecstatic gratification in, 133–34; function in imperial program, 7, 37–38, 225n29; and new graphic culture, 66–67; paradise imagery, 5–7, 34–35, 66; and Shah Abbas I's inaugural program, 32–36, 213n14
Nasira Hamadani (religious scholar and literati): as *dibacha* composer, 233n12; friendship letters, 137, 139–47, *145*, 155–56, 205, 228n1, 229n8; on letter writing, 137, 139, 228n3
Nasrabadi, Muhammad Tahir, 90–91, 108, 146–47
Navvab Isfahani, 78, 84, 221n53
New Friday Prayer Mosque: courtly imagery comparison, 49; imperial epigraphic program, *6*, *7*, 8–9, 40–46, *43*, 214n27; as second Ka'ba, 42, 130–31
Nizami, 229n18; *Khamsa*, 102; *Layli and Majnun*, 185, 186, 187, 193
Nuqtavi millenarian rebellion (1593), 18, 30–31

occult practices, 34, 81–83, 90, 166
Old Friday Prayer Mosque, 119, 131–32, 227n70

paper, 10–11, 76, 92, 94, 96, 97, 106, 110, 115–25, 134–35, 140–42, 148–53, 156, 158, 160, 162, 165–66, 168, 173, 181, 219n32
paradise: as eternal reward, 44–45; garden of, 5–8, 35, 63, 121; Isfahan as earthly, 118, 119–20, 121; in Isfahan visual program, 5–7, 34–35, 66
patrons: in *dibachas*, 172, 175–76; royal, 34, 40, 46, 100–102, 219n31; and scribes, 12, 172; soliciting, 97–100; varied clientele and services, 66–67, 217–18n10
Paul, Jurgen, 232n3
pedagogical discipline, 85, 92–96
Petrucci, Armando, 209n10
pilgrimage, 28, 60, 70, 73, 113, 185–88, 192; Isfahan as site of, 113, 133; of women, 94. See also Ka'ba; Mecca

poetry: epigraphic, 43–44; exchanging, 158, *159*; *ghazals*, 121, 137–44, 147–48, 151, 152, 228n2, 234n25; Muhammad Qasim's, 100, 222n77; realist school, 185, 187, 234n25. See also *shahrashub*
presence. *See* absence and presence
print *vs.* manuscript culture, 71
prostitution, 23
pubic hair, 88
public square. *See* Naqsh-i Jahan square
Puff, Helmut, 216n52, 228

Qarachaqay Khan, 102, 103
Qasim Tabrizi, 171
Qaysariyya. *See* bazaar, the
Qazvini, Muhammad Tahir Vahid, 211n40
Qizilbash, 47, 51, 214n33
Quran: apocalyptic imagery, 31, 213n4; divination, 81; duty of commanding right and forbidding wrong, 58, 74, 215n43; in New Friday Prayer Mosque epigraphic program, 5, *6*, 42–46; paradise imagery in maydan, 34–36, 39; preserved tablet reference, 173, 234n17
Qutb ibn Muy, *Tarikh-i Wassaf*, 229n18

rag sellers, 134–35, 202
Rancière, Jacques, 212n43
Raphaël du Mans, 71
rasa'il-i ikhvaniyyat. See male friendship letters
religion and spirituality: apocalypse, 18, 31–32; communal worship, 8–9, 41, 44, 131; and desire in sacred spaces, 130–33; diversity, 123; divination manuals, 81–83, 220n48; endowments, 37, 41–42, 80; Hajj pilgrimage, 70, 185–87, 192–94; leadership, 40–41, 131; and repentance, 130–32, 185, 187, 193–94, 227n64; sects, 226n39. *See also* God; Quran; Shi'ism; Sufism
repentance, 130–32, 185, 187, 193–94; declaration of (*tawbanama*), 74–75; 227n64
ritual gazing. *See* gazing
Riza Abbasi (painter), 19, *20*, 66, 91, *127*, 155, 160, 205, 219n35, 231n45
Riza Quli (scribe), 78, 80, 84, 203, 204, 220n40
romances, 25, 47, 74, 87, 89, 90, 102, 106, 111, 125, 147, 176, 184, 185, 186, 189
Roxburgh, David, 67, 68, 218n14
royal anthologies: *vs.* household, 68; and Persianate collecting tradition, 67, 218n14; workshops, 66, 67, 75–76, 219n29

Sa'di, 229n18; *Bustan*, 76
Safavi, Bahram Mirza, 219n31
Safavi, Ibrahim Mirza, 219n31
Safavi, Safi, Shah of Iran, 58, 102, 216n45
Safavi, Safi al-din, Shaykh, 215n39, 220n47
Safavi, Sam Mirza, *Tuhfat-i Sami*, 171, 224n6, 233n15
Safavi, Shah Sultan Husayn, Shah of Iran, 72
Safavi, Sulayman, Shah of Iran, 83, 150
Safavi, Tahmasb, Shah of Iran, 18, 46, 51–52
Safavi ancestry, 50–51, 215n39, 220n47
Sa'ib Tabrizi, 47, 63, 86, 139, 141, 171; *Safina-yi Sa'ib*, 70
Salman Farsi, 215n46

Saru Taqi, 169
secrecy: of homoerotic/homoeroticism, 19, 114, 117, 123, 135, 148–49, 178–80, 201–2; New Friday Prayer Mosque as secret Ka'ba, 42, 130–31; public secret, 30–31, 34, 42, 45–46; of the written word, 172, 173, 175
self-fashioning: and authorial status, 171; and bazaar as mirror, 122; as concept, 216–17n3; in letter writing, 160–62; as male youth, 85–86, 97, *98*; soliciting patronage through, 97–100, *98*, *99*
seminary libraries, 71–72, 75–76, 220n42
senses, cultivation of, 119–20, 123–26, 133–34
sexuality: and celibacy, 21, 59, 60–61, 88, 133; and self-regulation, 88; Shi'a promotion of heterosexual conjugality, 59–61; and sodomy, 61, 74, 135, 140, 216n52. *See also* homoerotic/homoeroticism
Shafi'a (friend of Mu'in Musavvir), 156, *157*
Shahnama, 68, 102, 125, 217n8, 228–29n5
shahrashub (city disturbance; literary tradition): sensitivity around production of, 108–9, 223–24n6; writing the city, 108–19, 224n9. *See also* Aqa Mansur Semnani, erotic city manual
shahsavani (shah loving), 50
Shamlu, Rustam Khan, 220n36
sharia law, 17, 22–24, 61, 74, 135, 180, 201
shaving beards, 22, 23, 24, 60, 88–89
Shaykh Lutfullah Mosque, 37–40, *39*, 214n19

Shaykh Najib, 220n36
Shihab al-Din Nuwayri, 232n2
Shi'ism: Aqa Husayn Khwansari as scholar of, 78–79; competition with and condemnation of Sufism, 22–23, 82–83, 84; imperial promotion of, 5, 8–9, 42–44; promotion of marriage, 59–61
Shiraz, 137, 139, 143–44, 149, 219n31
Shirazi, Baba Rukn al-Din, 83, 103
Shirazi, Ibn Muqla, 148, 230n29
sisterhood vows (*khwahar khwandagi*), 114, 180, 181
sociability. *See* female friendship; male friendship; male friendship letters; sworn friendship
social order: asymmetries of age and rank, 49–55, 56, 57, 89, 92–96, 212n42; and city disturbance (*see* Aqa Mansur Semnani, erotic city manual); homoerotic bonds as threat to, overview, 22–24; of letter writing, 150
sodomy (*livat*), 17, 57, 61, 74, 135, 140, 147, 200, 202, 216n52
sovereignty: and ritualized discipline of courtly love, 50–55, *51*, *53*, *55*, 95–96; shah as beloved cupbearer, 17–18, 46–50, *48*, 54, 58, 100–102, *101*; spectacle of, 30–36
spectacle, 12, 23, 24, 30–36, 108, 113, 119–20, 124, 125
spirituality. *See* religion and spirituality; Sufism
spiritual love. *See* mystic love
spring, letters in praise of, 84–85
square, the. *See* Naqsh-i Jahan square
Steedman, Carolyn, 234n22
sticks, disciplinary, 50–55, *51*, *53*, *55*, 85, 92–96, *93*

Sufism: divination, 82; epistemology, 8; mystic love and divine union, 19, 61, 121, 132–33, 185; ritual gazing, 19–21, *20*, 54, 119–20; and Safavi mystic brotherhood, 50–51, 215n39, 220n47; Shi'a competition with and condemnation of, 22–23, 82–83, 84; and sodomy, 61, 135, 140

Sultan al-Ulama (Khalifa Sultan, Mar'ashi), 23, 88, 233n15

Sunni, 8–9, 41

sworn friendship, 88, 114, 153, 180, 181

Tabib, Husayn ibn Nimatullah, 87–88

tables of contents, as innovation in household anthologies, 80, 168, *168*, 207–8

Takht-i Fulad cemetery, 83–84, 103

Talar-i Tavila, 126, 227n59

talismans, 75, 181–82, *182*

Taymuri, Mortiza, 219n34

tazkira (biography), 67

Timuri, Iskandar Sultan, 67

Timuri realm, 67, 218n12

tobacco stalls, 122–23

Traub, Valerie, 236n2

tribadism, 56

Tughra Tabrizi, 141–42

urbanity, imageability and legibility of, 2–4; *adab* of 11–12, 17, 19, 23–24, 62, 110, 140, 166, 198; in anthologies, 79–80. *See also* male friendship; masculinity

Urdubadi, Bahram Khan, 232n5

Urdubadi, Hatim Beg, 168, 169, 232n5

Urdubadi, Mirza Khalil, 167, 181, 184

Urdubadi, Mirza Talib Khan, 168, 169, 233–34n15

Urdubadi, Muhammad Mu'in, 165, 166, 167, 170, 171, 175–76. *See also* Urdubadi anthology

Urdubadi anthology, *168*, *169*, *170*, *174*; boat metaphor (*safina* and *jung*), 176, 177; contents, overview, 168–70, 171–72; dating, 167–68, 203; as family archive, 164–65; as materialized act of creation, 172–75; patronage, 175–76; rebinding and reassembly, 167–68, 171, 173, 204, 233nn13–14; social imaginary of the city in, 176–77; table of contents, 168, *168*

Urdubadi widow, 164–67, 181–97, 203: husband, 167, 181, 184, 187–88; love for husband, 187–88; pilgrimage to Ka'ba, 185–87, 192–94; preface to narrative of, 183, 184; tension between affective ties, 188–95

Ustad Ali Akbar Isfahani, 42

Ustad Muhammad Zaman, 217n10

Vahshi-yi Bafiqi, *Farhad and Shirin*, 89, 102

Vali Muhammad Khan, *48*, 49

Vali Tuni, 223n83

Walkowitz, Judith, 236n3

wine, prohibition of, 60, 74

women: as artist clientele, 105, 178; as entertainers, 55–56, *56*, 105, 215nn41–42; in Muhammad Qasim's portfolio, 105, 177–80, *179*, 181–83, *182*; prostitution, 23. *See also* female friendship

worship, communal, 8–9, 41, 44, 131

wrestling, 133–34

writing: composition manuals, 86–87; *dibacha*s, 171–77, *174*; poetic imagery

260 *Index*

of, 115, 120–21. *See also* male friendship letters

Yazdi, Sharaf al-Din Ali, 229n18
Yusuf (Joseph), 123, 226n41
Yusufi, Ustad, 30–31

Zahidi, Shaykh Abu Talib, 220n36
Zahid Khan, 147–49, 204
Zamani Nizhad, Ali Akbar, 221n56
Zuhuri Tarshizi, Mawlana, 222n59,60, 231n36, 233n12; *Gulzar-i Ibrahimi*, 86–87, 222n61